Portugal in the 21st Century

Portugal in the 21st Century provides a thorough yet accessible picture of contemporary Portugal in the first two decades of the 21st century.

It examines and elucidates Portugal's recent trajectory, its current position, and the main challenges it faces through an examination of the principal dimensions of cultural, economic, political, and social development in the country. Bringing together some of the foremost Portuguese experts in each of these areas, it draws on a diverse knowledge across the social sciences and humanities – including anthropologists, art historians, economists, historians, legal scholars, literary scholars, political scientists, biologists, and sociologists – to create a multidimensional portrait of contemporary Portuguese society.

Key features:

- Organised into nine substantive chapters – each of which covers a major area of Portugal's contemporary existence – from its national identity and political system to its economy, scientific, literary, and artistic production.
- Opens with a general introduction providing historical context, and a chapter on Portuguese national identity.
- Thematic chapters focus on social, political, economic, and cultural developments of the last two decades.

This book provides a comprehensive, erudite yet accessible introduction to contemporary Portugal and is essential reading for students, scholars, and readers interested in Portugal, Portuguese and Southern European politics and culture, Iberian, or Iberian-American studies and more broadly to European and Comparative Politics.

Nuno Monteiro was an Associate Professor of Political Science at Yale University, USA.

Patrícia Silva is an Assistant Professor and a researcher at the Governance, Competitiveness and Public Policies Research Centre (GOVCOPP), the University of Aveiro, Portugal.

Pedro C. Magalhães is a Senior Researcher at the Institute of Social Sciences at the University of Lisbon, Portugal.

"As a committed multilateralist, but also as a proud Portuguese, I'm delighted to see a book about my country that covers the fundamental aspects of contemporary Portugal in the 21st Century written by a highly competent group of scholars."

António Guterres, *UN Secretary-General*

"Portugal in the 21st Century is a book of remarkable breadth and depth, offering unique insight into the nation's history, politics, society, and culture. It is a must-read for anyone interested in Portugal's past, present, and future."

Charles A. Kupchan, *Georgetown University and Council on Foreign Relations, USA*

"The editors have gathered a stellar group of eleven of their colleagues to bring us a very timely analysis of Portugal in the 21st Century. This collection of remarkably succinct and accessible essays by some of Portugal's most eminent and articulate scholars is an exciting, enlightening, and essential read for anyone seeking to understand Europe's current dilemmas."

Kenneth Maxwell, *former Senior Fellow of the Council of Foreign Relations, author of The Making of Portuguese Democracy (2009).*

"This book is an absolutely invaluable guide for anyone interested in the political system of contemporary Portugal."

Constanze Stelzenmüller, *Director of Center on the United States and Europe, Brookings Institution, USA.*

Portugal in the 21st Century

Edited by Nuno Monteiro, Patrícia Silva,
and Pedro C. Magalhães

Designed cover image: Pedro Calapez, *Onimod 03 B*, 2015, © Pedro Calapez/
Luso-American Development Foundation Collection

First published 2025
by Routledge
4 Park Square, Milton Park, Abingdon, Oxon OX14 4RN

and by Routledge
605 Third Avenue, New York, NY 10158

Routledge is an imprint of the Taylor & Francis Group, an informa business

© 2025 selection and editorial matter, Nuno Monteiro, Patrícia Silva, and Pedro C. Magalhães; individual chapters, the contributors

The right of Nuno Monteiro, Patrícia Silva, and Pedro C. Magalhães to be identified as the authors of the editorial material, and of the authors for their individual chapters, has been asserted in accordance with sections 77 and 78 of the Copyright, Designs and Patents Act 1988.

The Open Access version of this book, available at www.taylorfrancis.com, has been made available under a Creative Commons Attribution-No Derivatives (CC-BY-ND) 4.0 license.

Open Access has been funded by FLAD - Fundação Luso-americana para o Desenvolvimento.

Trademark notice: Product or corporate names may be trademarks or registered trademarks, and are used only for identification and explanation without intent to infringe.

British Library Cataloguing in Publication Data
A catalogue record for this book is available from the British Library

Library of Congress Cataloging in Publication Data
Names: Monteiro, Nuno P., editor. | Silva, Patrícia Catarina de Sousa e, 1981- editor. | Magalhães, Pedro, 1970- editor.
Title: Portugal in the 21st century / edited by Nuno Monteiro, Patrícia Silva and Pedro C. Magalhães.
Other titles: Portugal in the twenty-first century
Description: Abingdon, Oxon; New York, NY: Routledge, 2025. | Includes bibliographical references and index.
Identifiers: LCCN 2024018492 (print) | LCCN 2024018493 (ebook) | ISBN 9781032784663 (hardback) | ISBN 9781032784632 (paperback) | ISBN 9781003488033 (ebook)
Subjects: LCSH: Portugal--Civilization--21st century.
Classification: LCC DP532 .P625 2025 (print) | LCC DP532 (ebook) | DDC 946.904/4--dc23/eng/20240514
LC record available at https://lccn.loc.gov/2024018492
LC ebook record available at https://lccn.loc.gov/2024018493

ISBN: 978-1-032-78466-3 (hbk)
ISBN: 978-1-032-78463-2 (pbk)
ISBN: 978-1-003-48803-3 (ebk)

DOI: 10.4324/9781003488033

Typeset in Sabon
by Deanta Global Publishing Services, Chennai, India

Contents

	List of Figures and Tables	*vi*
	List of Contributors	*ix*
	Preface	*xii*
	RITA FADEN	
1	Introduction	1
	PATRÍCIA SILVA AND PEDRO C. MAGALHÃES	
2	The nation	14
	JOSÉ MANUEL SOBRAL	
3	The welfare state	26
	RUI BRANCO AND PEDRO ADÃO E SILVA	
4	Politics	44
	CARLOS JALALI	
5	The economy	62
	SUSANA PERALTA	
6	Society	79
	ALICE RAMOS	
7	Science	99
	JOANA GONÇALVES-SÁ	
8	The arts	123
	ANTÓNIO PINTO RIBEIRO	
9	Literature	137
	HELENA BUESCU	
10	Portugal in the European Union	151
	ISABEL CAMISÃO AND SANDRA FERNANDES	
	Index	*169*

Figures and Tables

FIGURES

2.1	Being truly Portuguese (% responses "Very important" + "Important")	19
2.2	Sources of pride in being Portuguese (%response "Very important" + "Important")	20
3.1	Portuguese public debt interest rates and spread to German bunds	29
3.2	Public Expenditure by main functions 1995–2020 (% of the total)	30
4.1	Overview of the Portuguese political system	49
4.2	Combined PS-PSD vote share, 1975–2022	53
5.1	The Portuguese GDP	63
5.2	An indebted country	63
5.3	Selected EU countries in 2005: inequality, poverty, deprivation, and GDP per capita	76
5.4	Selected EU countries in 2020: inequality, poverty, deprivation, and GDP per capita	77
6.1	Population with completed tertiary education at the time of the censuses, by sex	82
6.2	Employment rates	83
6.3	Gender pay gap by qualification level	84
6.4	'When a mother works for pay, the children suffer' (% agreement in Portugal)	85
6.5	'A job is alright but what most women really want is a home and children' (% agreement in Portugal)	86
6.6	Residence permits, granting and extension of residence permits and extension of long-stay visas (1980–2021)	87
6.7	Openness to immigration in Portugal and Europe. (% of responses saying 'many '+'some' should be allowed to come and live here.)	90
6.8	Opinions on the impact of immigration in Portugal and Europe (averages)	91
6.9	Belief in racial or ethnic superiority	94
7.1	Calls for Projects in All Scientific Fields (PASF) between 2001 and 2020. Success rate (Projects approved/Projects submitted): grey bars, left axis; Total call budget in millions of euros (grey dots, right axis). "X" marks the years in which no calls were opened	102
7.2	FCT Investment. Total: black line; From the State Budget: grey line	103
7.3	R&D expenditure as a percentage of GDP	104

Figures and Tables   vii

7.4 Cumulative number of individual fellowships and contracts,
since 1998. Individual PhD Fellowships: Grey line; Total number
of funded postdoctoral contracts (fellowships and employment
contracts): Black line. Individual fellowships for doctoral
graduates: light grey, dotted line (superimposed on the black
line until 2012). Individual employment contracts for doctoral
graduates: dark grey, dashed line   104
7.5 Success rate of FCT calls for individual funding. PhD fellowships
(light grey) or postdocs (dark grey for fellowships and black for
contracts)—individual calls, see footnote 7   105
7.6 Human resources in R&D. Left axis: Number of university
professors (dark grey) and number of researchers in R&D (total)
(light grey and crosses). Note that yearly data is only available
from 2008 onwards. Right axis: New PhD graduates per year (black) 106
7.7 Researchers per thousand of the active population   106
7.8 Proportion of women by academic level in Portugal (dark grey)
and EU-27 (light grey). Grade D corresponds to postdoctoral
researchers, Grade C corresponds to assistant professors or similar,
Grade B corresponds to associate professors or equivalent, and
Grade A corresponds to full professors or equivalent. "Total"
shows weighted averages per grade. The values of "%Grade A"
(squares) indicate the percentage of all employed researchers/
professors at Level A (right axis). Data from 2018   107
7.9 Funding by main instrument of Horizon 2020 in millions of euros.
Left axis: Pillar 1: black; Pillar 2: dark grey; Pillar 3: light grey;
Widening; white. Right axis: Percentage of total funding secured by
Portugal per instrument: grey dots. Portugal's contribution to the
EU budget (1.2%): grey dotted line   108
7.10 Horizon 2020 funding attracted by Portugal by type of entity. Left
axis: proportion by entities: Higher Education Institutions and
Research Centres (HEIs-RCs); Industry; Others. Right axis: Total
funding per year in millions of euros   108
7.11 Articles in all scientific and engineering areas per million inhabitants 109
7.12 Ratio of citations per indexed document between Portugal and the
USA, and between Portugal and the EU-28 average   110
7.13 Proportion of all indexed publications by country reaching the top
1% of the most cited   110
7.14 Patents granted by European (EPO) and US (USPTO) patent offices
per million inhabitants   111
7.15 Results of the evaluations of R&D Units. Left axis: proportion
of R&D Units scoring each rating/grade (from 1 to 5), with 5
corresponding to the highest rating (darkest grey) and 1 to the
lowest rating (lightest grey). Right axis: number of units evaluated
in each round—date of publication of results (black dotted line) 113
7.16 Average amount funded per integrated researcher by R&DU
classification. Crosses mark the average value and bars the
standard deviation for the 2013 (light grey) and 2018 (dark grey)
classification   113

viii   *Figures and Tables*

7.17 PhD grants awarded by the FCT by the type of competition between 1994 and 2015. Lines mark grants to be carried out exclusively in Portugal (black), abroad (light grey), or mixed (between Portugal and abroad, dark grey)   115

TABLES

4.1 Alternation, innovation, and openness in government, 2000–2022   52
4.2 Vote and seat share (%) in legislative elections, with effective number of parties and volatility (2000–2022)   56

Contributors

Rui Branco is an Associate Professor at the Department of Political Studies, NOVA University Lisbon, and a senior researcher at IPRI/NOVA. His research focuses on comparative social and labour market regimes and policies. He has edited special issues and published in journals such as *Journal of Comparative Politics*, *Journal of Social Policy*, *New Political Economy*, *Politics & Society*, *Social Policy & Administration*, and *South European Society and Politics*. He has contributed chapters in books published by Cambridge University Press, Oxford University Press, Cornell University Press, and Notre Dame University Press, among others.

Helena Buescu is an Emerita Professor of Comparative and World Literature at U Lisboa. She has been a Research Professor and a Visiting Professor at various universities in Europe (King's College London, Cambridge), the USA (Columbia, Stanford, Princeton, Harvard, Wisconsin), Brazil, Macao, and China. She has published in Portuguese and international periodicals and has authored 11 books. Founder-director of the Centre of Comparative Studies (ULisboa), she has served in several international boards and evaluation committees. Member of Academia Europaea, St. John's College (Cambridge), and Academia das Ciências de Lisboa. She received a Doctor Honoris Causa from the U. Bucharest and won several national and international prizes.

Isabel Camisão holds a PhD in Political Science and International Relations. She is an Associate Professor and Director of the Master in European Studies at the Faculty of Arts and Humanities, University of Coimbra, and Deputy Dean of the same Faculty. She is also a researcher at the Research Center in Political Science, a founding member of the Section on European Studies of the Portuguese Political Science Association, of whose coordination team she is a member. Her main areas of research include EU governance and institutions and EU crisis management.

Rita Faden has a degree in Law from the University of Lisbon Law School and holds a postgraduate degree in European Studies from Universidade Católica Portuguesa (Portuguese Catholic University). She has vast experience in representing Portugal in international negotiations within the framework of the European Union and the United Nations, and a long career in the Portuguese Public Administration in the areas of Foreign Affairs, European Affairs, Justice, Security and Defence. She held several leadership positions, namely as Director-General in the Ministry of Foreign Affairs, in the Ministry of Justice, and in the Ministry of Interior. She was Chief of Staff to the Portuguese Prime Minister between 2015 and 2018, and the President of the Portuguese American Development Foundation (FLAD) since January 2019.

x *Contributors*

Sandra Fernandes is a Professor at the University of Minho and a researcher at the Research Centre in Political Science (CICP), holding a PhD in Political Science and International Relations from Sciences Po Paris. Her contributions to the field have received recognition, including the Jacques Delors Prize in 2005, the election as director of CICP, and invitations to a wide range of universities, namely in Belgium, Estonia, Finland, Poland, Slovenia, Türkiye, and Russia. Her research interests include the external action of the European Union and its relations with Russia, the post-Soviet space, multilateralism, foreign policy analysis, and international security.

Carlos Jalali is an Associate Professor of Political Science at the University of Aveiro and scientific coordinator of the Research Unit on Governance, Competitiveness and Public Policies. His research focuses on party systems, political campaigns and political institutions and has been published inter alia in *South European Society & Politics*, *West European Politics*, *Party Politics*, and *Government & Opposition*.

Pedro C. Magalhães is a Senior Researcher at the Institute of Social Sciences of the University of Lisbon. He holds a PhD in Political Science from the Ohio State University. His research focuses on public opinion, voting behaviour, and judicial politics, which has been published in journals such as the *American Journal of Political Science*, *Comparative Political Studies*, *European Journal of Political Research*, *Journal of European Public Policy*, and many others.

Nuno Monteiro (1971–2021) was an Associate Professor of Political Science at Yale University. He held a PhD in Political Science from the University of Chicago. His research focused on great-power politics, power transitions, nuclear proliferation, the causes of war, deterrence theory, nationalism, and the philosophy of science. He was the author of *Theory of Unipolar Politics* and *Nuclear Politics: The Strategic Causes of Proliferation* (with Alexandre Debs). His research and commentary appeared in numerous outlets including the *Annual Review of Political Science*, *Critical Review*, *The Guardian*, *Foreign Affairs*, *International Organization*, *International Security*, and *Perspectives on Politics*.

Susana Peralta is an Associate Professor at Nova School of Business and Economics. She holds a PhD in Economics from the Université catholique de Louvain. Since 2004 she has taught courses in public policy, poverty economics, and microeconomics. She is a specialist in Public Economics and Political Economy, and her research is published in international peer-reviewed journals such as the *Journal of Public Economics*, *Journal of Urban Economics*, *The Economic Journal*, or *Public Choice*.

Alice Ramos is a researcher at the Institute of Social Sciences, University of Lisbon. She is the National Coordinator of the European Social Survey-ERIC, Project Director, and Member of the Executive Committee of the European Values Study. Her research interests include the articulation between economic, social, and moral factors and their impacts on racial prejudice and discriminatory attitudes, and the methodology of longitudinal and cross-national studies. She has edited special issues and published in journals such as *Journal of Ethnic and Migration Studies*, *International Journal of Conflict and Violence*, and *Frontiers in Political Science*, among others.

António Pinto Ribeiro has combined his work as a cultural programmer with that of a senior researcher, now retired, at the Center for Social Studies/University of Coimbra. His areas of research and curatorship are contemporary art with a special focus on the relationship between Africa, Latin America, and Europe. He has been the artistic director of various cultural organizations – Culturgest, Calouste Gulbenkian Foundation, among others. He is currently an artistic advisor to FLAD. He has published many articles and books. Highlights: *Peut-on décoloniser les musées?* and *Novo Mundo - Arte contemporânea no tempo da Pós-memória.*

Joana Gonçalves de Sá is a researcher at LIP and the coordinator of the Social Physics and Complexity research group. She was an Associate Professor at Nova School of Business and Economics and a Principal Investigator at Instituto Gulbenkian de Ciência, Portugal, where she also coordinated the Science for Society Initiative and directed the Graduate Programme Science for Development. She has a degree in Physics Engineering from Instituto Superior Técnico – UL, and a PhD in Systems Biology from NOVA – ITQB, having developed her thesis at Harvard University. Her multidisciplinary research tackles complex problems at the interface between Biomedicine, Social Sciences, and Computation, with a large ethical and societal focus. She received two ERC grants (Stg_2019 and PoC_2022) to study human and algorithmic biases.

Patrícia Silva holds a PhD in Political Sciences. She is an assistant professor and a researcher at the Governance, Competitiveness and Public Policies Research Centre (GOVCOPP) of the University of Aveiro, where she has developed research work on political parties, the politicization of recruitment of appointed elites, public administration, and local governance. She has been involved in several research projects and published articles in journals including *Party Politics*, *South European Society and Politics*, *International Review of Administrative Sciences*, *Public Administration*, and *European Politics and Society*.

Pedro Adão e Silva is an Assistant Professor at ISCTE-IUL's School of Sociology and Public Policy, where he was also director of the doctoral programme in public policy. He was vice-president of IPPS-IUL and a member of the board of the collaborative laboratory, CoLABOR, where he coordinated the line of research dedicated to "social protection". Also at CoLABOR, he was part of the team responsible for developing the "DataLabor" platform. He has coordinated the publication of several volumes analysing public policies in Portugal and published several articles on the subject, particularly focusing on welfare policies, in national and international journals. From March 2022 to April 2024, he has been Minister of Culture in the Government of Portugal.

José Manuel Sobral, a historian and anthropologist, is a Senior Researcher, now retired, at the Institute of Social Sciences of the University of Lisbon. Among the topics he has researched are political clientelism, Portuguese rural society – dealing mainly with family and kinship, social structure, religion, conflict, and politics –, nationalism and national identity, racism, social memory, the history of anthropology in Portugal, food, and the Spanish flu. He was President of the Portuguese Association of Anthropology (APA) and Director of the journal *Análise Social*.

Preface

Rita Faden
President of FLAD's Executive Council

This book is the result of a series of conversations I had with Professor Nuno P. Monteiro in 2019 about the way to discuss and present modern Portugal in the United States. It became clear that, when speaking with someone in the United States, we could not find a reading to recommend that was at the same time comprehensive, accessible, and providing an overview of contemporary Portugal both to the general public and to academia.

This book aims to fill this gap in existing literature, providing a resource that until now did not exist. This is not a history book nor a book about Portuguese culture, identity, society, or politics. But it includes all those features, as it showcases the country's current reality and challenges in different fields, each covered in a separate chapter. We intend it to be informative to the general, interested public, as well as a valuable tool for students from different academic backgrounds.

As Nuno Monteiro wrote,

> *Portugal in the Twenty-First Century* provides a comprehensive yet accessible overview of Portugal's recent trajectory, its current position, and the main challenges it faces. It does so by examining the principal dimensions of cultural, economic, political, and social contemporary life in the country, focusing on the first two decades of the twenty-first century. With this goal, the volume draws on the knowledge of a diverse set of experts in the social sciences and humanities – including anthropologists, art historians, economists, historians, legal scholars, political scientists, and sociologists – to create a multidimensional portrait of contemporary Portugal.

Being a Portuguese Professor at Yale University, Nuno Monteiro had a profound knowledge both of Portugal and of the American public, and immediately set out to draft a book proposal.

When the pandemic began, the conversations about the book's structure, which topics to cover, and which authors to invite continued online. And they quickly evolved into conversations about politics, international relations, the United States, and the European Union, through which I witnessed Nuno's impressive knowledge and generosity in taking the time for this project. His enthusiasm was essential to the existence of this book.

Unfortunately, Nuno's untimely death put an end to these conversations. But not to the work that he started. FLAD decided to continue the project, not only as a way of honouring Nuno Monteiro and his work but also because, as Nuno did, I believe this is a necessary book.

This project is part of FLAD's (Portuguese American Development Foundation) mission as a Portuguese Foundation to contribute to the development of Portugal through cooperation with the United States. We want to bring the two countries closer by working with people and institutions across the Atlantic.

I am very grateful to Pedro Magalhães and Patrícia Silva for accepting FLAD's challenge of continuing Nuno Monteiro's work as co-editors of this book. They had the difficult task of building upon an existing project, respecting its initial plan, and enriching it with their own contributions.

I also want to thank Leonor Barroso from FLAD for her invaluable work in the completion of this book.

Lisbon, January 4, 2024

1 Introduction

Patrícia Silva and Pedro C. Magalhães

Portugal is at the same time a remarkably old and a radically new country. While its borders in Western Europe have remained the same for more than seven-and-a-half centuries, its contemporary identity as a European, modern, democratic country is less than 50 years old. After having endured decades of dictatorship, Portugal underwent two major transformations in the late 20th century. The first was a military coup leading to a social revolution, its attending decolonization process, and, ultimately, a transition to a democratic regime. Besides politically aligning the country with prevailing Western democratic values and institutions, this transformation ended the pluricontinental identity that had served as the organizing matrix of Portugal's worldview since the 15th century.

The second – Portugal's accession to the European Union – occurred a decade later and consolidated these previous processes. EU accession anchored the country firmly as a European social democracy while fostering economic development and bringing the country in line with – or at least closer to – Western European standards of living and cultural patterns. After this transformative – indeed, riveting – final quarter of the 20th century, Portugal entered the following century as a consolidated democracy and welfare state, with a firmly European identity, modern infrastructures and state bureaucracies, an economy that was fully EU-integrated, and an overall sense of achievement.

At the same time, with the EU enlargement towards the East, Portugal has also lost its privileged status within the bloc as one of the greatest per capita recipients of European funds. Furthermore, a series of bottlenecks – manifested in low human, institutional, and social capital – produced a series of mixed developments in the first two decades of the 21st century. While on some indicators – such as those related to health, inequality, diversity, or scientific and artistic production – the country continued to converge with Western standards, the same has not occurred in other domains – first and foremost in terms of economic, productivity, and wage growth. With the country diverging economically from Europe, populism (albeit belatedly) is on the rise, while many Portuguese citizens lack trust in the country's institutions and its political system more broadly. Meanwhile, over the last few pre-pandemic years, Portugal became a fashionable tourist destination, achieving renewed visibility globally. These dynamics reinforced processes of cultural exchange and globalization, while at the same time making the country more dependent on tourism revenue.

Taking stock at the beginning of the 2020s, Portugal finds itself at a crossroads: while it has achieved spectacular economic development and social transformation over the past half-century, much of this upward trajectory has been achieved in the closing decades of the last century. While civil society, private enterprise, and artistic and scientific production have blossomed to unprecedented levels, Portuguese citizens exhibit declining

DOI: 10.4324/9781003488033-1

This chapter has been made available under a CC-BY-NC-ND license.

2 Patrícia Silva and Pedro C. Magalhães

levels of trust in democratic institutions. Some see the country as a glass-half-full; others as a glass-half-empty.

1.1 A bird's-eye view of recent history

1.1.1 The longest dictatorship in Western Europe

It has become commonly acknowledged that historical antecedents leave relevant genetic imprints on social, political, economic, and cultural developments. The Portuguese case is no exception. The nature of political parties and their interactions, the structure of public administration and the quality of governance, or the wider economic environment can be traced back to the very specific nature of the previous regime and of the transition and democratization processes.

The Estado Novo, an authoritarian regime established in 1933, was Europe's longest-lasting right-wing dictatorship, characterized as 'non-democratic and anti-democratic' (Wiarda 1987, 292). António de Oliveira Salazar remained in power until 1968, when illness rendered him incapable, and Marcelo Caetano took his place. Beyond the reliance on instruments of repression such as censorship, a political police, and paramilitary forces (Portuguese Legion) – which were abolished after the Revolution of the Carnations in 1974 – the authoritarian regime relied heavily on the economic, military, and catholic elites to hold on to power (Magone 2003, 10). The state was central in economic activity by protecting certain companies from competition. Corporatism was crucial for regime stability. While political leaders publicly claimed they aimed to protect economic autonomy and portrayed the public sector as a mere regulator, government intervention in the economy was significant. Key private industries were shielded from competition either by granting them monopolies (under the 'industrial conditioning' policy – Garrido and Rosas, 2012) or through preferential treatment with trade tariffs. Business interactions were also highly regulated (in terms of prices and restricting workers' rights).

To a large extent, this became one of the main legacies of the Estado Novo, an uncompetitive economy (Pintado 2002). During the last decade of the regime, Portugal did witness a period of rapid economic expansion (Marques 2015, 1016), largely due to changes in international position and the lowering of trade barriers, with the country's accession to the European Free Trade Agreement (EFTA), in 1960. The trend towards convergence was not, however, consistently sustained after 1973. Despite impressive economic growth rates in the 1960s, structural weaknesses persisted (Corkill 1993). These included the composition of the industrial structure, with very few private economic groups coexisting with a traditional sector comprised of numerous small firms, which often were uncompetitive industries that still relied on the African market and were unprepared to face international markets; a very large but unproductive agricultural sector; an economy vulnerable to economic downturns; and an inefficient bureaucratic and centralized apparatus, designed to manage and regulate corporatist structures. This corporatist state created a conducive environment for the establishment of a relatively insular community of business leaders and high-ranking politicians (Marques 2015). In fact, after democratization in 1974, the pattern of the centrality of the state in economic activity continued and the new dominant political parties ended up becoming intermediaries between the state and public or private companies. This, in turn, also contributed to the consolidation of their position in the political system (Jalali 2007).

Another relevant legacy of the Estado Novo pertains to the centrality of public administration in the functions of coordination and control (Graham 1985). The exercise of long terms in office and the important role that the administrative leadership of the Estado Novo played in the policymaking processes (facilitated by the absence of restrictions on its involvement in political activities) left another difficult legacy for the political system that followed: a complex administrative structure and a culture of close relationship between the administrative and political elites. This had a strong impact on the first measures in the democratic period, marked by the need to renew the ruling elite, postponing political measures that promoted their professionalization.

In the meantime, the absence of political freedoms meant that even the limited societal pluralism found no articulation via political parties. The harsh repression by the regime has particularly affected the Communist Party. Facing systematic repression and brutal treatment, the PCP was considered a major ideological adversary, especially by conservative Catholics such as Salazar. The PCP operated clandestinely, as a structured opposition force, and became dependent for financial, political, and technical support on the Soviet Union, to which the party became increasingly loyal (Jalali 2007). To a large extent, this would explain the party's resistance to change, as seen in its continued adherence to Marxist-Leninist principles. These ties positioned the PCP as an anti-system party, which ultimately led to its permanent exclusion from national governance after democratization, in a sharp contrast to the fate of the Communist Party in Spain. But the consequences of repression of partisan activities left further legacies for the future which, as we will examine, manifested themselves in the strategies the new parties that emerged after democratization employed to overcome their almost non-existent social rooting

1.1.2 Toppling the dictatorship and the enduring imprints of the democratization process

In September 1968, Marcelo Caetano replaced the Estado Novo's founding leader, António de Oliveira Salazar. While he initially advocated a reformist approach to the regime, aiming at higher economic and political liberalization, internal resistance by the ultraconservative right led Caetano to abandon his most progressive initiatives. Beyond domestic factors, it was the colonial question which decisively contributed both to the failure of Caetanos's liberalization and to the end of the dictatorship. The colonial wars significantly strained Portugal's available resources, largely to the detriment of social and economic development programmes. Moreover, foreign investment was required to offset the drain on funds caused by the substantial defence budget (Vieira 2002, 144). It became increasingly contested that the wars in Africa could be militarily settled, with several higher-ranking members of the Armed Forces, as General António de Spínola, advocating for the negotiated autonomy for the colonies. Their public stances contributed to an increasing politicization of mid- and higher-ranking officers in the army, determined to end an unwinnable war and support a change of regime. Hence, the military ended up being a decisive protagonist in the downfall of the dictatorship, a unique case in the 20th century (Schmitter 1999).

The regime was overthrown in April 1974. The non-violent coup, which came to be known as the Revolution of the Carnations, took the international community by surprise (Teixeira 2002). It faced almost no resistance from the dictatorship's remaining loyalists, while it enjoyed large popular support. The two years that followed would be best characterized as a 'tortuous' transition period (Manuel 1996, 1), given the heated debates and social mobilization over the nature of the new regime and the decolonization processes.

Major tensions emerged, first and foremost, from the uncertainty about the kind of regime to be established in Portugal following the revolutionary period. The Socialist Party (PS, centre-left) and PSD (Social Democratic Party, centre-right) advocated a liberal and pluralistic democratic regime similar to Western European countries, as opposed to the Communist Party (PCP) preference towards a socialist regime and its lack of commitment to representative democracy (Jalali 2007). Given the volatility of the institutional environment after the revolution, all the political parties that then emerged or re-emerged – as in the case of the Communist Party – strived to capture a permanent position in the political vacuum left by the collapse of the previous regime (van Biezen 1998, 38). This was particularly acute for the parties in favour of liberal democracy, which needed to signal the existence of broad social support in order to 'block the PCP's organisational solidity' (Jalali 2007, 80).

In the light of the lack of clearly defined social divisions that political parties could readily activate, dominant parties directed their tactics towards offering tangible incentives rather than building robust foundations of ideological backing (Jalali and Lisi 2009, 449). As political parties assumed parliamentary and governing responsibilities even before structuring party organizations (Jalali 2007; van Biezen 1998), they were able to use their position in power to distribute positions in the public administration and thus secure the support and protection of their clienteles (Jalali 2007; Jalali and Lisi 2009).

In addition, the overload of state responsibilities (Aguiar 1985, 778), with the magnitude of the tasks entrusted to parties at the level of institutional reorganization and the formulation of public policies, largely prevented parties from becoming more actively involved in the construction of the party structure and its bases (van Biezen 1998, 39). Overall, then, the virtual dependence on state resources and the pressing burden associated with new structures and regime choices discouraged the development and consolidation of Portuguese party organizations.

After the resolution of the conflict regarding the choice of regime, parties strived for a continued access to government (Morlino 1995), through institutions that ensured their supremacy in several waysIn the Constitution, parties were exclusively entitled to present candidates in legislative elections (Lobo 2000). The electoral system, with its closed-list proportional representation and the d'Hondt formula, further strengthened party leaderships and mitigated proportionality (Morlino 1995). Material resources, including state funding for parties, were secured (Jalali 2007; van Biezen 2000). Finally, the constitutional revision of 1982 solidifiedthe partisan control over the Council of State, the Constitutional Court, the Assembly, and the public administration (Lobo 1996, 1087). These institutional reforms help in understanding the centrality of parties – particularly of the PS and the PSD – in the political system, despite their limited social roots. In addition, political parties relied on financial and technical assistance from prominent figures in the US administration and other European political families, particularly the German Social and Christian Democrats, who frequently acted as sponsors of, respectively, the PS and the PSD, enabling them to operate during times of crisis (Teixeira 2002, 9).

In this way, the powerful dynamics of the transition period left lasting impressions on the democratization process. The unstable and volatile nature of the transition to democracy generated 'internally mobilized' parties (as per Shefter's (1994, 31–32) typology), insofar as they were founded by elites who occupied important positions in the regime and used the state resources for the organizational construction of the party. Moreover, the intense disputes between the Socialist Party and the Communist Party throughout the transition made any collaboration between these two major left-wing parties unfeasible for nearly four decades (Lobo 2005; Lobo et al. 2016).

Another way in which events in this period affected future developments is visible in the role of the military. Having played a crucial role in toppling the dictatorship, the military was divided in its approach to decolonization. The conflicts between the coup leaders and conservative generals like General Spínola led to the rise of the MFA (Armed Forces Movement) as a political force. The MFA was far from being cohesive and coherent itself. Beyond the goal of ending the colonial wars, the movement did not have major political goals and had to face major internal struggles between the more moderate and the more radical members. These internal conflicts had a direct impact on the political landscape, leading to a division between those who aligned with the moderate and democratically liberal faction of the MFA (including PS, PPD/PSD, and CDS) and parties linked to the more radical military members, particularly the PCP. The entrenchment of the MFA in the state apparatus and provisional governments contributed to the state crisis, as it 'dispersed and paralyzed the classic mechanisms of legitimate state repression' (Lobo et al. 2016, 166) and prevented moderate elites from steering the swift institutionalization of democracy. Even as social and political tension gradually eased in 1976, when a new constitution was adopted, and the first legislative and presidential elections took place, the military still sought a role in the new democratic arena. After challenging negotiations, the military was granted a significant institutional role through the Council of the Revolution, a military body with important veto- and policy-making powers. Portugal was thus commonly acknowledged as a democracy, albeit one under the guidance of an undemocratic military institution (Teixeira 2002, 13). Only in 1982 was the Council of the Revolution dissolved.

Finally, the nature of the Portuguese transition also affected both the state and the economy quite deeply. As a transition by *rupture,* it was led by actors who had largely been excluded from Salazar and Caetano's political elite. 'Purges' of former political and administrative personnel followed, taken as a security mechanism to break the individual power of leaders over key activities.[1] Beyond these purges, which aggravated the shortage of trained and experienced staff, the democratic period witnessed a substantial transformation of the Portuguese state. The priority given to the expansion of welfare policies and strong economic interventionism of the post-1974 generated a huge expansion of the state sector. The growth of the civil service, where the number of personnel nearly doubled in the early years of democracy, reflected the role of the state in absorbing unemployment, particularly in the context of European recession and economic crisis (1973–74). Moreover, it also reflected political parties' endeavours to control the state apparatus while using public administration to cater to their party's followers (Barreto 1984, 206). This practice is often observed during democratic transition processes (*vide, inter alia,* the cases of Eastern Europe, as suggested by Grzymala-Busse 2003), a pattern that was also reported by former Portuguese ministers who acknowledged party pressures to promote their supporters within the public administration (Lobo 2000).

In the same vein, the effect of the nationalization of important economic sectors during the revolutionary period should not be disregarded. Approximately 10% of public jobs stemmed from the nationalization program itself, considered one of the 'conquests of the revolution' (Corkill 1999, 56). While it was not one of the objectives of the first provisional government, both the left-wing radicalization of the revolutionary process – particularly after the attempted coup on March 11, 1975 (Jalali 2007) – and the degradation of domestic and international economic conditions – which rendered several large companies unsalvageable – combined to produce this outcome. The 1976 Constitution assumed a highly interventionist role of the state and approved the irreversibility of the large nationalized sector. Even if this helped protect several social gains of the emerging democracy, prioritizing social and political concerns over economic ones generated substantial challenges for both productivity and public finances (Corkill 1999, 56–57).

The process of nationalizations that took place until the constitutional revision of 1976 tripled the size of the Portuguese state's business sector (Nunes, Bastien, and Valério 2005, 19), making it the largest among the member countries of the Organization for Economic Cooperation and Development (Baklanoff 1996, 925). This ensured the state's exclusive intervention in a wide range of economic domains. A wider public business sector did not, however, correspond to gains in productivity and performance. Quite the contrary, public enterprises were characterized by poor and dysfunctional performance due to the frequent turnover of managers (Gallagher 1986, 67–68), the 'excessive political interference' and a lack of consistency in decision-making among successive governments (Baklanoff 1996, 937). Furthermore, business interests sought to get closer to political decision-making bodies to understand their internal mechanisms and ensure their proper protection, while political actors approached businesses to ensure their survival or personal autonomy (Aguiar 1985). As a consequence, between 1978 and 1980, the set of public enterprises recorded one of the highest deficits among OECD countries (Baklanoff 1996, 939). The principle of the irreversibility of nationalizations was only eliminated with the second constitutional revision in 1989. This was an ambition of the Social Democratic Party, also pressured by the process of integration into the European Union (Barreto 1994, 1059–1060).

This period was also characterized by high executive instability, particularly during the first decade of the new democracy. There were nine constitutional cabinets, none completing a full four-year term. Coalition governments were fragile, with the shortest cabinet lasting three months and the longest lasting 29 months, while the average cabinet duration was just over a year (13 months). This political instability had considerable negative consequences, particularly visible in the decline of the growth rate of the Portuguese economy after 1973, while inflation and unemployment surged and public debt increased due to expanded social provision (Vieira 2002). The economy was also highly sensitive to the oil shocks. This led the government to seek assistance from the IMF and accept strict conditions for economic stabilization. While successful, the adjustment plan mostly occurred in the private sector, leaving the public deficit at around 10% of GDP. Another stabilization programme was imposed from 1983 to 1985, after a second agreement with the IMF in 1982. As Nataf and Sammis highlighted (1990, 114), fixing the underlying economic problems did not impact on long-term structural problems. Instead, 'governments were singularly ineffectual in reversing the deficiencies in Portugal's productive capacities, but they were quite successful in convincing austerity-oriented international lenders, budget-minded tourists, and high interest-seeking, stability-minded emigrants that the Portuguese economy was being corrected of its "excesses"'.

Only by the mid-1980s did this pattern begin to change. The first government led by Cavaco Silva (1985-1987) marked a significant shift in terms of partisan government composition, influenced by changes in electoral behaviour (Lobo, 2000) and the expanding scope of European governance. The party system gradually became more majoritarian, with a clear concentration of votes in two main parties, the Social Democratic Party and the Socialist Party, which strengthened their position as the main governing alternatives. These parties have monopolized government, with both achieving single-party parliamentary majorities, as well as large pluralities. While there are signs of a decline of this 'majoritarian change' – particularly considering the decline in votes for the two largest parties since the Eurozone crisis, it has not been translated in any way into the same kind of executive instability witnessed in the first years of democracy (Pinto 2020).

1.1.3 Stepping towards the European Union

Amid the challenging conflicts of democratization, Portuguese elites also faced increasing conflicts regarding the international strategic choices to be made by the new democracy. More specifically, provisional governments (with military ministers) were clearly in favour of the adoption of the Portuguese 'African vocation' (Teixeira 2002, 10). This pointed towards linkages with the former African colonies and their protected markets, a connection rooted in an authoritarian corporatist structure. The first constitutional government, however, was clearly inclined towards a foreign policy that would simultaneously be Atlanticist and European. These became the core principles of the new democracy's foreign policy. The Atlanticist perspective, rooted in Portuguese historical foreign policy, provided stability and directed the nation internationally. Simultaneously, establishing ties with the United States and strengthening NATO participation were clear signs of the new democracy's global positioning. After the revolutionary period, Portugal also wholeheartedly embraced the 'European option' from 1976 onwards when Prime Minister Mário Soares applied for European Economic Community membership in March 1977, marking a significant step in the country's pursuit of closer ties with Europe. This was a strategic and political choice: it was a safeguard towards the consolidation of Portuguese democracy and to ensure the country's modernization and economic growth – even if this narrative was not taken for granted across all sectors of society (Teixeira 2002, 12).

Soares and his government actively worked to meet the EEC's requirements and align Portuguese policies and institutions with European standards. European integration became a priority for all subsequent governments (Barreto 1994, 1058), with the adaptation of political, economic, and administrative structures to the European project. The EEC would impose relevant conditions that would solidify the first steps of the new democracy: 'the inauguration of free elections; the predominance of parties supportive of liberal democracy; the existence of a constitution; and evidence of a reasonably stable government led, if possible, by a political figure known and approved in European circles' (Pridham 1991, 234–35). Accession negotiations were, however, protracted, given the EEC's objections to the economic measures taken during the revolutionary period, particularly the nationalization of important economic sectors, and the institutionalization of the Council of Revolution, a body comprised exclusively of military officers, endowed with the authority to block any government legislation and enact its own laws. Both objections were solved with Constitutional reforms of 1982 and 1989, allowing a successful conclusion of the accession negotiations.

In 1986, integration into the European Union and joining the first wave of the common European currency in the late 1990s were fundamental not only to solidify Portuguese democracy but also to Portugal's modernization and economic development (Corkill 1993, 1999). EEC membership allowed Portuguese society and economy to enter a new phase. International trade increased as well as the level of foreign capital investment. Access to ECC's funding mechanisms – through the Regional Development Fund

8 *Patrícia Silva and Pedro C. Magalhães*

(FEDER) and the Cohesion Fund – significantly contributed to reducing regional disparities and fostering convergence within the EU (Royo 2007), by supporting investment, employment and formation policies, infrastructural development. Politically, it contributed to a wide political consensus on foreign policy, geared towards the European integration, a perception shared by elites (and the main political parties) and mass citizens.

However, embracing the European Union came with its own set of drawbacks. The new millennium marked the beginning of a decline in Portugal's eagerness for European integration. The Treaty of Nice and particularly the EU enlargement towards the East meant that Portugal would no longer enjoy a privileged status within the bloc as one of the greatest per capita recipients of European funds. Moreover, the 'moving Europe's centre of gravity to the East' (Teixeira 2002: 23) emphasized the Portuguese peripheral condition in the European context.

1.1.4 The 21st century: weathering the global crises

The problems of national debt and the Eurozone crisis plunged several nations into recessions in 2007–2008. Given its weak structural position – unsustainable public finances (high fiscal deficit of 3% of GDP) and a deficit that reached over 11% of GDP in 2010 – Portugal was one of the hardest hit Eurozone countries. Facing ever-increasing borrowing costs, a bailout package from the European Union (EU), the European Central Bank, and the International Monetary Fund – dubbed the *Troika* – was formally requested in April 2011, following the resignation of the Socialist prime minister, José Sócrates, after failing to win parliamentary support for the fourth and most severe package of austerity measures put forward by his minority government in less than a year. Portugal was to embark on austerity, implementing extensive fiscal consolidation measures aimed at curbing public expenditure.

The Memorandum of Understanding (MoU) was signed on 17 May 2011 and its actual implementation only began in earnest after the 5 June legislative elections. The PSD, led by Pedro Passos Coelho, obtained 40.3% of the vote and sought support from its usual partner, the Social and Democratic Centre-Popular Party (CDS-PP), to form a government enjoying majority support in parliament. This coalition government envisaged the bailout agreement as an opportunity to achieve major harsh and highly contested reforms to recover Portugal's credibility among international institutions and markets (Moury and Standring 2017).

Although the PSD and the CDS-PP (now forming a pre-electoral coalition) were the most voted party in the 2015 elections, following clear signs of economic recovery, they failed to muster enough support in parliament to form a cabinet. Instead, this fell on the Socialist António Costa who, with unprecedented cooperation between the parties on the left (Left Bloc, the Portuguese Communist Party and the Ecologist Party 'The Greens') sought to roll back austerity and return to growth while at the same time keeping fiscal discipline. This government proved to be resilient, successfully navigating political and economic challenges while maintaining stability and advancing its agenda (de Giorgi and Santana Pereira 2020).The downward path of Portuguese public debt caused Portugal to be presented as a model for struggling social democratic parties from other EU member-states. Mário Centeno, Finance Minister, became President of the Eurogroup in early 2018, the first southern European President and coming from a bailed-out country. At that time, Portugal's economic recovery was well established: a reported budget deficit of 0.5% of GDP in 2018 and the prospects for a continuous decrease in 2019, which would represent the lowest level registered within the democratic period. Also, the yearly GDP growth rate was kept above 2% and unemployment rates were low (6.7% in December 2019) (Eurostat 2020), standing in stark contrast with the preceding two legislatures, under bailout conditionality.

Despite the positive outlook, Portugal still grapples with high levels of public debt, ranking as the third highest in Europe, surpassed only by Greece and Italy. Moreover, fiscal consolidation has been achieved by bringing public sector investments to dismal levels and postponing a renewal of highly degraded public services, a problem particularly visible in the Health and Education arenas (Fernandes et al. 2018; Moury et al. 2021). While Portuguese government effectiveness – following the World Bank's indicator on the quality of policy-making formulation and implementation – is in line with other EU economies, it is the inefficient resource allocation that has been identified as the major issue in the public sector (Baer et al. 2013).

1.2 This volume

Portugal in the 21st Century takes these developments as a point of departure to lay out Portugal's recent trajectory, its current position, and the main challenges it faces. It does so by examining the principal dimensions of cultural, economic, political, and social development in the country. Bringing together some of the foremost Portuguese experts in each of these areas, this volume provides a thorough yet accessible picture of contemporary Portugal in the last two decades. In contrast with books in contemporary history, which draw on historical knowledge and methods to examine recent events, the present volume draws on the knowledge of a diverse set of experts in the social sciences and humanities – including anthropologists, art historians, economists, historians, political scientists, biologists, and sociologists – to create a multidimensional portrait of contemporary Portuguese society. It is organized into nine substantive chapters, each delving into a crucial facet of Portugal's modern landscape, from its national identity and political system to its economy, scientific, literary, and artistic production.

The book opens with a chapter on Portuguese national identity by anthropologist José Manuel Sobral, where he addresses the different processes that were at play in the construction of the Portuguese nation. Sobral shows that, way before the ideology of nationalism emerged in the late 18th century, the constitutive elements of a Portuguese national identity were already being shaped by processes that date back to the Middle Ages. Subsequent periods – empire-building, the liberal-monarchical regime of the 19th century, the short-lived First Republic, and the authoritarian Estado Novo – all left their imprint on Portuguese national identity. Today, the Portuguese display high and stable levels of national identification, with language as its most important pillar and the country's history as the primary source of national pride. However, Sobral also shows how democratization caused not only a reconfiguration of what it means to be 'Portuguese' but also increasing contestation around old nationalist narratives inherited from the authoritarian and imperial past.

The following chapter, by political scientists Rui Branco and Pedro Adão e Silva, focuses on the Portuguese state, particularly the welfare state, in the 21st century. With democratization in the 1970s, the notion of citizenship in Portugal came to be indissociably linked with socio-economic rights and a welfare state to protect them. Since then, Europeanization has brought both opportunities and constraints, fostering the expansion of the welfare system to previously underdeveloped areas but also retrenchment in

10 *Patrícia Silva and Pedro C. Magalhães*

other domains, as monetary integration and fiscal discipline forced cost containment. Branco and Silva then show how the Eurozone crisis, the financial bailout of the country, and the ensuing austerity measures halted what has previously been a slow but steady convergence with more advanced European welfare states. Since then, within the limited possibilities provided by an improved but still fragile fiscal position, governments have struggled to reconcile protection against new social risks – support for early and continuing education and balancing work and family, for example – with the demands of strong constituencies pressing for continued protection against 'old' ones (old age, unemployment, and invalidity).

In Chapter 4, political scientist Carlos Jalali focuses on the political system. Following the agitated first decade of Portuguese democracy, a remarkable stability in political institutions and the party system ensued. Static government formulas, alternation between the two main centre-right and centre-left parties, and lack of openness to new parties made the country into an unusual oasis of political uneventfulness in the European context. And yet, in the last two decades, signs of change successively emerged: the rise of independent mayoral and presidential candidates; the decline in vote shares for the two largest parties; and the unprecedented collaboration between the Socialists and the radical parties to its left. Finally, as the second decade of the century came to a close, newcomers in the party system successfully emerged, among them, following belatedly a trend common to almost all European countries, a populist radical-right party, which managed to become the third largest force in parliament in 2022.

Chapter 5, by economist Susana Peralta, traces the recent evolution of the country's economy. Following a remarkable convergence with the European advanced economies until the end of the previous century, the record since then has been rather mixed: reduction of poverty, inequality, and material deprivation, but also sluggish growth, external indebtedness, and stagnant productivity. Peralta reviews some of the factors behind the disappointing performance of the Portuguese economy in the last two decades. They include the scarcity of human capital; the presence of small firms with limited access to financial resources; low quality of governance and defective institutions; and lack of fiscal capacity of the state. While European cohesion funds could potentially alleviate these concerns, an examination of recent trends raises concerns that, once again, they might fall short of their intended impact.

In Chapter 6, sociologist Alice Ramos examines Portuguese society since the beginning of the 21st century, using three specific social groups – women, immigrants, and racialized people – as a lens through which to examine the dynamics of social change. Legal reforms such as the decriminalization of abortion, gender quotas in parliament and the public administration, the facilitated acquisition of legal residence and nationality for immigrants and their children, and the approval of anti-discrimination legislation reveal how the political mood has changed in the direction of a much greater concern with dimensions of equality that were previously neglected. However, the reality on the ground still lags the legal framework. The gender pay gap remains considerable, especially among the highly qualified, and its reduction has been minimal over time. Social attitudes, entrenched in stereotypes regarding the roles of women in both the workplace and family, persist. And while the openness of the Portuguese to immigration has increased substantially, beliefs in racial or ethnic superiority of some groups over others are among the highest in Europe, suggesting that anti-racist social norms are weak.

Chapter 7, by researcher Joana Gonçalves-Sá, focuses on the Portuguese scientific landscape. It describes, again, a mixed picture. Human resources – PhD graduates per million inhabitants – have converged with the European average, R&D expenditure and public funding have expanded in the first decade of the century, and the country still punches above its weight in terms of scientific outputs. However, signs of crisis have accumulated. Investment in science has begun diverging from the European average since 2009. Job insecurity in academia has increased, particularly among women. The impact of science made in Portugal is declining in relative terms, mostly through the inability to keep up with the much larger growth in other areas of the world. Islands of excellence and internationalization do exist. Science policy, however, lacks a clear long-term strategy and is unstable and politically cyclical. Furthermore, since the financial crisis, science has become chronically underfunded, even though there exists an ostensibly unanimous – but superficial – political and public acknowledgement of its significance.

Chapter 8, by curator and cultural studies scholar António Pinto Ribeiro, looks at the situation of artistic production. Today, cinema, theatre, and the visual and performing arts in Portugal provide a picture of great diversity and increasing cosmopolitanism and internationalization. This comes not only via the ability of Portuguese artists to establish themselves in the international scene but also via the role of Portugal – particularly its largest urban centres – as a hub for multiple cross-cultural exchanges. Pinto Ribeiro provides many examples of works and artists that represent this trend. At the same time, there are important challenges. The constraints on public funding for the arts mirrored, if not surpassed, those we previously discussed in relation to social policies, science, and education investment. Conversely, the population's low average wages and low (though rising) educational resources result in a limited audience for the arts. The challenge of scale stands out as a paramount concern.

In Chapter 9, literary scholar Helena Buescu addresses the main characteristics of Portuguese literary production in the last two decades. Immediately after democratization, the most notable examples of Portuguese literature involved self-questioning about the country and its identity in this now post-imperial and post-colonial setting. These themes remain important in many of the 21st-century novels discussed here. However, there is an increasing cosmopolitanism of Portuguese literature, which began to decidedly open itself to a much broader variety of themes, geographic contexts, and historical settings, from contemporary New York to a *Mitteleuropa* placed 'out of time'. This is also a period of consolidation of the female literary voice, as well as of increasing interaction between literature and other art forms, including theatre, cinema, and the visual arts. There are many diverse stops on this map provided by Buescu's chapter.

Finally, Chapter 10, by political scientists Isabel Camisão and Sandra Fernandes, places Portugal in the context of the European Union. In many respects, all previous chapters touch upon the different ways in which Portugal was transformed by increased political, economic, and even cultural integration in Europe. However, this 'Europeanization' is not completely unidirectional. Camisão and Fernandes show how, in spite of its relatively small size, Portugal has left its important imprint in several European policy areas: relations with Africa, the innovation and knowledge agenda, and maritime policy. They see climate change and the energetic transition as areas where the country can impact European policies in the future, reflecting the nation's strong record in renewable energy and its reputation as a trustworthy mediator.

12 *Patrícia Silva and Pedro C. Magalhães*

Note

1 Two months after the fall of the dictatorship, the Interministerial Commission was created, under the jurisdiction of the Prime Minister's Office, with the mission of coordinating the existing commissions of purges in different ministries (Pinto 2006). By February 1975, around 12,000 people had been removed or suspended from their previous jobs. The number is likely to have significantly increased by November 1975 when all forms of sanctions (including transfers and dismissals) are taken into account (Pinto 2008, 314). Furthermore, after Spínola's exile following the attempted coup of 11 March 1975, the purge movement was reinforced, also affecting those closest to Spínola (Nunes 2003, 118; Pinto 2000, 45). In fact, from that moment on, the purge process entered a second phase of radicalization, marked by frequent illegalities and which involved the removal of more than 20,000 people (Nunes 2003, 124–125).

References

Aguiar, Joaquim. 1985. "Partidos, estruturas patrimonialistas e poder funcional: A crise de legitimidade." *Análise Social* XXI, no. 87–89: 759–783.

Baer, Wolfgang, Dias, Daniel A., e Duarte, João B. 2013. "The economy of Portugal and the European Union: From high growth prospects to the debt crisis." *The Quarterly Review of Economics and Finance* 53, no. 4: 345–52.

Baklanoff, Eric N. 1996. "Breve experiência do socialismo em Portugal: o sector das empresas estatais." *Análise Social* 138, no. 4: 925–947.

Barreto, António. 1984. "Estado central e descentralização: antecedentes e evolução, 1974–84." *Análise Social* XX, no. 81–82: 191–218.

Barreto, António. 1994. "Portugal, a Europa e a democracia." *Análise Social* 29, no. 129: 1051–1069.

Corkill, David. 1993. *The Portuguese Economy Since 1974*. Edinburgh: Edinburgh University Press.

Corkill, David. 1999. *The Development of the Portuguese Economy: A Case of Europeanization*. London: Routledge.

De Giorgi, Enrico, and José Santana-Pereira. 2020. "The exceptional case of post-bailout Portugal: A comparative outlook." *South European Society and Politics* 25, no 2: 127–150.

Eurostat. 2020. Euro area unemployment at 8.3%. (available at https://ec.europa.eu/eurostat/documents/portlet_file_entry/2995521/3-01022021-AP-EN.pdf/db860f10-65e3-a1a6-e526-9d4db80904b9)

Fernandes, Jorge M., Pedro C. Magalhães, and José Santana-Pereira. 2018. "Portugal's leftist Government: From sick man to poster boy?." *South European Society and Politics* 23, no. 4: 503–524.

Gallagher, Tom. 1986. "Portugal's second decade of democracy." *The World Today*, 42 no.4, 67–69.

Garrido, António and Fernando Rosas, eds. 2012. *Corporativismo, Fascismos, Estado Novo*. Lisbon: Edições Almedina.

Graham, Lawrence. 1985. "Administração pública central e local: continuidade e mudança." *Análise Social* XXI, no. 87–89: 903–924.

Grzymala-Busse, Anna. 2003. "Political competition and the politicization of the state in East Central Europe." *Comparative Political Studies* 36, no. 10: 1123–1147.

Jalali, Carlos. 2007. *Partidos e Democracia em Portugal (1974–2005)*. Lisbon: Instituto de Ciências Sociais.

Jalali, Carlos, and Marco Lisi. 2009. "Weak societal roots, strong individual patrons? Patronage & party organization in Portugal." *Revista Enfoques: Ciencia Política y Administración Pública* 7, no. 11 : 443–472.

Lobo, Marina Costa. 1996. "A evolução do sistema partidário português à luz de mudanças económicas e políticas, 1976-1991." *Análise Social* XXXI, 139, no. 5: 1085 –1116.

Lobo, Marina Costa. 2000. "Governos partidários numa democracia recente: Portugal, 1976–1995." *Análise Social* XXXV, no. 154–155: 147–174.

Lobo, Marina Costa. 2005. *Governar em democracia*. Lisbon: Imprensa de Ciências Sociais.

Lobo, Marina Costa, Costa Pinto, Antóni and Pedro Magalhães. 2016. Portuguese democratisation 40 years on: its meaning and enduring legacies. *South European Society and Politics* 21, no. 2: 163–180.

Magone, José. 2003. *The Politics of Southern Europe*. London: Praeger Publishers.

Manuel, Paul Christopher. 1996. *The challenges of democratic consolidation in Portugal: political, economic, and military issues, 1976–1991*. Westport, CT: Praeger.

Marques, Pedro. 2015. "Why did the Portuguese economy stop converging with the OECD? Institutions, politics and innovation." *Journal of Economic Geography* 15, no. 5: 1009–1031.

Morlino, Leonardo. 1998. *Democracy Between Consolidation and Crisis: Parties, Groups and Citizens in Southern Europe*. Oxford: Oxford University Press.

Moury, Catherine, and Adam Standring. 2017. "Going beyond the troika: Power and discourse in Portuguese austerity politics." *European Journal of Political Research* 56, no. 3: 660–679.

Moury, Catherine, Elisabetta De Giorgi, and Pedro Pita Barros. 2021. "How to combine public spending with fiscal rigour? 'Austerity by stealth' in post-bailout Portugal (2015–2019)." In *The Exceptional Case of Post-Bailout Portugal*, edited by de Giorgi, Elisabetta, and José Santana-Pereira, 25–52. London: Routledge.

Nataf, Daniel, and Elizabeth Sammis. 1990. "Classes, Hegemony, and Portuguese Democratization." In *Transitions from Dictatorship to Democracy: Comparative Studies of Spain, Portugal and Greece*, edited by Ronald H. Chilcote, Stylianos Hadjiyannis, Fred A. III Lopez, Daniel Nataf and Elizabeth Sammis, 73–130. New York: Taylor and Francis.

Nunes, Ana Bela, Carlos Bastien, and Nuno Valério. 2005. "Nationalizations and de-nationalizations in Portugal (19th and 20th centuries): a historical assessment." GHES Working paper 22.

Nunes, Filipe. 2003. "Os directores-gerais: a elite administrativa portuguesa durante o XIV Governo Constitucional." In *Elites, Sociedade e Mudança Política*, edited by António C. Pinto e André Freire, 97–129. Oeiras: Celta.

Pintado, Vítor. 2002. *Structure and Growth of the Portuguese Economy*. Lisbon: Imprensa Ciências Sociais.

Pinto, António Costa. 2000. "O império do professor: Salazar e a elite ministerial do Estado Novo (1933–1945)." *Análise Social* XXXV, no. 157: 1055–1076.

Pinto, António Costa. 2006. "Authoritarian legacies, transitional justice and state crisis in Portugal's democratization." *Democratization* 13, no. 2: 173–204.

Pinto, António Costa. 2008. "Political purges and state crisis in Portugal's transition to democracy, 1975–76." *Journal of Contemporary History* 43, no. 2: 305–332.

Pinto, António Costa. 2020. "A elite ministerial da democracia portuguesa: Entre políticos e tecnocratas." In *45 Anos de Democracia em Portugal*, edited by Rui Branco and Tiago Fernandes, 143–161. Lisbon: Assembleia da República.

Pridham, Geoffrey. 1991. "The Politics of the European Community: Transnational Networks, and Democratic Transitions in Southern Europe." in *Encouraging Democracy: The Institutional Context of Regime Transition in Southern Europe*, edited by Geoffrey Pridham, 212–245. Leicester: Leicester University Press.

Royo, Sebastián. 2007. Lessons from the Integration of Spain and Portugal to the EU. PS: *Political Science & Politics* 40, no. 4: 689–693.

Schmitter, Philippe C. 1999. "The Democratization of Portugal in its Comparative Perspective." In *Portugal e a Transição para a Democracia*, edited by Fernando Rosas, 337–363. Lisbon: Colibri.

Shefter, Martin. 1994. *Political parties and the state: The American historical experience*. Princeton: Princeton University Press.

Teixeira, Nuno Severiano. 2002. "Introduction: Portugal and European Integration." In *The Europeanization of Portuguese Democracy*, edited by Nuno Severiano Teixeira and António Costa Pinto, 7–26. New York, Columbia University Press.

van Biezen, Ingrid. 1998. "Building party organisations and the relevance of past models: The communist and socialist parties in Spain and Portugal." *West European Politics* 21, no. 2: 32–62.

van Biezen, Ingrid. 2000. "Party financing in new democracies: Spain and Portugal." *Party politics* 6, no. 3: 329–342.

Vieira, Rui Jorge Oliveira. 2002. *Accounting and change in the financial services sector: the case of activity-based costing in a Portuguese bank*. Doctoral dissertation, University of Warwick.

Wiarda, Howard. 1987. "Portugal." In *Competitive Elections in Developing Countries*, edited by Weiner, Myron, and Ergun Özbudun, 283–326. Durham, NC: Duke University Press.

2 The nation

José Manuel Sobral

2.1 The medieval kingdom and the beginning of the nation-building process

An approach to the Portuguese nation implies that we combine an analysis of its past and its present. Nations are complex historical collectives. Their existence implies the widespread perception among their inhabitants of having a national identity, a collective sense of belonging, sharing most of the attributes that make it distinct from others (Guibernau 2007, 11). We could conceive of national identity as comprising several dimensions, such as the psychological, linked to the feeling of belonging to a group of like-minded people; the cultural, linked to the sharing of myths and symbols and, in most cases, a language; the historical, implying the selective construction of a past and of mythical ancestors; a territory, the homeland, to which it is linked materially and emotionally and which is a reference of social life and memory. And it implies a political dimension, of loyalty to the group (Guibernau 2013, 125–128). This implies neither that it is fixed or immutable nor that such attributes are shared equally by all (Crosby 2021, 2–3). National collectives are differentiated and permeated by conflict, notably around interpretations of the nation and its history (Hutchinson 2005).

The acquisition of the attributes of national identity is the product of historical processes. It is not an easy task trying to reconstruct a genealogy of the nation in a few pages. Thus, in this text, stripped of any pretension to exhaustiveness, we will limit ourselves to offer, on the one hand, a synthesis of the formation of the Portuguese nation and identity, and on the other, to look at some of its manifestations in the present, addressing dominant perceptions of Portuguese national identity, its relation to European identity, and recent tensions and conflicts around a central element, the representations of its history.

In the case of Portugal, the formation of the nation dates back to the struggles between Christians and Muslims for control of the Iberian Peninsula in the medieval period. In the 12th century, a prince issued from the Castilian-Leonese royal family, Afonso Henriques, heir to a county in the west of the peninsula, the *Condado Portucalense*, succeeded in expanding its territory by conquering Muslim-dominated territories to the south, asserting his autonomy and being recognized as king. The consolidation of the new state would continue under his successors, who expanded its territory up to its southernmost part, the Algarve. The borders of the medieval state at the close of the 13th century remained almost the same as they are today, which shows enormous territorial stability.

There are several processes at play – political-legal, economic, social, cultural, mythical-symbolic – in the construction of the Portuguese nation. On the political level, it is worth noting the growing assertion of royal power through legislation, the appointment of magistrates, the exercise of judicial power, as well as administrative action. The new

DOI: 10.4324/9781003488033-2

This chapter has been made available under a CC-BY-NC-ND license.

kingdom also comes into existence in economic terms with the formation of an internal space with its fairs and markets. It uses its own currency featuring the royal arms, symbols that would endure throughout the ages in Portuguese national symbology until the present. And within its territorial boundaries, a Portuguese national social space is slowly taking shape.

The new state soon acquired a name, Portugal, and a language, the Portuguese, which evolved from the language spoken in the Christian peninsular west, Galician-Portuguese. It became the official language of the new state since the late 13th century. In this way, some of the constitutive elements of a national identity were gathered in this period (Guibernau 2007, 11). We do not know, however, the pace of their diffusion in the process of national identification. The formation of the Portuguese nation as a multi-secular historical process is something recognized by the Portuguese historiography that has dealt specifically with the subject, although in different ways (Albuquerque 1974; Mattoso 1985; Sobral 2003). For historian José Mattoso, focusing on the medieval period, the "national consciousness" – in his understanding, an identification with the kingdom – already exists (still very incipient) at the beginning of the 14th century, making itself felt within a minority linked to the political power, from which it disseminated (Mattoso 1985 II, 211–212).

We must attribute an important role in this dissemination to the actions over time of the various state agencies, the church, and the literate people associated with them. But also, to the role played by the simple fact of coexisting daily along time with other similar people, since national belonging is a territorially based social relationship, of a certain type of "we" (Crosby 2021, 1) imbedded in other networks such as those of kinship, neighbourhood, and locality. And to that one should add the role of dramatic events, such as conflicts, which play a crucial role in the production and consolidation of national identities (Bloom 1990). We must also consider that continuity over time of a given relational core is fundamental to national identities, as is differentiation from others (Guibernau 1996), since all collective identities are based on the distinction between "us" and the "others" (Eisenstadt and Giesen 1975, 74–76; Hewer and Lyons 2018, 95–96).

At the end of the 14th century, a very important conflict took place, triggered by the fact that the only daughter of the late Portuguese King Ferdinand was married to the king of Castile. If she inherited the throne, Portugal could be absorbed by its more powerful neighbour, Castile. This dispute offers a rare occasion for observing the behaviour of popular groups, even if one considers that the information comes from a Portuguese source that was an adversary of Castile (Sobral 2012). On the side of the Queen of Castile, we find most of the great nobility; on the other side, second sons of this group, nobles of lesser status, and non-noble people from a wide social spectrum, ranging from local officers to bourgeois, tradesmen, journeymen, and peasants. The head figure of this faction was a natural brother of the late King, the future King John I. Information about the conflict attributed to this last group's attitudes and perceptions of hatred and resentment towards everything appearing to be Castilian or connected to them, expressed in violent actions and debasing group stereotypes (Albuquerque 1974, 226–228). These can be understood as manifestations of the existence of a consciousness of a Portuguese collective *us* opposed to a Castilian-foreigner *them*.

After this conflict there were repeated mentions to the so-called miracle of Ourique, that claimed that Christ appeared on the cross to the first Portuguese king on the eve of the mythical battle of the same name against Islam. In memory of this, the king would

16 José Manuel Sobral

have added specific symbols to the flag, such as the cross arranged in five shields (*quinas*) – as many as the legendary Moorish kings defeated at the battle – and, on these, the representation of the monies for which Christ would have been sold. The myth, only openly questioned from the 19th century on, as well as other subsequent representations, points to a special relationship between Portugal and Christianity, and to the Portuguese as the "chosen people" for the Christianization of the world (Albuquerque 1974, 340–358). This is a topic existing in other nationalisms as well (Smith 2003), that was still reproduced in the times of the authoritarian nationalist New State (*Estado Novo*) (1933–1974) in Portugal (Sobral 2010, 135), which claimed the existence of an essential link between the nation and Catholicism.

2.2 Empire and its persistent impact

With John I and the new dynasty of Avis, the construction of the Portuguese empire begins in the 15th century. The empire will endure, with varying configurations, over several centuries. It was an empire based on trade – from spices to slave trade – on plantations and extractivism in general. This was also the time of an enforced homogenization of the Portuguese population: the kingdom defines itself as exclusively Christian, forcibly converting, repressing, and expelling Jews and Moors at the close of the 15th century. The gypsies would also be persecuted, being only admitted as national citizens with the advent of liberalism in the 19th century.

The empire is of crucial importance to Portugal, not only in economic but also in political, symbolic, and social terms. One cannot understand the recovery of the Portuguese state's autonomy in the 17th century, after being unified with the Spanish crown in 1580 – a conflict in which, once again, there was a clash with the Castilian-Spanish power – without taking this imperial dimension into account. Empire and its resources, those of Brazil in particular, directly influenced the course of the events (Sobral 2012, 43–56). The Brazilian independence in 1822 meant the loss of the main part of empire, and a feeling of loss and decadence became widespread among the Portuguese political and cultural elites. But representations of the past greatness would permeate attempts for national revival, that included the building of a new empire in Africa from the second half of the 19th century onwards.

The very different and opposed regimes of the liberal first Republic (1910–1926) and the authoritarian New State (*Estado Novo*, 1933–74) inherited, developed, and defended this old imperial legacy in the 20th century. Facing the demands for decolonization, and the rise of African nationalisms, the latter regime spread the image of Portugal as a unique pluricontinental and multiracial nation, and denied the existence of racism, a structural feature of all colonialisms. That authoritarian regime perished for not accepting the demands for independence of the Portuguese colonies, sustaining a prolonged colonial war in its defence. It was the last legatee, in symbolic-ideological terms, of an official nationalist narrative that, since the 16th century, proclaimed the age of sea voyages and the construction of the Empire as the greatest moment in Portuguese history, its Golden Age (Smith 1996).

It is also during the imperial period that important pieces of the process of building a national identity appear, such as grammars dedicated to the Portuguese language – and extolling it – or histories of Portugal. In these, the Lusitanians, a peninsular people famed for the resistance offered to the Roman conquerors, featured as being the ethnic ancestors of the Portuguese. Printed at the end of the 16th century, and glorifying the Portuguese,

The epic poem *Os Lusíadas* soon became an enduring influential piece among representations of Portuguese national history (Sobral 2003, 1117–1118).

In social terms, the imperial period saw the beginning of emigration, a movement which led the Portuguese to various continents, and which continues today in radically different circumstances. Portugal is the European Union country with the highest number of emigrants in proportion to its population: a little over 20% (ACM n.d.). Thus, Portuguese are not only those who live in Portugal but also those who live outside the country and continue, like other diasporas, particularly in the first generations, to maintain multidimensional relations with Portugal and the other Portuguese. And some identification with Portugal persists among groups who claim a distant ancestry or connections in territories that were under Portuguese rule, such as Malacca or Goa. Successes in a tournament with clear nationalist connotations, such as the European soccer tournament in 2016, were celebrated in Portugal, among the Portuguese diaspora and in former Portuguese colonies (Jornal de Negócios 2016; Lusa 2016; MP/SB 2016).

Also rooted in the imperial reality are facts such as the generalization of the Portuguese language as an official language of several states other than Portugal, or the various creoles in which elements of the Portuguese language are inserted. The reference to language is a central element in the construction of the Community of Portuguese Language Countries (CPLP). The recent transformation of Portugal from an almost exclusively emigrant-producing country to an immigrant-receiving country is also partly a product of this history, since several of the main flows come from Brazil – by far the dominant nationality – and former Portuguese colonies, while the presence of Europeans is largely due to Portugal's recent integration into the European Union (Estrela 2021).

2.3 State, official nationalism, and banal nationalism in the reproduction of national identity

From the medieval kingdom to the present, the State played a decisive role in shaping national identity in Portugal, and this action intensified over time. The action of State agencies (and of literate elites often in their close dependence), geographical descriptions, population records and other social, economic, and juridical registers, historical narratives, literature, and the press: these were among the main instruments that made it possible to imagine the nation (Anderson 1983). In the first centuries of Portuguese history, this action was limited, since the overwhelming majority, being illiterate, could not directly access the written contents, although there was an important circulation of these mediated by oral communication, for example through religious preaching. Then, with the emergence of the printing press and its growing impact, through schooling and military service, it was possible to operate a more intense national socialization of the population. This was mostly achieved during the 19th and 20th centuries, during the liberal-monarchical regime (1834–1910) and the short-lived parliamentarian and intensively nationalist First Republic (1910–1926). Both shared an explicit cult of the nation, the extolling of its history and cultural specificities (Ramos 1994; Leal 2010; Sobral 2003). The spread of political and cultural nationalist ideologies of the 19th and 20th centuries further contributed to the strengthening of national identification.

These processes of "nationalization of the masses" (Mosse 1975) reached a culminating moment with the authoritarian regime of the *Estado Novo*, which was able to avail itself of the new means of cinema, radio, and television. It amplified the ritualization of national history that already came from the 19th century, exemplified by the

18   José Manuel Sobral

Exposition of the Portuguese World in 1940, explicitly dedicated to the commemoration of the centenary of the Portuguese independence and its restoration in the 17th century (Catroga 1996), and the nationalization of the public space through toponymy and monuments. The Exposition took place in the Belém area in Lisbon, where the Tower of the same name and the Jerónimos Monastery are located, infusing that area with nationalist meaning. This area remains today the main destination for visits to monuments by the Portuguese (Machado Pais, Magalhães and Lobo-Antunes 2022, 8).

However, the experience of national belonging is not merely a product of the socializing action of the State and the nationalist elites, who build the official nationalism, it is also based on daily living in a social universe identified as a nation and in the belief of people that they form a specific bounded "we". In this way, the national identification is naturalized by the routines of banal nationalism (Billig 1995), which involve the simple use of the national language, cooking and eating food identified as national (Sobral 2019), or cheering Portuguese sports teams, athletes, or teams. In short, through activities that do not even imply a conscious and thoughtful identification that this is something endowed with a national meaning (Edensor 2002, 28).

2.4 Recent expressions of national identification in Portugal

The Portuguese economy and society have changed profoundly since the advent of democracy in 1974, the end of the colonial regime in 1975, and the country's insertion in the European Union in 1986. Also, the democratic regime allowed the possibility of acquiring an in-depth knowledge of its inhabitants' ideas on society and politics, something impossible to achieve in the context of an authoritarian state, where that was deemed a major political risk.

Unlike what happened in the past, in which our sources for approaching the national reality are predominantly marked by their relationship with power and literate elites, today we can access the self-representations that the Portuguese have of Portugal and its history in more direct ways, far from that kind of biases. One of these ways is provided by surveys. Some of these also have the advantage of allowing the comparison of the Portuguese case with others.

In a recent edition of *Eurobarometer*, dedicated to a study of the values and identities of Europeans, Portuguese respondents were, among the citizens of the Union, those who attributed the highest score to their identification with nationality (93%, adding "strongly identifies" to "tends to identify"; the average for the EU countries is 73%). It is also worth stressing that such a strong identification with the nation is clearly higher than the identification with being European – Portugal average, 59%, European average, 56% – and almost coincides with the identification with their region (88%), in which case they are clearly above the European average (69%) (European Commission 2021).

These data are in line with what has been revealed in other studies such as the *European Social Survey* about the high degree of stability of the national identification of the Portuguese, among the highest in European countries (Sobral and Vala 2022). It should be noted that the fact that the Portuguese are, relatively speaking, the main country of emigrants in the European Union, and that some of their main destinations are countries belonging to this community, did not translate, for the Portuguese living in Portugal who responded to this survey, in a particularly relevant identification with being European.

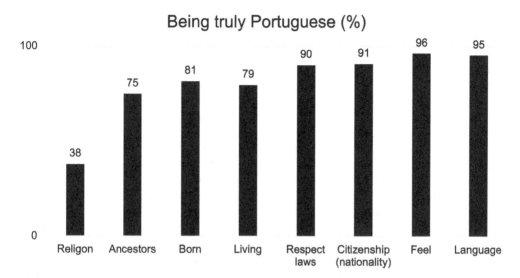

Figure 2.1 Being truly Portuguese (% responses "Very important" + "Important")

National identity is usually something unquestioned – something implicit – and taken as natural as breathing itself, and we cannot assume that its contents are something fixed, let alone shared homogeneously by all of them (McCrone and Bechhofer 2015, 52–53). However, it has been pointed out that there are several criteria or markers cited recurrently as its components – such as the place where one was born, the language one speaks, one's ancestors, and one's place of residence (Idem: 29). These markers are part of a larger range of attributes through which national identities were sought to be characterized in the *International Social Survey Programme* (ISSP 2013) (Figure 2.1).

The importance conferred upon language should come as no surprise, since it is seen as a marker of national identity everywhere (Edwards 2001), even when it is not exclusive to a single nation, as is the case with English, Spanish, French, or Portuguese, for example, which was adopted, through circumstances of history by nations other than those in which they first emerged. Language not only allows us to operate an immediate distinction between its speakers and others but also establishes continuity between the generations that reproduce it in the present and those of the past. In addition to its pragmatic dimensions as a system of communication, language is associated with emotional dimensions linked to the structuring role it plays in social life, socialization, and memory. If we add to this the importance the state itself confers to language teaching and its value as a pillar of national identity, we can well understand the importance given to it by respondents. High importance is also given to "feeling", which shows the emotional tone that is associated with national identification (Smith 1996).

Attributes such as citizenship and respecting the laws are also held to be very important and are derived from legal-political norms. Citizenship – or nationality – may not be original, that is, it may not come from being descended from Portuguese people, nor from being born on Portuguese soil – the criteria of *jus sanguinis* (blood law) and *jus soli* (soil law) – but derived, that is, acquired. Respect for the laws is something that relates to the behaviour of the individual, not something independent of the will of the subjects such as having ancestors, being born in a certain place, or even having one's own language.

National belonging entails both material elements – being a national citizen confers political, economic, and social rights – and emotional ones: belonging to a nation allows one to belong to a broader community than those formed by family, kin, friends, or working colleagues (McCrone and Bechhoffer 2015, 196). Having a Portuguese ancestry is an important attribute for many, which is not surprising, as nations are represented in the image of families, with multiple generations (Zerubavel 2012). The claim of an ancient and prestigious ancestry is something recurrent in nationalist manifestations – as it happens with other peoples, there is an old belief of the Portuguese having the Lusitanians as mythical ancestors, as already noted. It should be noted that this survey shows less relative weight given to this attribute, which potentially tends to exclude from the collective anyone who is not a descendant, compared to that represented by citizenship, which is more inclusive.

The low weight given to religion may reflect the decreasing importance of the dominant Catholic religiosity for the Portuguese (Teixeira 2012), reflecting perhaps a more global trend of decline of religion (Inglehart 2020). In any case, it marks a rupture not only with recent representations disseminated by the *Estado Novo*, in which Catholicism appeared as a vector of the official image of national identity, but also with previous representations, which associated Portugal with Christianity since its medieval matrix was forged in the context of the Peninsular confrontation between Christianity and Islam (Figure 2.2).

The data on the various dimensions of an emotion such as "national pride" are very interesting when one tries to analyse the various elements associated with identification today. One can see a huge asymmetry between the value conferred to history, literature, and the arts, or to science and technology or sports, and the judgements marked by

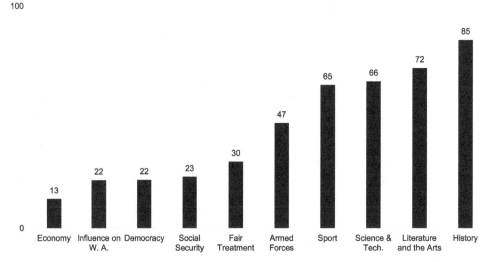

Figure 2.2 Sources of pride in being Portuguese (%response "Very important" + "Important")

The nation 21

negativity attributed to the economy or democracy, for example, while the armed forces occupy an intermediate position. It must be said that we must ponder in these hierarchizations the impact of old representations of the Portuguese economy and society, seen as defective, combined with other, more recent ones, which have reinforced them – while other dimensions seem linked to very different dynamics. Indeed, we cannot separate the low valuation of the economy or the country's influence, democracy, or unfair treatment, from the possible influence of old and persistent negative images of the country's decadence, as already signalled, spread among the intellectuals and in the media (Serrão 1990). The perception of the distance that separates Portugal from countries deemed more advanced fuels those enduring images.

Recent crises, which showed the continued dependence of the country on external decision centres – notorious at the time of the intervention of the Troika made up of the International Monetary Fund, the European Central Bank, and the European Commission (2011–2014) – will have probably accentuated these perceptions, which constitute a negative judgment of the state of the country in economic, political, and social terms. At the other pole, we find very different results, with the great weight given to sports fuelled by some triumphs in soccer – the most recent, the victory in the 2022 Futsal World Cup. Or the pride manifested in science and technology, a reflection of the investment made in this sector and its visibility in the media in recent times.

As for the pride manifested in literature and the arts, there seems to be some continuity between past and present – particularly if we are referring specifically to literature. Here we can go back to the celebration of the poet Camões, which was greatly intensified in the 19th century, when *Os Lusíadas* was enshrined in the nationalist context of the time as the major narrative of Portuguese history, and he was made an exemplary symbol of being Portuguese. The nationalist extolling of literary figures from the past has contributed to a national self-image of excellence in this field, reinforced by the importance given by the international recognition of figures like Fernando Pessoa, José Saramago, or António Lobo Antunes. Other media-recognized figures, from painting – such as Paula Rego – to architecture – Siza Vieira, Souto Moura – may also have contributed to this frankly positive image of the sector, the same happening in sports, with world-famous footballers like Eusébio or Cristiano Ronaldo.

However, nothing compares to the pride shown by the Portuguese in their history, which is among the highest among the countries in this type of survey (Sobral 2010). A very old pride in a history deemed exceptional of which *Os Lusíadas* is a major expression. We must take into consideration that the past is a component of identity formation, personal or collective (Hewer 2018, 209–211). As a collective, the Portuguese acquired through mnemonic socialization (Zerubavel 1996) – operating through narratives, monuments, the architecture of certain spaces – a very exalting idea of their history, which seems to remain stable while the state and society in Portugal underwent profound changes.

2.5 Confrontations in a time of change

The establishment of democracy in 1974, decolonization in 1975, and integration into the European Union in 1986, represented crucial changes in the configuration of the country. The independence of the former colonies marked a complete rupture with old conceptions of Portuguese identity as pluricontinental, which had been sustained by the *Estado Novo*, but which predated it by a long way – the Constitution of 1822, the first

22 José Manuel Sobral

Portuguese constitutional text, already defined the "Portuguese Nation as the union of Portuguese residents in both hemispheres" (article 20, Title II). Excluded from citizenship were all slaves, a fundamental part of the population of the territories under Portuguese rule (Constituição de 1822).

However, the break with the centuries-old colonial past did not imply the abandonment of a narrative centred on the maritime expansion, but rather adaptations and reconfigurations. Sites and buildings located in spaces that had been erected to build an official memory linked to these achievements were used to symbolically mark new national policies noticeably different from previous ones. The 1998 Expo, the most important intervention in a Portuguese urban space and a marker of the desired cosmopolitan modernity, opposed to the nation-centred view of the *Estado Novo*, took place in a riverside area of the Tagus, under the aegis of a celebration of the Portuguese discoveries, as it coincided with the Fifth Centennial of Vasco da Gama's arrival in the Indian subcontinent in 1498. The Cultural Center of Belém was built as a monument to the desired European condition in an emblematic area, already strongly infused with a nationalistic meaning by the *Estado Novo*, as said before. And the temple of Jerónimos, built to glorify the dynasty of Avis and the overseas expansion, was the place chosen to sign Portugal's accession to the European Economic Community, future European Union, in 1985. Under the sign of a symbolic historical continuity between past and present, the affirmation of a new path for the Portuguese state and society was underlined.

The persistence in the present of narratives, sites, and monuments erected by the *Estado Novo*, infused with past nationalist symbolism, has been a source of contestation. This is not a specifically Portuguese phenomenon but also echoes political-ideological conflicts on an international scale, such as those concerning monuments to figures in the United Kingdom, the United States, Belgium, the Netherlands, and France, among other countries, associated with slavery and the defence of white superiority. The *Padrão dos Descobrimentos*, an unequivocal celebration of what has been secularly claimed by the Portuguese as their greatest achievement, has been the object of controversy between those in favour of its demolition and those who favour its preservation (Simões 2021). This controversy continues when it is used to disseminate critical knowledge about African slavery, one of the pillars of the colonial endeavour, and about the Portuguese role in it (Sá 2021a). This is just one sign – one could speak of others, such as the botanical representation of the old political-administrative symbolism linked to the colonial State in the Praça do Império (Sá 2021b) – of the conflict between apologists of old narratives of national identity, renewed and consolidated under the *Estado Novo*, and those who postulate attitudes of critical and even iconoclastic rupture with them. Without, of course, reducing the space of the polemic to these polarized positions.

This type of open confrontation has many sources, one of them being claims of descendants from the former colonized. But is also the result of living in a democratic regime, which allows for the conflict of opinions and for the criticism of official narratives, starting in academia, that the *Estado Novo* prohibited. At the time, the navigations were exalted, and a vision of the Portuguese as being unique among the colonizers in the tropics as they were non-racist was widespread by the propaganda (Sobral 2010). Enslavement and racism were taboo, as shown by the banning of a work on race relations by an outstanding historian of the Portuguese empire, who questioned the non-racism of the Portuguese (Boxer 1963). After the end of the regime, it became possible to openly question the official rhetoric and this confrontation became more recently very public. It has found expression in polemics such as the ones mentioned above, or through artistic interventions, such as the installation and performance of a play, "O Barco" (The Boat), a metaphorical representation of the slave trade (Coelho 2021). And, although they are somehow less visible than these recent polemics, we must ponder the impact over time of the historical analytical approaches to the past developed under the democratic regime, which have drawn attention to formerly hidden dimensions of the official Portuguese national narrative, such as colonialism, slavery, and racism.

Sharing a national identity does not imply any consensus regarding its definition. As pointed out at the beginning, nations are "zones of conflict", and representations of the past are the stage for clashes over definitions of a collective "we". "Cultural wars" are not new (Hutchinson 2004, 7–113). It suffices to remember the conflict that opposed, in the first Republic (1910–1926), many republican Portuguese, who saw religion a main factor of national decay, and all those who looked at the country as being essentially Catholic. In the case of Portugal, as in the case of other national collectives, the past is inseparable from the present and its conflicts and of the projects for the future.

As was recently pointed out, historical narratives lie at the heart of memory and national identities. They are characterized by the selective and apologetic way in which they represent the national past, and, being inculcated from an early age, they become resistant to change (Wertsch 2021). It remains to be seen what effects the ongoing critical questioning we mentioned will have on the dominant historical representation of the Portuguese national past.

References

ACM, Alto Comissariado para as Migrações. nd. *Saber mais sobre as migrações portuguesas*, retrieved on 28.2.2022 from: https://www.acm.gov.pt/-/saber-mais-sobre-as-migracoes -portuguesas

Albuquerque, Martim. 1974. *A Consciência Nacional Portuguesa*. Lisboa: Edição do Autor.

Anderson, Benedict. 1983. *Imagined Communities: Reflections on the Origins and Spread of Nationalism*. London: Verso.

Billig, Michael. 1995. *Banal Nationalism*. London: Sage.

Bloom, William. 1990. *Personal Identity, National Identity and International Relations*. Cambridge: Cambridge University Press.

Boxer, Charles Ralph. 1963. *Race Relations in the Portuguese Colonial Empire, 1415–1825*. London: Oxford University Press.

Catroga, Fernando. 1996. "Ritualizações da História". In *História da História em Portugal nos Séculos XIX e XX*, edited by Fernando Catroga, José Maria Amado Mendes and Luís Reis Torgal, 221–361. Lisboa: Círculo de Leitores.

Coelho, Paulino. 2021. "'O Barco' de Grada Kilomba é uma metáfora para 'produzir nova memória da escravatura'". *Agência Lusa*, Sep, 3, 2021. Retrieved on 28.2.2022 from: https://www.lusa.pt/culture/article/2021-09-03/34251648/-o-barco-de-grada-kilomba -é-uma-metáfora-para-produzir-nova-memória-da-escravatura

Constituição de 1822. Retrieved on 28.2.2022 from: https://www.fd.unl.pt/Anexos/Investigacao /7511.pdf

Crosby, Steven. 2021. *Nations and Nationalism in World History*. Oxford: Oxford University Press.

Edensor, Tim. 2002. *National Identity, Popular Culture and Everyday Life*. Oxford: Berg.

Edwards, John. 2001. "Language and Nation". In *Encyclopaedia of Nationalism*, edited by Athena S. Leoussi, pp. 169–173. New Brunswick (U.S.A.) and London (U.K.): Transaction Publishers.

Eisenstadt, Shmuel Noah, and Bernhard Giesen. 1995. "The construction of collective Identity". *European Journal of Sociology* 36 (1): 72–102. doi: doi.org/10.1017/S0003975600007116.

Estrela, Joaquim, ed. 2021. *SEF, Relatório de Imigração, Fronteiras e Asilo, 2020*. Oeiras: Serviço de Estrangeiros e Fronteiras. Retrieved on 28.2.2022 from: https://sefstat.sef.pt/Docs/Rifa2020 .pdf

European Comission. 2021. *Special Barometer 508. Summary. Values and Identities of EU Citizens*. Retrieved on 28.2.2022 from: https://publications.jrc.ec.europa.eu/repository/handle/JRC126943

Guibernau, Montserrat. 1996. *Nationalisms: The Nation-State and Nationalism in the Twentieth Century*. Cambridge: Polity Press.

Guibernau, Montserrat. 2007. *The Identity of Nations*. Cambridge: Polity Press.

Guibernau, Montserrat. 2013. *Belonging: Solidarity and Division in Modern Societies*. Cambridge: Polity Press.

Hewer, Cristopher J. and Evanthia Lyons. 2018. "Identity". In *Political Psychology: A Social Psychology Approach*, edited by Cristopher J. Hewer and Evanthia Lyons, 93–113. Hoboken, NJ: Wiley.

Hutchinson, John. 2004. *Nations as Zones of Conflict*. London: Sage.

Inglehart, Ronald F. 2020. "Giving up on God: The Global Decline of Religion". *Foreign Affairs* 99 (5): 110–118.

ISSP, International Social Survey Programme. (2013). *National Identity III*. Retrieved on 28.2.2022 http://www.issp.org/data-download/by-year/

Jornal de Negócios. 2016. "De Paris ao Marquês, foi assim que os portugueses celebraram o título". *Jornal de Negócios*, Nov 11, 2016 Retrieved on 28.2.2022 from: https://www.jornaldenegocios.pt/empresas/desporto/detalhe/fotogaleria___de_paris_ao_marques_foi_assim_que_os_portugueses_celebraram_o_titulo

Leal, João. 2000. *Etnografias Portuguesas (1870-1970): Cultura Popular e Identidade Nacional*, Lisboa: Publicações Dom Quixote.

Lusa. 2016. "Malaca gritou "sou português, sou campeão" já ao nascer do dia". *Record, 11-07-2016*. Retrieved on 28.2.2022 from: https://www.record.pt/internacional/competicoes-de-selecoes/europeu/euro-2016/detalhe/malaca-gritou-sou-portugues-sou-campeao-ja-ao-nascer-do-dia)

Machado-Pais, José, Pedro Magalhães, and Miguel Lobo-Antunes, eds. 2022. *Inquérito às Práticas Culturais dos Portugueses 2020*. Lisboa: ICS.

Mattoso, José. 1985. *Identificação de Um País: Ensaio sobre as Origens de Portugal, vol. II, Composição*. Lisboa: Editorial Estampa.

McCrone, David and Frank Bechhofer. 2015. *Understanding National Identity*. Cambridge: Cambridge University Press.

Mosse, Georg L. 1975. *The Nationalization of the Masses: Political Symbolism and Mass Movements in Germany from the Napoleonic Wars through the Third Reich*. Ithaca e London: Cornell University Press.

MP/SB. 2016. "Entusiasmo com Portugal percorre a Ásia em 'fenómeno incrível' 'inexplicável'". *Agência Lusa*, Jul 10, 2016. Retrieved on 28.2.2022 from: _https://24.sapo.pt/noticias/internacional/artigo/entusiasmo-com-portugal-percorre-a-asia-em-fenomeno-incrivel-e-inexplicavel_20982828.htmlMP/SB. 2016

Ramos, Rui. 1994. *A Segunda Fundação (1890–1926)*. Lisboa: Círculo de Leitores.

Sá, Paula. 2021a. "Carta aberta contra filme sobre racismo no Padrão dos Descobrimentos. 'É um insulto'". *Diário de Notícias*, Oct 1, 2021. Retrieved on 28.2.2022 from: https://www.dn.pt/sociedade/carta-aberta-contra-filme-sobre-racismo-no-padrao-dos-descobrimentos-e-um-insulto-14181337.html

Sá, Paula. 2021b. "Deixem-me arranjar a Praça e depois logo se vê", diz Sá Fernandes. *Diário de Notícias, Feb 16, 2021*. Retrieved on 28.2.2022 from: https://www.dn.pt/local/deixem-me-arranjar-a-praca-e-depois-logo-se-ve-diz-sa-fernandes-13355121.html

Serrão, Joel. 1990. "Decadência". In *Dicionário de História de Portugal, III*, edited by Joel Serrão, 270–274. Porto: Livraria Figueirinhas.

Simões, Ascenso. 2021. "O Salazarismo não morreu". *O Público*, Feb 19, 2021. Retrieved on 28.2.2022 from: https://www.publico.pt/2021/02/19/opiniao/opiniao/salazarismo-nao-morreu-1951297

Smith, Anthony D. 1996. "LSE Centennial Lecture: The Resurgence of Nationalism? Myth and Memory in the Renewal of Nations". *The British Journal of Sociology* 47 (4): 575–598. https://doi.org/10.2307/591074

Smith, Anthony D. 2003. *Chosen Peoples: Sacred Sources of National Identity*. Oxford: Oxford University Press.

Sobral, José Manuel. 2003. "A Formação das Nações e o Nacionalismo: os Paradigmas Interpretativos e o Caso Português". *Análise Social* 37 (165): 1093–1126. http://www.jstor.org/stable/41011752

Sobral, José Manuel. 2010. "Dimensões Étnicas e Cívicas e Glorificação do Passado em Representações da Identidade Nacional Portuguesa". In *Identidade Nacional, Inclusão e Exclusão Social,* edited by José Manuel Sobral and Jorge Vala, 81–110. Lisboa: Imprensa de Ciências Sociais.

Sobral, José Manuel. 2010. "Representações Portuguesas e Brasileiras da Identidade Nacional Portuguesa no Século XX". *Revista de Ciências Sociais* 41 (2): 125–139.

Sobral, José Manuel. 2012. *Portugal, Portugueses: uma Identidade Nacional.* Lisboa: Fundação Francisco Manuel dos Santos.

Sobral, José Manuel. 2019. "Salt Cod and the Making of a Portuguese National Cuisine". In *The Emergence of National Food: The Dynamics of Food and Nationalism,* edited by Atsuko Ichijo, Venetia Johannes and Ronald Ranta, 17–27. London: Bloomsbury.

Sobral, José, and Jorge Vala. 2022. "Portuguese National Identity: Historical Constructions and Contemporary Expressions". In *The Oxford Handbook of Portuguese Politics,* edited by António Costa Pinto, Pedro Magalhães and Jorge M. Fernandes, 227–243. Oxford: Oxford University Press.

Teixeira, Alfredo, ed. 2012. *Identidades Religiosas em Portugal: Representações, Valores e Práticas.* Lisboa: CESOP-Universidade Católica Portuguesa.

Wertsch, James V. 2021. *How Nations Remember: A Narrative Approach.* Oxford: Oxford University Press.

Zerubavel, Eviatar. 1996. "Social memories: Steps to a Sociology of the Past". *Qualitative Sociology* 19: 283–299. https://doi.org/10.1007/BF02393273

Zerubavel, Eviatar. 2012. *Ancestors and Relatives: Genealogy, Identity and Community.* Oxford: Oxford University Press.

3 The welfare state

Rui Branco and Pedro Adão e Silva

3.1 Introduction

The consolidation of the Portuguese democracy rested on the mutual implication between democratic politics, social citizenship, and integration in the European community. The welfare state came to embody a substantive democratic citizenship based on the provision of social and economic rights, legitimized by the normative aspiration to be a part of the 'European social model'. In the aftermath of the revolutionary period of 1974 to 1976, the simultaneous transition to a pluralist democracy and welfare capitalism, which combined political democratization with the expansion of social protection and economic liberalization, followed a path that has been described as 'social democratic' (Pereira and Przeworski 1993).

The evolving architecture of the welfare state over the democratic period brings together diverse protection principles and political logics. Whereas the new National Health Service (NHS) is the result of a deep institutional reorientation in a social-democratic (or Beveridgian) direction, the same cannot be said of the financially burdensome social security system, which kept the Bismarckian, occupational design, carried over from the authoritarian period. Since the 1990s, demographic ageing and the 'new social risks' associated with the changes wrought by the employment patterns typical of a post-industrial society have intensified the tensions within this hybrid construct. Over time, the main expenditure items, the NHS and the pension system, along with the sphere of labour market regulation, have sustained a constant pressure to reform originated from European integration and the financial markets.

This chapter studies the transformation of social policies in the early decades of the 21st century under the European linkage, understood in terms of a constraint but also capabilities inherent in the process of Europeanization, membership in the EMU/ Eurozone and the insertion in international financial and debt markets. This linkage conveys no overriding single, homogeneous, and constant policy direction. Rather, the valence of the European link has changed direction and scope over time, as governments and domestic actors jostle to shape the content of social policies by mobilizing European material, institutional, and cognitive resources.

The next section presents the theoretical and analytical framework. Then follow three empirical sections dedicated to the reform of social policies over different time periods. The first looks at the period ranging from accession to the Economic and Monetary Union (EMU) in 1992, through joining the euro zone, up until the sovereign debt crisis in 2010. The second deals with the Great Recession in which social policy reforms were carried out under external conditionality by a centre-right coalition to bring about internal

DOI: 10.4324/9781003488033-3

This chapter has been made available under a CC-BY-NC-ND license.

devaluation, from 2011 to 2015. Finally, we shall look at the post-Troika period, in which external pressures wane and a centre-left government with the parliamentary support from the radical left takes office, only to break down by the end of 2021, giving way, after the 2022 snap elections, to a centre-left, single-party majority government. The conclusion reiterates the main empirical findings and discusses the significance of the recent 'social turn' in European governance.

3.2 Social policies and the European *Vincolo Esterno*: modes and mechanisms

European integration followed from the start the institutional settlement 'Keynes at home and Smith abroad' (Gilpin 1987, 355), leaving 'market-making to the EC, market correcting to the member states' (Ferrera 2005, 113). The Treaty of Rome gave social policy more of a productive role, that is, one geared to easing the integration of product and labour markets by harmonizing the terms of competition and removing hurdles to the 'four freedoms'. The social policy function of protecting against, or compensating for, the social risks typical of the industrial economy (old age, unemployment, and sickness) and market-based inequalities was the charge of member states. However, the route followed by European integration since Maastricht, the EMU and Stability and Growth Pact's rules, step by step brought more and more social policies under the remit of the European shadow.

European social policy became ever more important to the reform of *national* welfare states, through European primary law mechanisms as well as the adoption of modes of governance, such as the open method of coordination, relying on benchmarking through 'diffusion of best practices' and 'scorecards' (Silva 2011). The sphere of social protection, once the almost exclusive province of the national state, has been Europeanized within the framework of an expansive *vincolo esterno*, to recall Dyson and Featherstone's moniker (1996).

The scope of social policy Europeanization has only ever risen, starting from a modest core concerning the social security of mobile workers and gender pay equality by the 1970s. It then gained steam from early 1990s with the setting up of the EMU all the way to the Next Generation EU recovery and resilience facility, both in intensity and scope: from social protection (social safety net and social minima, pensions, and unemployment protection) to labour market regulation (anti-discrimination, job security, activation, gender equality, and lately minimum wage and collective bargaining), to cross-border policies (including poverty, social exclusion, and recently even healthcare) to regional cohesion policies. Decision-making in these policy areas moved from being exclusively national to show some European influence by 1993, and then to a more mixed pattern, sometimes with national, other times with European predominance, by 2017 (Schmidt 2021, 406).

Social policy-making within the European multi-level governance implies direct and indirect (or adaptive) pressures. The former grew as each new Treaty have conferred more social competencies onto the Union; the latter have stemmed from the process of economic and monetary integration, along with the insertion of national economies in the international financial markets.

Governments must abide by primary European law, directives, and regulations, always careful to respect market compatibility requirements with freedom of movement for workers, products, services, and capital. Such modes of governance perform harmonizing functions, scraping differences in order to ease economic cooperation ('negative integration' process), and the coordination of social security systems to guarantee worker and patient mobility within the common market. This type of social policy intent on the integration and efficient working of markets is thus 'market making'. A different type of social policy, historically underdeveloped at the European level, works through 'positive integration', performing redistributive and cooperative functions, and is of the 'market correcting' type, that is, oriented towards correcting market outcomes in line with political standards of social justice. Here, redistribution does not work between social strata or risk groups (as with national welfare states) but between regions through structural funding to underdeveloped regions.

Indirect pressures trigger adaptive responses from the more burdensome expenditure items, such as healthcare and pensions, but also in policies that impact economic competitiveness, such as labour market regulation. The SGP has wrought a constant deflationary pressure, a form of permanent austerity affecting expenditure. Here, the predominant mode of governance is voluntary cooperation through soft law mechanisms (Streeck 1995), offering incentives and cues for policy reform via benchmarking, surveillance, and the promotion of best practices. Two decades apart, the European Employment Strategy (1997) and the European Pillar of Social Rights (2017) offer apt examples.

In the original formulation by Dyson and Featherstone (1996), the European link worked as an externally imposed economic and financial discipline empowering governments to overcome domestic veto points. Since then, the literature has underlined how it also operates as a mechanism for institutional capacity building (Silva 2016).

European pressures have changed direction and scope over time. On the one hand, it has helped the expansion of historically underdeveloped areas of the Portuguese welfare system, such as non-contributory benefits, via financial and cognitive resources (Guillén, Alvarez and Silva 2003). Such expansive impact, as we shall see, was felt in combating poverty and gender inequalities, promoting social inclusion, balancing work and family, and activating employment policies, thereby driving a recalibration of the welfare state towards new social risks and underserved social strata. On the other hand, the permanent need to rationalize resources and improve efficiency in the context of economic and monetary integration was influential in pushing for retrenchment and in offering governments of different hues a way to offload the cost of austerity according to a blame-shifting logic.

The Great Recession and the sovereign debt crisis triggered a qualitative change: a more comprehensive and intrusive *vincolo esterno* (Magone 2021). As was the Portuguese case in 2011, a more extreme governance mode was set up for countries in need of financial assistance, part of the European Stability Mechanism (hard law), non-compliance to which may end up in sovereign debt default. Moreover, the European Semester cycle was strengthened. Country-specific recommendations combine the soft law of voluntary compliance with the hard law of penalized non-compliance in certain areas under the purview of the SGP and, since 2012, the Procedure for Macroeconomic Imbalance (PMI). Intensification was coupled with an increase in scope to policy areas such as labour market regulation (Jordan, Maccarrone and Erne 2021), healthcare systems (Baeten and Vanhercke 2017), or pensions (Guardiancich, Guidi and Terlizzi 2022).

There is a hierarchy of imposed constraints, depending on the severity of sanctioning mechanisms, ranging from the hardest Memoranda of Understanding for SGPs and PMIs, to the softest 'Europe 2020 Strategy'. Let us recall that Portugal was under a MoU from 2011 to 2014, under Excessive Deficit Procedure in 2002–04, 2006–08, and 2009–17 (and 2021–2022, but with suspended SGP); and in 'excessive' macroeconomic imbalance from 2015 to 2017 moving to 'moderate' from 2019 to 2021.

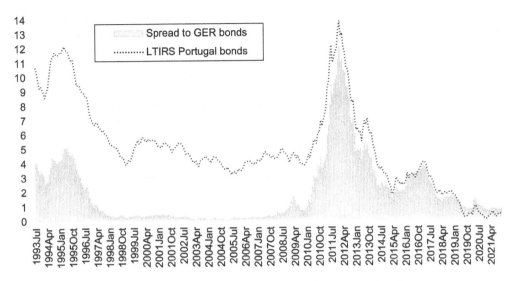

Figure 3.1 Portuguese public debt interest rates and spread to German bunds

Source: European Central Bank – Statistical Data Warehouse, own elaboration based on series for Portugal and Germany from 'Long-term interest rate for convergence purposes, 10 years maturity, denominated in Euro' (https://sdw.ecb.europa.eu/home.do, accessed on 3.2.2022).

At the same time, the crisis made clear that international economic governance institutions, such as the European Central Bank or the International Monetary Fund, and financial markets in general, were also sources of indirect pressure towards cost containment and deregulation, perceived as favourable to economic competitiveness.

The current and capital account balance and the spread relative to German debt securities (*bunds*) are widely used to assess fiscal sustainability and gauge investor and creditor confidence. The former determines external exposure, indicating, when negative, a lack of external competitiveness. This risk is measured by the requested interest on long-term debt financing and by the spread between this and the long-term *bunds*.

Figure 3.1 clearly delineates three major periods in terms of external financing needs and conditions since the mid-1990s, which we shall use to anchor our subsequent empirical analysis. From the setting up of the EMU until 2009, Portugal benefited from propitious financing conditions, with low interest rates *and* a short spread to German bunds, despite growing external deficits, on average around 8% of GDP.[1] The crisis period from 2010 set up a new regime with maximum external pressure: the hike in interest rates triggered the Troika loan under formal conditionality. Since then, the interest rate has been similar to the spread, a sign that German debt is financed at almost no cost. In the third phase, roughly from the end of 2014, Portugal has once again benefited from low interest rates *and* low spreads, close to the lower limit since the end of 2019. Let us also recall that since 2012 the valence of the external exposure has been reversed, becoming positive (an average of +1.4% between 2012 and 2021) thus contributing to a relief in pressure. However, a new period of greater pressure may be approaching, as the temporary suspension of budgetary discipline rules, activated in March 2020 to facilitate public responses to the pandemic crisis, will come to an end in 2024. The pressures from the

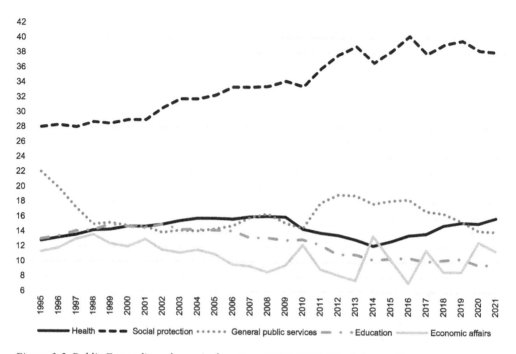

Figure 3.2 Public Expenditure by main functions 1995–2020 (% of the total)

Source: Eurostat, General government expenditure by function (COFOG) [GOV_10A_EXP], accessed on 26.9.2023 at https://ec.europa.eu/eurostat/databrowser/view/gov_10a_exp/default/table?lang=en.

markets are particularly impactful when combined with European governance rules in critical junctures such as the Great Recession.

The larger items of public expenditure are the most susceptible to cost containment pressures (Figure 3.2), while being politically harder to cut. From 1995 to 2021 the combined weight of social protection and healthcare expenditure always exceeded 40% of total public outlays, peaking at 55% by the eve of the COVID-19 pandemic. Social protection (of which pensions are about one-half) has led healthcare (mostly the NHS) on average by roughly 2:1.

The literature on the Troika era has shown that reform policies are never mechanically imposed from the top down, even in the case of the MoUs. The direction of reforms depends on how external pressures are filtered by domestic politics and actors (Graziano, Jacquot and Palier 2011). There is some room of manoeuvre for the expression of interests and ideological preferences, for deploying power resources, and for the agency of political actors and institutions (Silva and Pereira 2017; Moury, Ladi and Cardoso 2021; Branco and Cardoso 2022).

Governments, parties, trade unions, employers' associations, interest groups, civil society organizations, or municipalities use European resources and frameworks as strategic levers to further their agendas. From their point of view, the European link can be used as a facilitator of reforms by legitimizing claims. This is especially the case in countries such as Portugal where there is an overlap between the social concertation and the European agendas, around themes such as pension sustainability, adequate minimum

The welfare state   31

income, labour market segmentation, or minimum wage. It can also be used as 'policy sword', in which case European recommendations are deployed to overcome domestic veto points or blockages, including putting pressure on the government 'from the outside in'. Finally, it can be deployed as a 'problem prevention' strategy when domestic actors participate in European governance cycles to block initiatives that are harmful to their objectives or autonomy, or to influence European social policy itself (Pavolini and Natili 2020).

3.3 Dualization and recalibration before the crisis (1990s to 2010)

Until the accession to the Eurozone, workers' protection relied more on job security than on the replacement of income in the event of unemployment. The worker with a permanent contract's position was protected from dismissal by constitutional and legal provisions, and by the collective bargaining regime, set up in 1979, that enshrined the principle of *favor laboratoris*,[2] the continuity of expired collective agreements until joint replacement and the sectoral extension of collective agreements by ministerial ordinance.

Since membership in the Eurozone prevents the traditional adjustment via exchange rate devaluation ('crawling peg'), labour (wages, productivity, non-wage costs) became a main economic adjustment variable. There followed a major re-orientation in the mode of economic intervention through the social protection system, from the demand side (income replacement as protection) to supply side management by encouraging labour market participation and economic competitiveness. Ever since, state intervention shifted from a protective role to one of enabling the liberalization of job security offset by improved unemployment protection. The European Employment Strategy (1997) and the Lisbon Agenda (2000) encouraged job creation by easing dismissals and better unemployment protection and activation, that is, by facilitating labour market participation through lifelong training. This was done through deploying the open method of coordination via tripartite agreements with the buy-in of social partners. However, job security and unemployment protection for permanent contracts (so-called 'insiders') remained higher than that of atypical workers ('outsiders'), giving rise to a dual labour market.

Such was the background for Portuguese labour law revisions before 2010. The 2003 reform cut employment protections for permanent and temporary contracts, derogated the *favor laboratoris* principle and the ultra-activity of expired collective agreements, allowing employers to present unilateral expiry claims. In so doing, the union's bargaining position was weakened. Neither the government or employers' confederations (in favour of the reform) nor trade unions (against the reform) employed European resources. The reform delivered a liberalization across the board and not, as the Lisbon Agenda envisioned, the piecemeal liberalization of permanent contracts compensated by improved job security for temporary workers, better unemployment protection, and activation policies. The trade unions criticized the reform for violating, first and foremost, the Constitution, and only secondarily the European directives (UGT, 2003). One should note that the reform took place under the external constraint from the excessive deficit procedure opened in 2002 for non-compliance with the SGP criteria.

The 2009 reform did not fully restore the *favor laboratoris* principle. Rather, it enumerated some areas in which collective agreements could not deviate from the law for the worse, but not as regards overtime work, nor temporary employment. The expiry regime of collective bargaining was kept. Flexibility increased for permanent contracts, both external (easing dismissals) and internal (individual hour bank). Unlike in 2003, both trade unions deployed European cognitive and normative resources, such as the concept of 'flexicurity', and European recommendations, to criticize the reform's liberalizing orientation as driven by employers' demands and contrary to the 'European social model' (Zartaloudis 2011, 191).

As regards unemployment protection, the focus shifted from income replacement to labour market participation, stressing the requirement of active job search or participation in training programmes. A reform in 2006 showcased this activation turn: while access to the unemployment benefit was limited, it prioritized up-skilling the workforce, long-term unemployment, and the activation of outsider groups such as youth, elderly workers, women, ethnic minorities, and people with disabilities.

The labour market developed a dual segmentation pattern or 'liberalization at the margins': comparatively higher job security for permanent contracts contrasting with a growing segment of temporary workers (around one in every four employees), with less job security and worse income protection when unemployed (Moreira et al. 2015; Marques and Salavisa 2017).

Social protection reforms focused, in an initial stage, on the universalization of personal and risk coverage. Then followed a path of recalibration geared towards containing costs in the 'old social policies', such as pensions, while 'new social risks' were looked after by new non-contributory benefits, such as the guaranteed minimum income, early education and childhood services, old age support services, and reconciliation policies for balancing work and family, such as parental leaves. Such movement towards the protection of 'new social risks' was nevertheless thwarted by insufficient levels of expenditure and remained comparatively modest (Branco 2022).

Portugal set up the NHS in 1979. Southern European countries set up universal healthcare services comparatively late, Italy in 1978; Greece in 1983; and Spain in 1986. These are, along with the United Kingdom, Ireland, and the Nordic countries, the only NHS in Europe. The remaining countries, including France, Germany, and the Netherlands, have kept health insurance systems, combining a public component with private, occupationally based elements. The NHS breaks with the past by replacing the corporatist 'insurance funds' by the 'social-democratic' logic of universal public provision financed by general taxation. The system also includes an important private sector and generous insurance schemes for civil servants. The concentration in certain groups or social strata of overlapping schemes generates a pattern in which peaks of protection for some coexist with deficits in access and coverage for others. The NHS's weaknesses show, for example, in congested hospital emergency care or in the long waiting lists for surgeries.

Public healthcare expenditure grew from 1006 euros in 2000 to 1175 in 2010 (OECD 2021), to which should be added the fiscal expenditure on healthcare which peaked at 610 million euros in 2010 (Branco and Costa 2019). Ever since the 1990s reforms sought cost containment by acting upon the supply and demand of health services. If there was limited success in cost containment, recalibration efforts towards primary care and hitherto unaddressed needs were more successful. The generic market for drugs was expanded, price controls were set up and co-pays were hiked. User fees were created to repress the use of hospital emergency services. From 2005 to 2008 there was a sizeable cut of 12% in expenditure, mostly on drug spending and contracting with private providers (Campos and Simões 2014, 58–59). Then, expenditures shot up again. All the while, funding was separated from the provision by contracting between public hospitals and private providers, and a network of health primary care centres was created, but in an incomplete manner and poorly integrated within the hospital network. The setting up of the National Network of Long-Term Care in partnership with private actors and the third sector filled an important gap in provision.

From 1991 to 2011 the number of pensioners jumped from around 2.5 million to 3.5 million, while the average pension value increased by 44% and pension expenditure rose from 9.2% to 13.7% of GDP. Rapid population ageing downgraded the ratio between active workers and benefit recipients from 4.7 per pension paid in 1974 to 1.4 in 2012. Concerns with financial sustainability emerged, to which we must add transnational and European pressures, ranging from the World Bank[3] and the OECD,[4] to the White Book from the Commission for Social Security Reform in 1998 (Campos 2022, 23), and those imposed by the discipline inherent in the EMU rules, putting downward pressure on public expenditure.

The policy response was cost containment. The minimum contributory period and the reference period for the pension formula were extended, and the legal retirement age of women was aligned with that of men (at 65). Early retirement was penalized and there was an openness in 2002 to consider capping contributions to the public system to promote partial privatization, under an excessive deficit procedure. The 2007 reform, again under an excessive deficit procedure, indexed pensions to a new sustainability factor, adjusting the retirement age to life expectancy, greatly reducing long-term generosity. The Minister of Labour and Social Solidarity Vieira da Silva argued that the government sought to 'reform old-age pensions by whittling down generosity that would be incompatible with the future increase in life expectancy'. This would gradually bring 'the pension replacement rate (the ratio between the first pension and the last wage) in line with the European standard within 40 years'.[5] The European Commissioner for Employment, Social Affairs and Inclusion, Lazlo Andor, praised the reform for being *adopted before the sovereign debt crisis*, and for contributing to the sustainability of public finances.[6] The ongoing EMU budgetary restrictions have provided governments with ways to legitimize and, at the same time, 'shift the blame' for potentially unpopular measures.

The European link can act as a brake, but also as an engine for expansion. The EU pressures member states to engage with social problems and often new social risks that otherwise would remain invisible. Such was the case with poverty and social exclusion. Similarly, with improving the market position of part-time, fixed-term and temporary agency workers (European Directives in 1997, 1999, and 2008); and in early education and child support policies to balance women's labour market participation and family life. Case in point, the shift in the approach to care for the elderly that took place from late 1990s culminating with the creation of a Network of Integrated Long-Term Care in 2008. More than setting up new services and facilities, a new structure was created in which the state acts primarily as coordinator and funder leaving the provision of services to private institutions, commercial and nonprofit. The shift came as a response to the calls from different international forums such as the OECD or the European Commission that had been raising awareness among national states for the topic of integration of health and social care (Lopes 2016).

Similarly with the expansion of the social safety net. The guaranteed minimum income was created in 1996 as a means-tested non-contributory benefit to combat poverty in old age, social exclusion, or unemployment. In 2002, under an excessive deficit procedure, access was limited, and the benefit was renamed Social Insertion Income (SII). European legal, financial, and cognitive resources were decisive, as the creation was based on the 1992 European Council Recommendation on sufficient resources and benefits in social protection systems (92/441/EEC). The new benefit covered an extant gap in protection

34 *Rui Branco and Pedro Adão e Silva*

typical of Bismarckian systems, with an eye to activation and not just 'passive' income replacement. Politically, it helped the centre-left Socialist Party differentiate from the centre-right Social Democratic Party at the 1995 general election, mobilizing the large network of 'third sector' civil society organizations, most of which of Catholic affiliation, as well as the main union confederations General Confederation of Portuguese Workers (CGTP) and General Workers' Union (UGT) (Silva 2009). This European policy orientation towards social inclusion has long been reiterated, from the Lisbon Strategy all the way up to the European Parliament resolution of 15 March 2023 calling on member states to swiftly implement Directive 2022/2041 on adequate minimum wages in EU.

3.4 The great internal devaluation (2010–2014)

Finance Minister Teixeira dos Santos had warned: 'If debt interest rates reach 7%, the Government has to consider resorting to the IMF and the European fund'.[7] When the interest rate exceeds the lowest comparable interest rate in the eurozone – the German *bunds* – by more than 4 p.p. that conveys financial markets' reservations about the state's solvency. In February 2011 both criteria were met for the first time. On 23 March the fourth round of austerity measures was rejected by Parliament and the minority Socialist Prime Minister resigned; on 6 April the socialist caretaker government asked for international financial assistance. Snap general elections ensued, won by the centre-right coalition of PSD and CDS-PP.

The Memorandum of Understanding (MoU) signed with the Troika of creditors (ECB, EC, and IMF), in exchange for a €78 billion loan, set up cuts in public sector wages and healthcare, tax increases, and structural reforms in social protection, including the labour market, held to be responsible for the lack of economic competitiveness.

The MoU prescribed liberalization to reform a 'rigid' labour market due to the 'excessive' protection of permanent contracts, 'generous' unemployment benefits and collective bargaining unable to align wage growth with productivity and competitiveness. On the other hand, it avowedly sought to fight dualization by improving the position of temporary workers, the long-term unemployed, and active labour market policies (Cardoso and Branco 2018).

There was a qualitative change in the mode of the external constraint, now more intrusive and far-reaching, but also a clear policy direction: internal devaluation seeking to boost exports by relying on cost-competition ('competitive impoverishment'). European Commissioner László Andor acknowledged that the EMU

> excludes unilateral adjustment of its member economies through the exchange rate or interest rate (by definition), as well as by inflation or fiscal expansion (by design). The only remaining adjustment mechanism is so-called internal devaluation, which involves social damage: it is an effort to restore price competitiveness by reducing costs, including through layoffs and wage cuts in both the public and private sectors.
> (Andor 2013)

In essence, wage-setting mechanisms and collective bargaining were reformed to reduce labour costs, generating downward wage adjustment. Job security and unemployment protection for permanent contracts worsened. The protection offered by collective bargaining was cut down by restricting sectoral extensions and the ultra-activity of collective agreements, and by giving firm-level agreements priority over sectoral or higher levels.

Yet, combatting dualization and recalibrating social protection towards outsiders were left by the wayside (Branco and Cardoso 2022).

The generosity and duration of the unemployment benefit was cut, plunging the income of the unemployed by 25% from 2010 to 2013 (Moreira et al. 2015). Young workers were targeted: the benefit's duration was cut from 270 to 150 days for workers under 30 with less than 15 months of contributions. Other measures expanded coverage to bogus independent workers. However, neither offset the drop in income nor was dual segmentation resolved. According to the European Commission (2016), from 2007 to 2014, the gap in quality of protection between the more and the less entitled to unemployment benefits rose. Coverage remained low due to large numbers of unprotected long-term unemployed (Pereirinha and Murteira 2020). In other words, the reform degraded the position of insiders without improving that of outsiders.

The MoU did not initially include any pension structural reform. Yet, pensions suffered nominal cuts, indexation freeze, and higher taxation. From 2010 to 2015, pensioner's income dropped significantly, albeit in a progressive manner (Silva and Pereira 2017). Before the end of the Adjustment Program, in early 2014, the executive passed a more profound reform: a 1-year increase in the legal retirement age; convergence of the public sector fund (Caixa Geral de Aposentações) with the general social security fund by adjusting the replacement rate; and a new ad hoc contribution levied on public sector pensions. After the Constitutional Court struck down the new contribution and convergence rules, the government dropped any plans for an ambitious reform.

The social safety net was retrenched by restrictions in access and cuts in generosity. From 2010 to 2015 the minimum income scheme lost one-third in value and 40% in the number of recipients. The same with the benefit supplementing the income of poor elderly pensioners, triggering a 23% drop in beneficiaries. Family allowances were retrenched by stricter means-testing and the exclusion of higher incomes, leading to a 30% drop in expenditure, and a loss of 500,000 recipients. While protection became less generous, covering fewer people, with the shrinking of public responsibilities, civil society organizations were given more responsibilities and a larger role in the welfare system. For instance, the 2011 Social Emergency Program signed by the government and the third-sector peak confederation National Confederation of Solidarity Institutions opened services such as social canteens and funerals to Catholic charities.

A concern with the NHS sustainability marked the MoU, triggering years of severe austerity. Per capita expenditure fell from €1175 to €967 from 2010 to 2013. Spending on drugs dropped 12%. Salaries, career progressions, and recruitment were frozen, and overtime pay was cut. Except for the case of long-term and palliative care networks (in partnership with the private and 'third'sectors), austerity undermined universal access, transferring costs to individuals and families at a time when private spending was reduced by the economic crisis and unemployment. The shrinking of public responsibilities led to an increase in unmet healthcare needs, especially among the unemployed, pensioners, and inactive population (Pavolini et al. 2023).

3.5 The *Geringonça* reforms: direction and limits (2015–2022)

After the 2015 general elections, a centre-left PS minority government took office with the support in parliament of radical left Communist Party (PCP) and Left Bloc (BE). This was a form of contract parliamentarianism (Bale and Bergman, 2006) based on *ex ante* political agreements setting the terms under which the cabinet was allowed to take office

(Fernandes, Magalhães and Santana-Pereira, 2018). This Left coalition of sorts came to be known in political parlance as '*geringonça*', which translates as 'rickety contraption'.

The context of resumed growth with good labour market performance, waning pressure from financial markets, and a gradual social turn in European governance presented an opportunity to reverse Troika-era measures and reform social policy.

The first order of business in 2015 was the reversal of austerity measures, restoring public sector wages and career progression, increasing the minimum wage, hiking public pensions and other social benefits, and lowering taxes for the middle and working classes, small- and medium-sized businesses. This triggered a broad-based recovery of incomes that pushed internal demand, which, coupled with increasing exports (mostly low-end manufactures and tourism), drove economic growth before the onset of the COVID-19 pandemic.

One important measure was the step increase in the minimum wage, from €505 in 2015 to €655 in 2021, backed by tripartite agreements in social concertation. Such a rise was not detrimental to labour market performance given the 8% growth in the employed population and the drop in the unemployment rate from 12.4% to 6.5% from 2015 to 2019. The initial caution in the European Semester country-specific recommendations (hikes would hurt employment creation) was countered by a domestic coalition including trade union and employers' confederations (Perista and Perista 2019) drawn by the importance of boosting incomes to drive consumption and internal demand.

Not surprisingly, given the origin story of the '*Geringonça*' as an anti-Troika austerity coalition, labour market regulation took centre stage. In the short term, the expiry regime of collective agreements was suspended for 18 months, with a return to an unbridled state-supported sectoral extension mechanism (decided by tripartite agreement). However, the long-awaited labour code reform in 2019 exposed an internal fracture: it was passed in parliament against the opposition of PCP and BE, based on a tripartite agreement signed in 2018 by the moderate trade union UGT and employers' confederations.

The reform increased the regulation of temporary contracts and bogus self-employment. At the same time, as a nod to employers, the use and duration of short-term contracts was liberalized and the trial period for first-time jobseekers and the long-term unemployed was doubled. On the social protection side, various measures granted independent workers access to cash benefit assistance for children and broadened the coverage of unemployment benefits for bogus self-employed.

However, the bill fell short of reversing certain previous reforms, a deal-breaker for both radical left parties (which voted against the bill) and their trade union ally CGTP, which had not signed the 2018 tripartite agreement. Besides opposing the flexibilization of short-term contracts and the longer trial period, left parties and CGTP demanded the full reinstatement of the *favor laboratoris* principle and the return to the ultra-activity of collective agreements, both lost in the 2003 labour law reform (the Constitutional Court struck down the trial period extension for first-time jobseekers in Ruling 318/2021).

The reform, despite increasing employment protections for atypical workers, stopped short of a two-pronged regulatory movement including both labour market segments, the line taken by the centre-left Socialist Party, the social-partnership-oriented UGT, and employers' organizations. The policymaking process, unfolding during the initial stages of the European social turn, but prior to the EU-wide response to the pandemic, gave social dialogue pride of place over parliament. Indeed, the misalignment between the preferences of radical left parties and trade union allies and the policy direction settled in the tripartite agreement is the reason why it passed in parliament only due to the abstention of right-wing parties.

Nevertheless, the rickety political situation held until the end of the legislature in the Fall of 2019. What made it palatable to radical parties was a form of broad political exchange including trade unions and employers. The former got compensation in income, welfare, and public sector policies (minimum wage, end of the cuts in public sector wages and pensions, redrawing income tax brackets, pro-outsider reforms, and full-time integration of precarious workers in the public administration). Employers assented to an expansionary income policy but forcefully signalled that no further reversals of core labour reforms were acceptable.[8] The political exchange set *Geringonça*'s policy limits to its left, as the Socialist Party in office did not wish to forego the support of employers in the social partnership policy model, and therefore its eventual fall (Branco and Cardoso 2023).

Changes in unemployment protectionincreased the replacement rate, coverage, and access of the social insurance benefit. In addition, the non-contributory social assistance benefit was extended in terms of duration and updated in terms of value, while also broadening access to the self-employed and long-term unemployed. However, the government did not heed the demand from radical left parties to reverse the Troika-era shorter insurance benefit duration.

This broadly inclusive recalibration was matched in other social protection areas, historically underdeveloped, such as minimum income, safety net, and disability (Branco et. al 2024). The minimum income scheme value and access criteria, as well as those for the non-contributory supplemental benefit for the elderly, were restored, improving coverage and income security (Pereirinha et al. 2020). The protection of people with disabilities was improved by creating a new benefit, Social Assistance for Inclusion, in 2017. As for work/life balance and gender equality, new laws in 2019 reinforced the parental leave regime. All these measures were aligned with European social policy guidelines, framed in a wide range of instruments, from the open method of coordination of the 'European Disability Strategy 2010–2020' (COM 2010/636),[9] to the Directive for Reconciliation between work and family for Parents (2019/1158 of 6/20/2019).[10]

Healthcare expenditure increased and changed composition. Per capita expenditure rose from €967 in 2015 to €1143 in 2019, and then to €1211 in 2020. All the while, it shifted from hospital care to primary and outpatient care, and to long-term care. The NHS staff and payroll returned to pre-2010 levels. From 2015 to 2020 NHS professionals increased by 24.618, bridging the emigration of the Troika years. Even so, the NHS faced the pandemic with personnel shortages, including of nurses and diagnostic technicians, with few intensive care beds and a deficient primary care network pushing demand onto hospital emergencies, in addition to worrying long-standing socio-economic access inequalities (Pavolini et al 2023).

As noted, the economic surveillance of health systems carried out within the European Semester was ramping up (Baeten and Vanhercke 2017). Portugal's country-specific recommendations included ensuring the long-term sustainability of the health sector without compromising access to primary care (2016); strengthening controls over spending and budgeting to reduce accumulated debt (2017, 2018, and 2019) and, already in the pandemic context, reinforcing the resilience of the system to guarantee equal access to quality health and continuous care.

Despite increasing the electoral score in the Fall 2019 elections, the incumbent Socialist Party remained minoritarian. Radical left parties either kept their score (BE) or faded (PCP), further undermining the political conditions for a renewal of the *Geringonça*.

Soon afterwards, the COVID-19 pandemic hit. Over the next 18 months a wide array of responses focused on economic, labour market, and social recovery, the protection of workers and the workplace, income protection beyond short-term work, and preventing social hardship, backed up by European financial resources via SURE, Pandemic Crisis Support, and the European Guarantee Fund. Differently from prior crisis responses, risk-sharing between member states was the defining feature of such programmes, so that solidarity between member states took the form of joint guarantees with elements of fiscal solidarity.

Authorities quickly expanded the coverage and scope of sickness benefits. A 'simplified furlough' scheme allowed companies to shed working hours or fully suspend work contracts all the while offering employees a payment worth two-thirds of gross salary and exempting employers from social contributions. Strengthening the safety net for those who lost their jobs or earnings, with entitlement to unemployment insurance and unemployment assistance, the minimum income scheme and the benefit for poor pensioners were extended (Moreira et al. 2021). These broadly inclusive and egalitarian policy responses protected insiders' income with demand-side and supply-side interventions *and* protected atypical workers and vulnerable strata by raising the minimum wage and non-contributory pensions, extraordinary income support and assistance for people in economic hardship, and unemployment benefits.

The result of a coordinated European response to the pandemic against the backdrop of suspended SGP budgetary rules, the 2021 Recovery and Resilience Plan (RRP) illustrates the *vincolo esterno*'s enabling influence. Following in the footsteps of earlier pandemic responses, the Next Generation EU changed the orientation of European social policy in that it supports solidarity without conditionality. By deploying the largest European budget ever, supported for the first time by the issuance of common debt, it conveys a solidaristic logic. By loosening the link between financial assistance and budgetary requirements and by fomenting public investment, it sheds the austerity orientation that marked policy responses to the Great Recession. Finally, it strengthens the social dimension in European governance by adopting the European Pillar of Social Rights as a compass in the road to recovery, interlinking the green and digital 'just transitions' of the European Green Deal (Petmesidou et al. 2023).

Social interventions in the Portuguese RRP recalibrate protection towards labour market outsiders, young people, women, excluded strata, and the elderly. The Plan draws direction and legitimacy from the CSRs, though much less from the European Pillar of Social Rights, eliciting worries that market-making measures overpower market-correcting interventions, especially when inequalities of voice (namely of trade unions) in policymaking may concomitantly skew the balance from the protective to the productive dimensions of social policy (Petmesidou et al. 2023).

Pandemic politics froze political conflict for a long while. When politics thawed, the *Geringonça* unravelled in October 2021 around the same labour market reform divergences that had surfaced in 2019. Following the collapse in parliamentary support, a snap election was held in January, which the PS won with an absolute majority, taking office in April 2022. According to PCP and BE, the programmatic disagreements about labour market regulation were crucial for the breakup. Issues such as reversing the liberalization of dismissals, the expiry regime of collective agreements, the full reinstatement of the *favor laboratoris* principle, and a quicker and more generous national minimum wage increase.[11]

Since then, a relevant labour market reform was enacted in March 2023, one of the reforms laid down in the RRP, the 'Decent Work Agenda'. A follow-up of the 2019 effort, it further regulates atypical employment and digital/platform work, slightly increases protections against collective dismissal, and sets up an arbitration mechanism that constrains, but does not derogate the expiry regime of collective agreements. Because there was no tripartite agreement, employers have voiced low-key criticisms regarding process and content. After all, in October 2022 employers' confederations had signed with UGT and the government a medium-term agreement until 2026, setting up a 4.8% average wage increase for the private sector and an 18.4% minimum wage step increase (to €900), offset by better tax and regulatory treatment of business enterprises.

3.6 Conclusion

This chapter evinced how the European external linkage has influenced the direction and scope of social policy reform in Portugal. Since joining the EMU and the creation of the euro, Portugal benefited from favourable financing conditions to modernize the welfare state. This period is marked by a catch-up recovery towards the European pattern in volume, coverage, and composition of expenditure. A first stage of expansion with universalization of coverage and risks was followed by an emphasis on recalibration, accompanied by cost containment in the largest expenditure items, more thorough in the case of pensions, and more episodic in that of the NHS. At the same time, new social risks were attended to by non-contributory benefits and services such as the minimum income benefit, in addition to policies to reconcile work and family, though at a level still far from the European average.

In this first period, the concern of European institutions that countries with higher protection standards would suffer the competition from 'socially laggard' southern countries through 'social dumping' made possible the creation of a social dimension in cohesion policies through structural funds. This effort was politically sustained by a coalition between donor governments in central and northern Europe and centre-left and conservative parties in recipient countries in the south.

The eurozone sovereign debt crisis raised the opposite concern, that overly generous or misdirected social protection standards triggered economic stagnation, budgetary imbalances, and lack of external competitiveness across Southern Europe. A new European policy orientation followed driven by a different political dynamic across Europe, the cleavage between creditor countries and debtor countries in the southern periphery. The enactment of the Memorandum of Understanding in Portugal triggered a sharp decline in public expenditure, retrenching social protection according to a logic of negative, or subtractive, recalibration (Ferrera 2012). In this period of maximum external constraint, Portugal reversed years of convergence to initiate a divergence relative to social Europe (Guillén et al 2021). By the end of the economic adjustment, the welfare regime was more 'pension-centric', less concerned with new social risks, and the access to, and the ability to provide by, the most important universalist institution, the NHS, had been jeopardized, as witnessed by the rise in access inequalities and unmet needs. The deregulation of job security for workers with permanent contracts was not coupled with an improvement in the market position of 'outsiders' – in contrast to the stance advocated in the 2013 'Social Investment Package' (regulation of temporary work, investment in early education and child services, access to healthcare, active employment, and family support) (European Commission 2013).

40 Rui Branco and Pedro Adão e Silva

The European social investment thrust was already a sign of a change of valence in the European connection. Correcting course after counter-productive policy responses to the eurozone crisis, European institutions triggered since 2016 a 'social turn' in European governance. This rebalancing of the EU's economic and social dimensions includes the Commission's ambitious social agenda, the setting up in 2017 of the European Pillar of Social Rights (followed by the Action Plan in 2021) as the European Semester's social compass, the directive on minimum protection for workers in precarious jobs (2019/1152), the directive on decent minimum wage and collective bargaining coverage (2022/2041), and the forthcoming Platform Workers Directive. The 2021 Next Generation-EU embodies this turn to solidarity without conditionality. This 'social turn' has been driven by the Von der Leyen Commission and has received broad political support in the European Parliament, which went beyond left-wing parties (Greens, GUE, and S&D) to include large sectors of the centre-right EPP and of the liberal ALDE (Keune and Pochet 2023, 8).

Mobilizing such financial, legal, and cognitive resources, the minority socialist government, supported in parliament by PCP and BE, gave a central place to social protection and income policies. It reversed the cuts and labour market measures from the Troika era – although, crucially, not all – and renewed the focus on new social risks and outsider strata, always within the confines of European budgetary rules (the excessive deficit procedure was closed in 2017).

The fact that it was when the European economic governance made a propitious social turn, and in a moment when SGP budgetary rules were suspended, that divergences within the Left political majority about labour market regulation and the NHS brought down the *Geringonça* goes to show the ongoing importance of programmatic differences based upon competing power resources within Left parties and trade union allies.

Notes

1 Portugal: current and capital account balance (1999–2020) (actual balance in % of the GDP), available at https://bpstat.bportugal.pt/serie/12517408, accessed on 3.2.2022.
2 The *favor laboratoris* principle sets up a hierarchy within multilevel collective bargaining systems: 'if the terms and conditions in the individual contract are more favourable to the employee than the provisions of the relevant collective agreement, then the former prevail'. Standards set in the general labour law or concluded at a higher level can be improved on (for employees) but not worsened at a lower level. https://www.eurofound.europa.eu/observatories/eurwork/industrial-relations-dictionary/favourability-principle, accessed 24.7.2023.
3 World Bank, *Averting the Old Age Crisis: Policies to Protect the Old and Promote Growth*, 1994.
4 OECD, *Ageing Populations, Pension Systems and Government Budget*, 1996.
5 The Minister of Labor and Social Solidarity, José Vieira da Silva, 'Falemos Então de Estado Social' (So Let's Talk about the Social State), *Diário de Notícias* 14.8.2006, https://www.dn.pt/arquivo/2006/falemos-entao-de-estado-social-644633.html, accessed on 19.1.2023.
6 'Bruxelas diz: Reforma do sistema de pensões português "é um exemplo"' ('Brussels says: Reform of the Portuguese pension system "is an example"'), *Jornal de Negócios*, 7/7/2010, https://www.jornaldenegocios.pt/economia/europa/detalhe/bruxelas_diz_reforma_do_sistema_de_pensotildees_portuguecircs_quoteacute_um_exemploquot?act=0&est=Aberto, accessed on 4.5.2022
7 https://www.publico.pt/2011/05/16/jornal/o-caminho-ate-a-aprovacao-da-ajuda-22061169, accessed on 4.2.2022.
8 António Saraiva, the Chairman of CIP (Confederation of Portuguese Business) made it clear in 2016 that 'the government has to pay a price for an agreement' on the minimum wage. To this end, 'you cannot change labor legislation', nor increase holidays to 25 days, extend the 35 hours of weekly work to the private sector, or eliminate the individual hour bank. Available at:

https://www.jornaldenegocios.pt/economia/politica/detalhe/cip_disponivel_para_um_aumento_do_salario_minimo_mas_exige_contrapartidas, accessed on 5.1.2023.

9 This, however, was replaced in March 2021 by the 'Union of Equality: Strategy for the rights of persons with disabilities 2021-2030', which expanded the general orientation. See https://ec.europa.eu/social/main.jsp?catId=1484&langId=en, accessed on 20.1.2023.

10 This was the result of the European Commission's political initiative, and its work dating back to 2015 to break the European legislative blockade on the 'Maternity Leave Directive' that had been presented in 2008. This proposal for a Directive was later withdrawn by the Commission and replaced by another in 2019.

11 See https://pcp.pt/sobre-reuniao-do-comite-central-do-pcp-de-24-de-outubro-de-2021, and https://www.esquerda.net/artigo/quais-sao-9-propostas-do-bloco-para-o-orcamento/77418, accessed on 7/12/2021.

References

Andor, Lazlo. 2013. *Developing the social dimension of a deep and genuine Economic and Monetary Union.* Policy Brief: European Policy Centre.

Baeten, Rita, and Bart Vanhercke. 2017. "Inside the black box: The EU's economic surveillance of national healthcare systems." *Comparative European Politics* 15, no. 3: 478–497.

Bale, Tim, and Torbjörn Bergman. 2006. "Captives No Longer, but Servants Still? Contract Parliamentarism and the New Minority Governance in Sweden and New Zealand1." *Government and Opposition* 41, no. 3: 422–449.

Branco, Rui, 2022. *Protecção Social no Portugal Democrático. Trajetórias de Reforma.* Lisbon: Fundação Francisco Manuel dos Santos.

Branco, Rui and Daniel Cardoso. 2022. "The Politics of Change. Coalitional politics and labour market reforms during the sovereign debt crisis in Portugal", *Journal of Social Policy* 51, no. 1: 39–57.

Branco, Rui and Daniel Cardoso. 2023. "Solidarity in Hard Times: The Politics of Labour Market and Social Protection Reform in Portugal (2010–2020)." In *Inscribing Solidarity in the era of gig economy*, 145–169, edited by Julia Lopéz. Cambridge: Cambridge University Press.

Branco, Rui, Daniel Cardoso, Ana Guillén and David Luque Balbona. 2019. "Here to stay? Reversals of structural reforms in Southern Europe as the crisis wanes." *South European Society and Politics* 24, no. 2: 205–232.

Branco, Rui and Edna Costa. 2019. "The golden age of tax expenditures: Fiscal welfare and inequality in Portugal (1989–2011)." *New Political Economy* 24, no. 6: 780–797-.Branco, Rui, Joan Miró, and Marcello Natili. 2024. "Back from the Cold? Progressive Politics and Social Policy Paradigms in Southern Europe after the Great Recession." *Politics & Society* 0(0). https://doi.org/10.1177/00323292241226806.

Campos, António Correia de. 2022. *Gaveta de Reformas.* Lisbon: Caminho.

Campos, António Correia de, and Jorge Simões (eds) 2014. *40 Anos de Abril na Saúde.* Coimbra: Almedina.

Dyson, Kenneth and Kevin Featherstone. 1996. "Italy and EMU as a 'Vincolo Esterno': empowering the technocrats, transforming the state". *South European Society and Politics* 1, no. 2: 272–299.

Cardoso, Daniel and Rui Branco. 2018. "Liberalised dualisation. Labour market reforms and the crisis in Portugal: A new departure." *European Journal of Social Security* 20, no 1: 31–48.

European Commission. 2013. Towards Social Investment for Growth and Cohesion - including implementing the European Social Fund 2014-2010, COM (2013) 83.

European Commission. 2016. *Employment and social developments in Europe 2015*, Publications Office. https://data.europa.eu/doi/10.2767 /42590

Fernandes, Jorge, Pedro C. Magalhães and José Santana-Pereira. 2018. "Portugal's leftist Government: From sick man to poster boy?" *South European Society and Politics* 23, no. 4: 503–524.

Ferrera, Maurizio. 2005. *The Boundaries of Welfare. European Integration and the New Spatial Politics of Social Protection.* Oxford: Oxford University Press.

Ferrera, Maurizio. 2012. "Verso un welfare più europeo? Conclusioni". In *Alle radici del welfare all'italiana: origini e futuro di un modello sociale squilibrato*, edited by Maurizio Ferrera, Valeria Fargion and Matteo Jessoula, 323–344. Padova: Marsilio.

Gilpin, Richard. 1987. *The Political Economy of International Relations*. Princeton: Princeton University Press.

Graziano, Paolo, Sophie Jacquot and Bruno Palier. (eds) 2011. *The EU and the Domestic Politics of Welfare State Reforms: Europa, Europae*. London: Palgrave Macmillan

Guardiancich, Igor, Mattia Guidi, and Andrea Terlizzi. 2022. "Beyond the European Semester: The supranational evaluation cycle for pensions." *Journal of European Social Policy* 32, no. 5: 578–591.

Guillén, Ana, Matteo Jessoula, Manos Matsaganis, Rui Branco and Emmanuele Pavolini. 2021. "Southern European Welfare Systems in Transition". In *Mediterranean Capitalism Revisited: One Model, Different Trajectories*, edited by Emanuele Pavolini, Luigi Burroni and Marino Regini, 149–171. Ithaca: Cornell University Press.

Guillén, Ana, Santiago Álvarez and Pedro Adão e Silva. 2003. "Redesigning the Spanish and Portuguese welfare states: the impact of accession into the European Union." *South European Society and Politics* 8, nos. 1–2: 231–268.

Jordan, Jamie, Vincenzo Maccarrone, and Roland Erne. 2021. "Towards a socialization of the EU's new economic governance regime? EU labour policy interventions in Germany, Ireland, Italy and Romania (2009–2019)." *British Journal of Industrial Relations* 59, no. 1: 191–213.

Keune, Maarten, and Philippe Pochet. 2023. "The revival of Social Europe: is this time different?" *Transfer: European Review of Labour and Research* 29, no. 2: 173–183

Lopes, Alexandra. 2016.Long-term care in Portugal: quasi-privatization of a dual system of care. In *Long-term Care for the Elderly in Europe*, edited by Bent Greve, 73-88, New York: Routledge.

Magone, José. 2021. *Constraining Democratic Governance in Southern Europe: From 'Superficial' To 'Coercive' Europeanization*. Cheltenham: Edward Elgar Publishing.

Marques, Paulo, and Isabel Salavisa. 2017. "Young people and dualization in Europe: a fuzzy set analysis." *Socio-Economic Review* 15, no. 1: 135–160.

Moreira, Amilcar, Ángel Alonso Domínguez, Cátia Antunes, Maria Karamessini, Michele Raitano, and Miguel Glatzer. 2015. "Austerity-driven labour market reforms in southern Europe: eroding the security of labour market insiders." *European Journal of Social Security* 17, no. 2: 202–225.

Moreira, Amílcar, Margarita Léon, Flavia Coda Moscarola and Antonios Roumpakis. 2021. "In the eye of the storm… again! Social policy responses to COVID-19 in Southern Europe." *Social Policy & Administration* 55, no. 2: 339–357.

Moury, Catherine, Stella Ladi, Daniel Cardoso, and Angie Gago. 2021. *Capitalising on constraint*. Manchester: Manchester University Press.

OECD. 1996. *Ageing Populations, Pension Systems and Government Budget*. Paris: OECD.

Pavolini, Emmanuele, and Marcello Natili. 2020. "Towards a stronger relationship between national social dialogue and the European Semester." *Analytical Report Work Package 3*, European Social Observatory.

Pavolini, Emmanuele, Maria Petmesidou, Rui Branco and Ana Guillén, 2023. "From crisis to opportunity? Recalibrating healthcare in Southern Europe in the wake of the pandemic". In *European Social Policy and the COVID-19 Pandemic: Challenges to National Welfare and EU Policy*, edited by Stefanie Börner and Martin Seeleib-Kaiser, 107–130. Oxford: Oxford University Press.

Pereira, Luiz Carlos Bresser, and Adam Przeworski. 1993. *Economic reforms in new democracies: a social-democratic approach*. Cambridge: Cambridge University Press.

Pereirinha, José António, and Maria Clara Murteira. 2019. "The Portuguese welfare system: A late European welfare system under permanent stress." In *Routledge handbook of European Welfare systems*, edited by Sonja Blum, Johanna Kuhlmann, and Klaus Schubert, 424–444. Abingdon: Routledge.

Pereirinha, José António, Francisco Branco, Elvira Pereira, and Maria Inês Amaro. 2020. "The guaranteed minimum income in Portugal: a universal safety net under political and financial pressure." *Social Policy & Administration* 54, no. 4: 574–586.

Perista, P., and Heloísa Perista. 2019. ""Just being heard"? Engaging in the European Semester in the shadow of macroeconomic surveillance–Case study Portugal." *Observatoire social européen Research Paper 41*.

Petmesidou, Maria, Rui Branco, Emmanuele Pavolini, Sergio González Begega, and Ana Guillén. 2023. "The EPSR and the Next Generation EU: Heralding a reconfiguration of social protection in South Europe?" *Social Policy & Administration*. https://doi.org/10.1111/spol.12892.

Schmidt, Manfred. 2021. European and National Social Policy. In *The Oxford handbook of the welfare state*, edited by Béland, Daniel, Kimberly J. Morgan, Herbert Obinger, and Christopher Pierson, 397–416. Oxford: Oxford University Press.

Silva, Pedro Adão e. 2009. *Waving the European flag in a Southern European welfare state: factors behind domestic compliance with European social policy in Portugal*, PhD thesis, European University Institute.

Silva, Pedro Adão e, 2011. "The Europeanization of Social Policies in Portugal." *Portuguese Journal of Social Science* 10, no 1: 3–22.

Silva, Pedro Adão e. 2016. "A política social europeia: da esperança à desesperança." In *União Europeia, Reforma ou Declínio*, edited by Eduardo Paz Ferreira, 231–244. Lisbon: Nova Vega.

Silva, Pedro Adão e, and Mariana Trigo Pereira. 2017. "O Estado Social português: entre a maturação e os constrangimentos externos." In *O Sistema Político Português. Uma Perspetiva Comparada*, edited by Conceição Pequito Teixeira, 431–456. Cascais: Principia.

Streeck, Wolfgang, 1995. "Neo-voluntarism: A new European social policy regime?" *European Law Journal* 1, no 1: 31–59.

Zartaloudis, S., 2011. A compass or a spear? The partisan usage of Europe in Portuguese employment-friendly reforms. In *The EU and the domestic politics of welfare state reforms: Europa, Europae*, edited by Paolo Graziano, Sophie Jacquot and Bruno Palier, 175-200. London: Palgrave Macmillan

4 Politics

Carlos Jalali

4.1 Introduction

It is something of a cliché to highlight Portugal's role as the precursor of the 'third wave of democratisation' with its transition to democracy in 1974. Yet this cliché is not without significance. Almost 50 years on, Portugal's democracy is not only the oldest 'third wave democracy' but also one of the most stable, with its political institutions largely unchanged since democratisation and a seemingly resilient party system in terms of its composition and the main dimension of competition.

This is noteworthy on both comparative and domestic grounds. Comparatively, it contrasts with the electoral volatility and party system de-institutionalisation of many democracies during the new millennium, not to mention the growing spectre of democratic backsliding. Domestically, the stability of the current democratic period belies historical precedent, with previous attempts at democracy proving fractious and short-lived.

This chapter examines this stability, assessing the main institutional features of this highly centralised political system, notably the political leadership of the government within its semipresidential system; the relatively high levels of disproportionality in its electoral system; and the main patterns of the party system. Yet the chapter also highlights the considerably less constant undercurrent beneath the surface of this stability, with increasing signs of fraying in the party system's strength and control, making the future trajectory considerably more open-ended than might otherwise appear.

4.2 Historical and institutional context

10 May 2017 marked a significant milestone in Portugal's political history, as the democratic regime established with the 1976 Constitution surpassed the 41 years and 14 days of duration of its predecessor, the Estado Novo. The authoritarian Estado Novo collapsed on 25 April 1974, with a largely bloodless military coup by junior officers. At its demise, it held two deleterious records: as the most enduring non-democratic regime of 20th-century Western Europe; and the longest regime in Portugal in over 150 years.[1]

The coup generated a complex revolutionary dynamic, marked by a conflict over the nature of the regime that would replace the Estado Novo, notably between liberal democracy vs. a radical left popular democracy. This period placed one of Europe's oldest and ethnically and religiously most homogeneous nation-states on the verge of civil war, before the option for liberal democracy was settled and enshrined in the 1976 Constitution. As we shall see next, the lines of division generated by this period were reflected in the party system.

DOI: 10.4324/9781003488033-4

This chapter has been made available under a CC-BY-NC-ND license.

4.2.1 Party system

Four parties dominated Portuguese politics from democratisation until the 21st century and consistently secured parliamentary representation until 2022. The two largest are broad-church parties: the centre-right Social Democratic Party (PSD) and the centre-left Socialist Party (PS). PSD aligns with the European People's Party and the Centrist Democrat International, while PS is affiliated with the Party of European Socialists, the International Socialist, and the Progressive Alliance network. The other two parties are the conservative Democratic Social Centre (CDS), positioned to the right of PSD and affiliated with the European People's Party and the International Democrat Union. To the left of the Socialists is the Marxist-Leninist Communist Party (PCP), affiliated with the International Meeting of Communist and Workers' Parties and part of the Left in the European Parliament parliamentary group.

These four parties emerged as significant forces during the 1974–75 revolutionary period. In the 1999 legislative elections, the party system expanded with the emergence of the Bloco de Esquerda (BE, Left Bloc), formed from a coalition of smaller radical left parties and groups. BE is affiliated with the Party of the European Left and is a founding member of the Now the People! alliance.

Party systems can be defined as the interactions between parties. The central interaction pertains to the formation of government: how parties compete (and cooperate) to form governments (Mair 1997). Indeed, this centrality is evidenced in the classic definition of relevant parties of Sartori (2005 [1976]): parties' coalition or blackmail potential hinges on their ability to enable – or, conversely, block – governmental majorities and survival.

Regarding party interactions until the new millennium, three stand out. First, the competition between the two centrist parties, PS and PSD, for government leadership – i.e., the principal dimension of competition in the party system, following Mair's (1997) framework. PS and PSD have consistently headed every party government since 1976. Second, the exclusion of the PCP (and later of the BE) from national government, preventing left-wing coalitions. Third, the blackmail and/or coalition potential of CDS, PCP, and BE, enabling or blocking parliamentary majority support for the former two parties when they failed to reach single-party majorities.

These three interactions emerged almost immediately after democratisation and largely derived from Portugal's democratic transition.

The revolutionary period fostered lasting divisions in the party system into the late 20th century and beyond. It pitted the PCP and smaller extreme-left parties, some of which later formed the BE, advocating 'popular democracy', against a liberal democratic camp comprising PS, PSD, and CDS, advocating Western liberal democracy. This conflict helps explain the PCP's (and, post-1999, the BE's) exclusion from national government. The Socialist Party – which did not win any single-party parliamentary majorities in the 20th century – often formed minority governments when it held the largest parliamentary share in 1976, 1995, and 1999. In coalition governments, it aligned with right-wing parties like CDS in 1978 and PSD in 1983, avoiding coalitions with the Communists.

The principal dimension of competition emerged early on and strengthened in the second decade of constitutional governments. From 1987 on, the combined vote share of PS and PSD increased, enabling these parties to form single-party governments more easily, at times with single-party parliamentary majorities. Their average combined vote

46   *Carlos Jalali*

in the four legislative elections from 1987 to 1999 was 78%, almost 20 percentage points above the 59% average combined vote share in the previous five elections.

The Portuguese party system quickly institutionalised, demonstrating remarkable stability and predictability regarding relevant parties and key interactions. Applying Mair's (1997) framework, which gauges the closure of competition structures to evaluate party system institutionalisation, reveals a lack of openness to new parties in government since 1980. Government formulas remained static after 1985, and from 1987 onwards, the pattern of government alternation consistently indicated wholesale or non-existent alternation. These three characteristics firmly establish the Portuguese party system, from the latter half of the 1980s onwards, within Mair's closed structure of competition (Mair 1997, 212), reflecting the system's institutionalisation.

4.2.2 Political system

In terms of its political system, we can highlight three central aspects: first, its semi-presidentialism, albeit one where political leadership rests with prime ministers and their cabinets, generating a quasi-parliamentary system; second, the electoral system, which is comparatively disproportional for a proportional representation system; and third, its comparatively weak subnational government.

With regard to the first, Portugal features a popularly elected, fixed-term head of state who coexists alongside a prime minister and government who are responsible to parliament, meeting Elgie's (1999, 13) definition of semipresidentialism. This element was established in the 1976 constitution, with Portugal not only pioneering the third wave of democracy but also heralding one of its main institutional characteristics: semipresidentialism (Elgie, Moestrup and Wu 2011, 271).

In its current format, and since 1982, Portugal fits the premier-presidential subtype of semipresidentialism, with prime ministers and their cabinets accountable solely to parliament, in a hierarchical relationship (Shugart 2005). The relationship of the prime minister and cabinet with the president is largely a transactional and horizontal one, where neither can operate unilaterally, but rather requiring cooperation (Shugart 2005, 328). This is evidenced by the president's veto powers over governmental decrees (which cannot be overturned) and parliamentary legislation (which can be overturned with a 50%+1 or 2/3 majority of parliament, depending on the domain of the proposed legislation).

The Portuguese constitution grants presidents comparatively wide-ranging legislative and non-legislative powers. Portugal presents the highest score of presidential powers for premier-presidential regimes, and the second highest score overall, in Europe (Tavits 2008, 53).

However, formal presidential powers do not necessarily correlate with presidential practice. In Portugal, political leadership within the political system has rested with the prime minister and cabinet, not with the president, a pattern also perceived by voters (Magalhães 2008). This contrasts with French semipresidentialism, where political leadership resides primarily with the president, despite Portuguese presidents holding wider formal powers than their French counterparts.

As Jalali (2011) shows, two related factors explain this. First, the process of Portugal's entry to semipresidentialism. An implicit requirement for the first president to issue from the military after the 1974–75 revolution largely removed the presidency from party competition in the first decade of democracy. Second, and related, presidential practice to date, with presidents not controlling parliamentary majorities and positioning themselves as supra-partisan figures, unlike France.

The initial (military) president did not have a parliamentary party till the very last year of his term. This lack of parliamentary leverage explains the failure of his attempts at imprinting greater presidential control in the executive, when he appointed non-partisan governments in 1978–79, which were blocked by the parties in parliament. It also helped institutionalise the role of the president as a moderating, supra-partisan figure, that can act as a 'safety-valve' in the political system (Cruz 1995, 224; Feijó 2001).

This military requirement lapsed in 1986[2] and led to the full integration of the presidential level in the party system. However, political leadership has remained primarily with the government. The four post-1986 presidents all had strong ties with PS and PSD; indeed, all were former party leaders. However, none retained leadership within their party at the time of election as president, and thus could not command parliamentary support. Moreover, for the most part, they had to face a parliament with a majority that was not congruent with their own.

This very much remains the case in the 21st century. The presidential and parliamentary majorities have been congruent for 36% of the time from the beginning of 2000 till the end of 2021. Moreover, when there has been congruence, the parliamentary group has been beholden to the party leader (who was the prime minister), not the president.

The fact that political leadership rests overwhelmingly with the prime minister places Portugal in the quasi-parliamentary operational sub-type of semipresidentialism of Wu (2011). Despite coexisting with an elected president, the Portuguese prime minister (PM) is a comparatively powerful one, as Silveira and Silva (2023) demonstrate. As their study demonstrates, prime ministerial autonomy and power within the executive has, if anything, increased during the period at hand, due to three factors: first, a decline in cabinet collegiality, with cabinet serving to rubberstamp decisions that are coordinated by the PM's office or decided bilaterally between the PM and ministers; second, a strengthening of the informal inner cabinet in policy coordination, alongside a weakening of party control over this structure with the greater inclusion of non-partisan ministers; and third, the strengthening of the PMs private office, in terms of resources and influence (Silveira and Silva 2023).

At the same time, the Portuguese experience in the 21st century belies Bahro, Bayerlein, and Veser's (1998) expectation that semipresidential presidents are 'void of influence' and akin to indirectly elected presidents in contexts of incongruence. Presidents wield considerable influence, even when facing a government backed by a solid (and rival) parliamentary majority. Presidential vs. prime ministerial influence thus appears to be better captured as a continuum rather than a dichotomy (as suggested by Sartori 1997), with presidents acting largely as a moderating power (Feijó 2021).

This can be seen in two distinct dimensions. The first is in the leveraging of their formal and informal powers to influence government decisions, especially when facing a minority government. A sizeable proportion of legislation emanating from the government is negotiated ex ante between the president and government rather than being formally vetoed (Feijó 2021, 102).

It is also seen with the presidential power of parliamentary dissolution, which can be a significant bargaining chip for presidents, especially when the government fears it will lose power with dissolution (Shugart 2005, 18). While not frequent in the period at hand, it has been significant, notably in 2003 over the Iraq war. As Jalali (2011) notes, then Prime Minister (and later European Commission president) Barroso intended to include

48   *Carlos Jalali*

Portuguese troops in Operation Iraqi Freedom, after hosting the March 2003 summit between Bush, Blair, and Aznar in the Portuguese Azores. However, the prime minister had to back down when President Sampaio informed him that, as supreme commander of the armed forces, he would not endorse sending troops to Iraq without an EU or UN mandate. While Sampaio did not explicitly threaten Barroso with dissolution if he persisted with his plans, he made clear that he would use his full range of constitutional powers. It did not exercise Barroso's political instinct much to realise that an election over the deeply unpopular Iraq war would not be a winning one (especially when his government was unpopular enough due to a growing economic crisis).

Second, presidents wield influence by shaping public and media agenda. Presidential statements have substantial media and public repercussion. Presidents leverage this, with their constitutional powers, generating considerable salience for issues they favour or accentuating opposition to government proposals they disagree with.

This practice was established early on in Portuguese semipresidentialism. Barroso (1983, 236–7), assessing semipresidentialism between 1979 and 1983, characterised presidential speeches and public statements as 'a new weapon of the president', noting the endogenous capacity of a president to manage his public visibility and speeches, reinforcing his power to influence public and media agenda.

This pattern has remained in the period at hand. For instance, President Cavaco Silva was instrumental in derailing the government's preferred location for a new international airport for Lisbon, even though the government had a single-party parliamentary majority. His public expression of doubts in mid-2007 reinforced opposition to the government's choice and maintained the issue in the limelight, ultimately forcing the government to change tack.

The Cavaco Silva presidency also highlights how a president's capacity to influence fundamentally hinges on his popularity. Cavaco Silva's second term was marked by a significant drop in his popularity, which made it less costly for other political actors to ignore his preferences (Fernandes and Jalali 2017). The subsequent president, Marcelo Rebelo de Sousa (2016–), has re-established high levels of presidential popularity and re-established presidential influence, not least during the Covid pandemic (Feijó 2021, 93–4, 121–2).

Given the quasi-parliamentary nature of semipresidentialism, parliament-executive relations play a central role in Portugal, in terms of government formation and survival, executive scrutiny, and legislation.

Regarding the first, the president has constitutional autonomy in appointing a prime minister. However, the government must then survive an investiture vote in the unicameral parliament. As Section 4.3.2 details, this became relevant after the 2015 parliamentary elections.

Parliament can oust governments with no-confidence motion (*moção de censura*), needing support of over half of all MPs to be approved. While only one such vote succeeded, in 1989, the new millennium has seen a substantial increase in these motions: 22 from 2000 to 2022, compared to five from 1976 to 1999.

All but two of the no-confidence in the 21st century were bound to fail from the outset, as they targeted governments with apparent parliamentary majority support. Nevertheless, their occurrence reflects parliament's shift to a greater emphasis on scrutinising the executive in the period at hand, alongside other tools like regular prime minister debates or a greater role for parliamentary committees (Goes and Leston-Bandeira 2023).

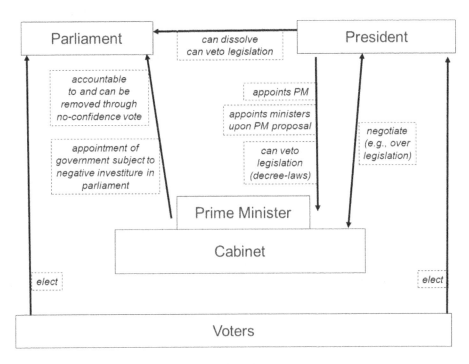

Figure 4.1 Overview of the Portuguese political system

Concerning legislation, parliament has fairly wide powers to initiate, amend, and reject legislation. Yet, the executive also wields considerable legislative powers. As Goes and Bandeira (2023, 140) note, the balance of power between parliament and government ultimately hinges on the government's parliamentary support rather than constitutional stipulations, with parliamentary influence greater when facing a minority government. Figure 4.1 provides an overview of the Portuguese political system.

4.2.3 Electoral system

As political leadership rests primarily with the government, tied to parliamentary support, legislative elections become the central political arena. Portugal employs a closed list proportional representation (PR) electoral system with one-tier districting, the d'Hondt formula, and no formal electoral thresholds. This system, used since the constituent assembly elections of 1975, has only seen modifications in the size of parliament: 263 in the first legislative elections of 1976; then 250 till the 1987 elections; and 230 from the 1991 legislative elections on.

District magnitude, a significant determinant of an electoral system's impact, averages relatively high at 10.5 MPs per district. However, this conceals a broad variance, with districts split into three groups. The first comprises two sizeable districts, Lisbon and Porto, with 48 and 40 seats each in the most recent 2019 and 2022 legislative elections. The second comprises the remaining seven districts in the more populous coastal regions, averaging 12.9 seats with a range of 9 to 19. The final group includes the remaining 13 electoral districts of the less populated interior; the insular regions of Azores and

50 *Carlos Jalali*

Madeira; and two districts for foreign residents, a reflection of Portugal's large diaspora. In the 2019 and 2022 elections, these had an average district magnitude of 4.4, ranging from 2 to 8 deputies, with only three exceeding a magnitude of 5.

This variance contradicts Lijphart et al.'s (1988, 19) claim that 'Portuguese PR can be regarded as basically proportional'. Smaller parties (polling under 5%) can only compete for seats in Lisbon and Porto, where the average effective threshold – i.e., the expected percentage of votes required to have a midway chance of winning a seat – was 1.5% in the 2019 and 2022 elections. In medium-sized districts, it was 5.6%; in smaller districts, it exceeded 18%.

This variance also contributes to the considerable seat bonus awarded by the electoral system to the more voted lists. From 1976 to 2022, the most voted party or list, on average, gained 7 percentage points more seats than its share of votes. The second most voted party or list received a smaller but still significant bonus: an average of 3.7 percentage points. This seat bonus bolsters PS and PSD within the principal dimension of competition. Moreover, it has strengthened in the 21st century, with an average of 8 percentage points compared to 6.5 percentage points from 1976 to 1999. In the two most recent elections of 2019 and 2022, it has exceeded 10 percentage points (10.6 and 10.8, respectively), enabling a single-party majority with 41.4% of the vote in 2022.

4.2.4 Subnational government

The final institutional dimension to highlight concerns the subnational government. Portugal is a unitary state. Regional government is restricted to the two insular regions of the Azores and Madeira. The main subnational structure is local government, at municipal and submunicipal levels, with the main executive body being the mayor and the municipal council (Freire 2005, 822). These are elected through an unusual mixed electoral system, which combines, in the same vote, first-past-the-post plurality for the election of the mayor and closed-list PR for the remaining municipal councillors.

Portugal has 308 municipalities ('*concelhos*'),[3] with substantial population disparities, ranging from almost 500,000 to a few hundred voters. A significant proportion of municipalities are small, with 39% having less than 10,000 registered voters in the 2021 local elections. Those with fewer than 50,000 voters represented 84% of all municipalities, though only 41% of the voting population. In contrast, the largest municipalities, with over 100,000 voters, constituted 8% of all municipalities yet 43% of the voting population.

Differences in population yield variations in resources. Nonetheless, Portugal remains one of the most centralised countries in the developed world. Subnational government expenditure in Portugal was 13.5% of total public expenditure in 2019, well below the OECD weighted average of 40.2% and the OECD weighted average for unitary states of 28.8% (OECD 2022). Subnational expenditure represented 5.7% of GDP, vs. 16.2% for the OECD as a whole (OECD 2022).

4.2.5 Political system evolution

Portugal's political system did not present any significant changes in the period of 2000–2022. However, there is one noteworthy dynamic to highlight. Since the 2001 local elections, non-party lists can contest local elections. With this change, parties' monopoly of representation became limited to legislative and European Parliament elections.

Politics 51

This has undermined parties' control of voter support, revealing a less-than-complete party loyalty among voters. In both 2017 and 2021, independent candidates garnered more votes than all but the three largest parties. Moreover, they won the mayoral race in several municipalities (16 in 2017 and 19 in 2021), including the second most important city of Porto.

The rise of independent candidates reflects both diminished external control of voter support by parties and a loosening of internal control over their members. Many of these candidates are often referred to as 'false independents' – politicians from within parties who run as independents (Jalali 2014).

There is a high level of internal factionalism, usually over who gets offices rather than policy or ideology, particularly in the two main parties (Jalali 2015). Prior to 2001, conflicts over local candidates were settled inside the parties. With the rule change of 2001, rival party contenders can bring their disputes to the electorate, by competing as independents. Party structures are thus less capable of containing intra-party conflict.

This weakening of party control is also evident in the post-2000 presidential elections. Although these elections are technically individual contests, candidates are typically supported by political parties. In the four elections spanning the civilianising election of 1986 till 2001, 14 out of 15 candidates were officially backed by parties with parliamentary representation.[4] Subsequently, this pattern has shifted significantly. In the four elections between 2006 and 2021, there were 28 candidacies, of which 8 were without endorsement of parties with parliamentary seats.[5] Moreover, independent candidates came second in 2006, and third in 2011, significantly outvoting several party-supported candidates.

As we shall see in the next section, this weakening party loyalty appears to be gradually filtering through to the parliamentary party system.

4.3 Party system dynamics in the 21st century

We begin by characterising the Portuguese party system during this period using Mair's framework of structures of competition. Table 4.1 presents the patterns of alternation, innovation, and openness of government in the eight governments in the period of 2000–2022.

The party system's structures of competition remain highly stable. Government formation is dominated by the two centrist parties, the PS and the PSD, maintaining the pattern established since democratisation. As in the previous periods, the Socialist Party continued to form minority governments when it didn't attain a single-party majority; while the PSD maintained the pattern of coalition governments with the CDS when it failed to reach a majority. The period does not present any openness to new parties or innovation in governing formulas, with patterns of wholesale and non-alternation.

Party system interactions cannot be dissociated from electoral results, with parties' vote serving, in a way, as the currency by which they leverage their position vis-à-vis each other, influencing patterns of interaction. The stability evidenced in Table 4.1 is also found in levels of electoral volatility and the effective number of electoral and parliamentary parties (Table 4.2).

PS and PSD remain the two largest parties, with a notable gap vis-à-vis the remaining relevant parties. Despite a growing number of different lists elected to parliament, peaking at 9 in 2019 before dropping to 8 in 2022, parliamentary fragmentation has not increased. Indeed, there was a small decline in the number of effective parliamentary

52 Carlos Jalali

Table 4.1 Alternation, innovation, and openness in government, 2000–2022

Legislature	Period	Government composition and prime minister	Alternation	Innovation	Openness to new parties
VIII	1999–2002	PS; exactly 50% of seats (Guterres)	Non-existent	No	No
IX	2002–4	PSD-CDS majority (Barroso)	Wholesale	No	No
	2004–5	PSD-CDS majority (Santana Lopes)	Non-existent	No	No
X	2005–09	PS majority (Sócrates)	Wholesale	No	No
XI	2009–11	PS minority (Sócrates)	Non-existent	No	No
XII	2011–15	PSD-CDS majority (Passos Coelho)	Wholesale	No	No
XIII	Oct.–Nov. 2015	PSD-CDS minority (Passos Coelho)	Non-existent	No	No
	Nov. 2015–2019	PS minority (Costa)	Wholesale	No	No
XIV	2019–22	PS minority (Costa)	Non-existent	No	No
XV	2022–	PS majority (Costa)	Non-existent	No	No

parties in these two elections. The continued stability of the Portuguese party system is also evidenced in electoral volatility, with an average of 11.1 for the 2002–2022 elections and a standard deviation of 1.9. This is lower than the overall average since democratisation and is close to that of the previous decade, a high point of stability, with an average of 9.9 in the three legislative elections of 1991–1999.

However, beneath the surface of this apparent stability, there are some signs of change. We can identify three noteworthy trends: first, a decline in support for the two main centrist parties; second, greater openness in government formation and cooperation on the left; and third, the emergence of new parties.

4.3.1 Decline in support for the two main parties

While Portugal did not have an electoral earthquake in this period (unlike several other European countries), the combined vote share of the two main parties has gradually eroded since 2009. In the 2002 and 2005 legislative elections, their average combined vote share was 75.9%, similar to the average for the 1987–1999 elections. For the five

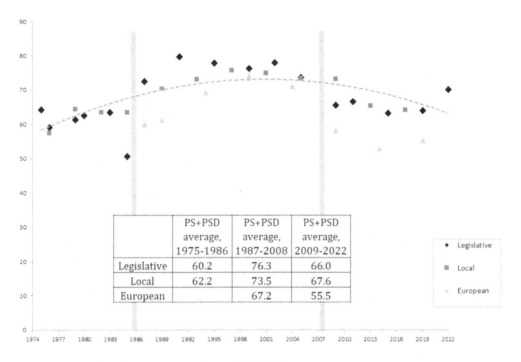

Figure 4.2 Combined PS-PSD vote share, 1975–2022

legislative elections from 2009 to 2022, this average fell to 66%, closer to the early years of democracy (average of 61.6% in the first four legislative elections) than to the 1987–2005 period. As Figure 4.2 shows, this decline is also evident in local and European elections.

The gradual decline of the two main parties is evidenced in the rising effective number of electoral parties (ENEP). The average ENEP for 2009–2022 is 4.2, vs. 3.2 for the first two elections of the 21st century. That stands closer to the average of the 1976–85 period (4.3) than that of the 1987–2005 period (3.1). This increase in the ENEP is moderated in terms of seats, not least due to the electoral system characteristics noted in the previous section. Nevertheless, the effective number of parliamentary parties (ENPP) also increases somewhat after 2009, with an average of 2.9 for the 2009–2022 elections, vs. 2.5 for the 1987–2005 period.

4.3.2 Greater openness in government and cooperation on the left

The second trend pertains to changes in interactions over government, arguably stemming from the erosion of PS-PSD votes. For the PSD, this has resulted in its participation solely in coalition governments during this period – whereas, in the 1987–2002 period, the PSD was able to govern with single party majorities. It also allowed the CDS to return to government, in 2002–5 and 2011–15, after being out of cabinets for almost 20 years.

More significantly, it has generated unprecedented cooperation on the left, notably during the 21st constitutional government of António Costa of 2015–19. On the surface, this government was hardly exceptional. It was formally a minority Socialist government,

54   *Carlos Jalali*

just as most previous Socialist governments. In terms of the structures of competition, typically measured through a government's party composition (Bértoa and Enyedi 2016), the Costa executive did not represent any openness or innovation in the governing formula, as Table 4.1 highlights.

However, party interactions regarding this government differed significantly from previous Socialist minority governments. The Costa executive reached and remained in office with the parliamentary support of the parties to its left, PCP and BE. The significance of this cooperation cannot be overstated. As noted above, a central characteristic of the party system was the historical divide between PS and the parties to its left.

This had historically precluded any cooperation over government formation on the left. It also generated an asymmetry in government formation, a pattern that Freire (2009, 224) describes as a 'party system bias to the right'. Of the 12 legislatures in Portugal between 1976 and 2015, seven had a parliamentary majority of parties to the left. However, only when the PS gained a single-party parliamentary majority, in 2005, did this translate into a left-wing government with the support of a parliamentary majority. In contrast, all five legislatures with right-wing majorities in this period led to governments with majority support in parliament, with the PSD coalescing with the CDS when it did not have a single-party majority.

The 2015–19 legislature reverted this rightward bias, with unprecedented cooperation on the left. Perhaps the clearest example of how innovative this was can be seen in the approval of the state budget, the central policy instrument for Portuguese governments. All annual state budgets of the PS government in the 2015–19 legislature were approved with the support of PS, BE, and PCP (and the opposition of the PSD and CDS).

Previously, BE and PCP had consistently voted against all Socialist budgets. The BE had done so in every budget since it was first elected to parliament in 1999. The PCP also voted against all budgets in its 40 previous years in parliament, only deviating from this position once: the first budget of 1976, when an abstention was irrelevant in terms of ensuring approval. Consistent with this 'rightward bias' of the party system, previous minority Socialist executives had sought budget approval from the parties to their right, usually through the latter's abstention, confirming the divide between the PS and the parties to its left when it came to key government decisions.

The exceptionality of the cooperation between PS, PCP, and BE was reflected in the designation that it received: the 'contraption' ('geringonça'). This term was initially advanced by the opposition in a depreciative manner, seeking to emphasise its likely instability. Yet the designation stuck and gradually gained a more positive connotation as the government endured, serving to highlight the innovative character of this unlikely entente.

The apparent success of the Portuguese 'contraption' made it a reference for many European social democratic parties (Jalali, Moniz, and Silva 2020, 230). It also seemingly gained popular support. Polls immediately prior to the 2019 legislative elections showed that the 'contraption' was voters' most preferred governing option, surpassing all other options combined (RTP 2019). The 2019 election results were consistent with this reading, as the combined vote and seat share for the three left-wing parties increased.

Yet, despite its stability in the 2015–19 legislature and popular backing for a renewed 'contraption' in the 2019 parliamentary elections, the left-wing cooperation had practically evaporated by late 2022. What explains this reversal?

To answer this question, it is necessary to assess why the 'contraption' emerged in 2015. I would argue it reflected the interplay between Portugal's semipresidentialism with a unique parliamentary configuration, which in turn reflected the declining vote share of PS and PSD noted above. As Table 4.2 shows, the electoral alliance between the PSD and CDS – which had governed together from 2011 to 2015 – gained the largest share of votes and seats in the 2015 elections, with the PSD having the largest parliamentary group, with 89 seats. However, with 107 seats combined, the PSD and CDS were nine seats short of a parliamentary majority. More significantly, this occurred in a parliament where left-wing parties (PS, BE, and PCP) held a majority, with these parties' combined seats totalling 122. With a partial exception of the 1985 elections,[6] this was the first time that the most voted list and largest party came from one political bloc while the majority in parliament was held by parties of the opposing bloc.

In the aftermath of the elections, President Cavaco Silva appointed, on the 22nd of October, the leader of the PSD and prime minister from 2011 to 2015, Pedro Passos Coelho, as prime minister, who subsequently formed a minority PSD-CDS coalition cabinet. The president explained that this appointment followed previous precedent, namely that 'winners' of elections be given the opportunity to form government (Cavaco Silva 2015).

As noted in Section 4.2.2, the executive must then secure parliamentary investiture. Investiture in Portugal presents a weak regime (Cheibub, Martin and Rasch 2015): it is reactive, *ex post*, requiring a negative majority to block investiture. The investiture centres on the presentation of the government's programme to parliament. For there to be an investiture vote, a motion to reject this programme must be tabled. If no such motion is tabled, the government takes full office. If a motion is presented, its approval by an absolute majority of all MPs triggers the government's automatic resignation.

On November 10, a majority of 123 MPs of PS, BE, PCP, and PAN rejected the programme of the minority PSD-CDS government, thus obliging its resignation. Constitutional rules precluded a presidential dissolution of parliament at that time on two grounds: the president was in the final six months of his term and the parliament was still in the first six months of its own term.

Prior to this vote, the PS formalised separate agreements (termed as 'joint positions') with the BE and PCP, ensuring a set of common policy options and their support for a Socialist government to take office. These agreements were the culmination of a negotiation process between the parties that began on the night of the October 4 elections. In the aftermath of the dismissal of the Passos Coelho government, the President appointed the Socialist Party leader, António Costa, as prime minister, with his government being sworn in on November 26.

With these election results and the President giving the first opportunity as formateur to PSD, 'necessity [became] the mother of the "contraption"' (Jalali, Moniz and Silva 2020, 248). Given investiture rules, the only means PS, PCP, and BE had to block the PSD-CDS government was to cooperate.

The three parties had significant incentives to enter this unprecedented cooperation. For PCP and BE, not blocking the PSD-CDS government risked provoking their voters' ire, all the more so given that the initial PSD-CDS government nominated by the president was the same that had imposed significant austerity measures during the bailout of 2011–14. For the PS, it offered a way to return to power and allowed its leader to preserve his political career, especially after failing to 'win' the 2015 elections.

This cooperation proved stable throughout the 2015–2019 Costa government. The literature describes this as an instance of contract parliamentarianism (Fernandes, Magalhães and Santana-Pereira 2018), i.e., where the relationship between a minority

Table 4.2 Vote and seat share (%) in legislative elections, with effective number of parties and volatility (2000–2022)

	2002		2005		2009		2011		2015		2019		2022	
	Vote	*Seat*	*Vote*	*Seat*	*Vote*	*Seat*	*Vote*	*Seat*	*Vote*	*Seat*	*Vote*	*Seat*	*Vote*	*Seat*
PS	37.8	41.7	45	52.6	36.6	42.2	28	32.2	32.3	37.4	36.3	47.0	41.4	52.2
PSD	40.2	45.7	28.8	32.6	29.1	35.2	38.7	47	(31)	38.7	27.8	34.3	28.8	33.5
CDS	8.7	6.1	7.2	5.2	10.4	9.1	11.7	10.4	(7.6)	7.8	4.2	2.2	1.9	0
PCP	6.9	5.2	7.5	6.1	7.9	6.5	7.9	7	8.2	7.4	6.3	5.2	4.3	2.6
BE	2.8	1.3	6.3	3.5	9.8	7	5.2	3.5	10.2	8.3	9.5	8.3	4.4	2.2
Portugal Ahead (PSD+CDS alliance)	-	-	-	-	-	-	-	-	38.6	(46.5)	-	-	-	-
Others	1.5	0	2.1	0	3.1	0	4.4	0	6.9	0.4	10.9	3	16.6	9.6
Effective number of parties	3.1	2.6	3.3	2.6	4.1	3.1	4	2.9	4.6	3.2	4.7	2.9	3.8	2.6
Electoral volatility	8.6		12.4		8.4		12.6		14.3		10.5		10.6	
Turnout	61.4		64.2		59.7		58		55.9		48.6		51.4	

Notes:
1. The PSD and CDS ran together in most electoral districts in 2015, under the label Portugal Ahead (*Portugal à Frente*, PàF). To calculate the individual votes shares of PSD and CDS, the alliance's votes are split in a 4:1 ratio, following the practice adopted in the literature (e.g., Jalali and Lobo 2006). This ratio is applied in other instances where the two parties ran together.
2. The effective number of electoral parties for 2015 is calculated by separating the PSD-CDS.
3. Volatility is calculated by aggregating the votes of other parties.

government and the parties that support it in parliament is 'so institutionalised that they come close to being majority governments' (Bale and Bergman 2006, 422). However, it is perhaps better described as an instance of weak contract parliamentarianism (Jalali, Moniz and Silva 2020), as the agreements did not guarantee PCP and BE support for the government in confidence and supply votes. That the cooperation proved stable suggests that parties will avoid rescinding contracts when the economy is growing and the government is popular (Jalali, Moniz and Silva 2020, 234–5).

Would there have been a 'contraption' had the Socialists been the most voted party in the 2015 elections? As with any counterfactual, an absolute answer is not possible. But the probability of an entente on the left appears to be significantly smaller. A key driver for the 'contraption' would no longer be present: the PS, PCP, and BE would not have to reach agreements to avoid a PSD-CDS government. As the winner of the election, the PS would have the first chance as formateur. As noted, government programmes are not necessarily voted on: only if a motion of rejection is presented. Most likely the BE and PCP would not have to position themselves on the Costa government's programme: out of five previous minority party governments, only two saw motions of rejection be tabled. And, if a motion was presented, PCP and BE abstentions would be sufficient for the government to survive, signifying a very different level of commitment with the government's programme.

In such a scenario, both sides would have fewer incentives to reach an agreement. The PCP and BE could maintain a more maximalist strategy in terms of policy, as they would not need to compromise to avoid a PSD-CDS government. The PS (and Costa personally) would also have fewer incentives to compromise with the parties to the left, as they would no longer be needed to reach government.

This counterfactual reading is not disconfirmed by the party interactions after the 2019 elections. As noted above, election results and pre-electoral polls suggested that voters supported the continuation of the 'contraption'. However, the post-2019 did not result in agreements between the three parties. Paradoxically, it was the electoral strengthening of the left that made the agreements redundant. With the PS being the most voted party and first formateur, the three parties no longer needed to formally agree to prevent a right-wing government. In the absence of such agreements, the pressure to compromise with each other also diminished.

The post-2019 period thus sees a relatively rapid erosion of this cooperation on the left, until its ultimate breakdown in 2021. The PCP excluded the possibility of renewing a formal agreement with the PS prior to the 2019 election; and while both PS and BE stated they were ready to renew a formal agreement, negotiations ended mere days after the election, amid mutual acrimony (Jalali, Moniz and Silva 2020, 247).

The previous cooperation did not immediately disappear. The 2020 budget, voted in February 2020, was approved thanks to the abstention of BE and PCP. The budget for 2021, voted in October 2020, was rejected by BE, but the PCP repeated its abstention, thus enabling approval. However, the re-emerging divisions on the left came to the fore over the 2022 budget proposal, with both PCP and BE voting against it and driving its rejection by parliament in October 2021. This was interpreted by the President as a breakdown in the parliamentary backing for the government, leading him to dissolve parliament and call new legislative elections, held in January 2022.

The 2022 elections were to give the Socialists a single-party parliamentary majority. Benefiting from the electoral system's disproportionality, the PS won 120 of the 230 parliamentary seats with 41.4% of the vote, allowing it to dispense with the need for

58   Carlos Jalali

parliamentary allies. Conversely, the election saw significant losses for BE and PCP, their parliamentary groups reduced by three-quarters and one-half, respectively.

The initial months of the post-2022 legislature point to a hardening of divisions between PS and its erstwhile allies on the left, very much reminiscent of pre-'contraption' days. The significant divides over economic policy were reflected in the BE and PCP rejection of the 2023 budget proposal, with both parties stating that the Socialists proposal betrayed left-wing principles. Meanwhile, Russia's invasion of Ukraine exposed the chasm between the parties over foreign policy, especially with the PCP's vocal anti-NATO stance and opposition to supporting Ukraine, decrying President Volodymyr Zelensky as the embodiment of a 'xenophobic and warmongering power, surrounded and sustained by fascist and neo-Nazi forces' (PCP 2022). Yet the experience of the 'contraption' has generated at least one important dynamic in the party system: that cooperation on the left is no longer seen as inconceivable, even if it appears unlikely in the near future.

4.3.3 Emergence of new parties

The third notable trend in the party system pertains to the emergence of new parliamentary parties, outside the hitherto pentagon of main parties. The combined vote share of other parties, beyond the five main parties, has grown throughout the 21st century, increasing over tenfold from 1.5% in 2002 to 16.6% in 2022.

The 2022 election is a good example of a seemingly calm surface that conceals more turbulent undercurrents. A cursory glance would suggest a reinforced party system after this election, with volatility being the third lowest of the 21st century; the effective number of electoral parties the lowest since 2005; and the effective number of parliamentary parties equalling, at 2.6, the lows of 2002 and 2005.

Yet this election marked the most significant shake-up in the composition of the party system since the mid-1980s,[7] marking the first time since democratisation that neither PCP nor CDS was among the five most-voted parties. The former came sixth, falling below 5% for the first time in history; the latter was ousted from parliament.

Taking their place in the five most voted parties were two relative newcomers. First, the radical-right populist Enough (*Chega*), formalised in 2019, whose 7.2% of the vote made it the third largest party in parliament. This result also put paid to the quaint notion that Portugal was somehow immune to radical right populism (Silva 2018), an impression also echoed by many of the country's politicians, including the secretary-general of the UN (and former Portuguese prime minister) António Guterres (Dias 2017). The second was the economically and socially liberal Liberal Initiative (*Iniciativa Liberal*), formalised in December 2017, which became the fourth largest party with 4.9% of the vote. Both parties had won a single seat in the 2019 elections. In addition, the 2022 election saw two other parties obtain parliamentary representation, the People-Animals-Nature party (*Partidos-Animais-Natureza*), a pro-animal rights and environmental party that has been in parliament since 2015; and the left-libertarian pro-European Free (Livre), which had also won a seat in 2019.

While the quantitative indicators of the party system remain stable, its composition shows signs of considerable fraying. Until the 2022 election, this was most perceptible in the erosion of the combined vote share of the two largest parties, PS and PSD. In 2022, it struck the other historically established parties, PCP, BE, and CDS. Their combined vote in 2022 stood at 10.6%, less than half of their average in the previous five elections (average 23.1%, max. 26% in 2015, min. 18.4% in 2002).

Politics 59

This pattern is significant. As noted earlier, the Portuguese party system became institutionalised early on after democratisation. This occurred despite the absence of mass parties. Except for the Communist Party, political parties did not seek deep social anchors nor politicise existing social cleavages, rather adopting broader catch-all strategies (Jalali 2015). Yet, despite the relative absence of these sociological constraints, aggregate voting behaviour has been relatively stable since democratisation. Part of the explanation for this resides in the institutionalisation of the party system: by becoming institutionalised, it generated constraints on voters, narrowing the set of parties perceived as viable.

The 2022 election suggests these constraints have weakened significantly, increasing voters' readiness to consider a wider range of alternatives at elections. If this pattern remains, we are likely to see more, not less, volatility and shifts in the composition of the party system. Moreover, the victims of this volatility may include some of the new parties that have emerged in the past three elections. The People-Animals-Nature party partly illustrates this: after winning four seats in 2019 and seemingly consolidating its position in the party system (Fernandes and Magalhães 2020, 1046), it only narrowly avoided falling out of parliament in 2022, winning a single seat by a mere 1,600 votes. It is not inconceivable that some of the parties that have recently emerged may yet prove short-lived, with the greater availability of voters being a boon but also potentially a bane.

4.4 Conclusion

The Portuguese political system is seemingly very stable. Its political institutions largely date back to the country's complex democratisation. Its party system has avoided the political earthquakes that have marked several other West European democracies, presenting relatively stable levels of parliamentary fragmentation and volatility. Likewise, the choice between the centre-right PSD and the centre-left PS to lead government remains the principal dimension of competition in the 21st century, continuing a pattern that was established in the first democratic elections.

However, as this chapter has shown, this apparent stability masks a significantly more turbulent undercurrent. The party system shows signs of fraying, with voters increasingly willing to consider options beyond the parties that have hitherto dominated Portuguese politics. This is reflected in an erosion in the support for the two largest parties, and, in the most recent 2022 election, in a sharp decline in the support for the other three mainstays of the party system.

If the parties that have historically dominated Portuguese politics fail to deliver in terms of policies and results vis-à-vis citizens' expectations in the coming years, this submerged turbulence may well come to the fore and engulf the existing party system. As the 50th anniversary of Portuguese democracy approaches, its political and party system stand at a potential crossroads.

Acknowledgements

This research was supported by the Research Project 'Into the Secret Garden of Portuguese politics: parliamentary candidate selection in Portugal, 1976–2015' financed by the Portuguese Foundation for Science and Technology (PTDC/CPO-CPO/30296/2017).

Notes

1 The period of the constitutional monarchy from 1822 to 1910 was assailed by numerous coups, revolts, and civil wars that yielded significant discontinuities in terms of the actual regime in

60 Carlos Jalali

place (Mata 1991, 765). Taking this into account, the constitutional monarchy does not surpass the current democratic regime (nor the Estado Novo).

2 This is reflected in the nature of presidential candidates. While eight out of ten candidates were military men in the first two presidential elections of 1976 and 1980, from the third (1986) election till the most recent (2021) election, not a single military candidate has come forward.

3 These, in turn, have submunicipalities. After a reform in 2013, there are a total of 3091 of these submunicipalities (*freguesias*). Previously there were 4259.

4 The exception was Maria de Lourdes Pintasilgo, the only female prime minister of Portugal. She ran in the 1986 presidential elections without backing from parliamentary parties and finished last in the first ballot.

5 2006: Manuel Alegre. 2011: Fernando Nobre. 2016: Henrique Neto; Cândido Ferreira; Jorge Sequeira; Vitorino Silva; Paulo de Morais. 2021: Vitorino Silva.

6 In the 1985 elections, the newly formed Democratic Renewal Party (PRD, *Partido Renovador Democrático*), won 18.7% of the vote. This party is typically placed on the centre-left. If we include it, the left had a parliamentary majority in 1985, despite the centre-right PSD winning the most seats. However, the PRD had an ambiguous political positioning, especially at its outset. In the investiture vote for the 1985 PSD minority government, the PS and PCP opposed the government programme, while the PRD and the CDS abstained, securing the government's approval. The PRD was to disappear from parliament by 1991.

7 See footnote 6 above.

References

Bahro, Horst, Bernhard H., Bayerlein, and Ernst Veser. 1998. "Duverger's concept: Semi-presidential government revisited." *European Journal of Political Research* 34, no. 2: 201–224.

Bale, Tim, and Torbjörn Bergman. 2006. "Captives no longer, but servants still? Contract parliamentarism and the new minority governance in Sweden and New Zealand." *Government and Opposition* 41, no. 3: 422–449.

Barroso, José Durão. 1986. "Les conflits entre le Président portugais et la majorité parlementaire de 1979 à 1983." In *Les Régimes Semi-Présidentiels*, edited by Maurice Duverger, 237–254. Paris: Presses Universitaires de France.

Bértoa, Fernando C., and Zsolt Enyedi. 2016. "Party system closure and openness: Conceptualization, operationalization and validation." *Party Politics* 22, no. 3: 265–277.

Cavaco Silva, Aníbal. 2015. "Comunicação ao País do Presidente da República sobre a indigitação do Primeiro-Ministro." October 22, 2015. https://anibalcavacosilva.arquivo.presidencia.pt/?idc=21&idi=97250

Cheibub, José Antonio, Shane Martin, and Bjørn Erik Rasch. 2015. "Government Selection and Executive Powers: Constitutional Design in Parliamentary Democracies." *West European Politics* 38, no. 5: 969–996.

Cruz, Manuel Braga. 1995. *Instituições Políticas e Processos Sociais*. Venda Nova: Bertrand.

Dias, Ana Sousa. 2017. "O pêndulo de Guterres: entrevista ao novo secretário-geral das Nações Unidas, António Guterres, para o DN/JN." *Diário de Notícias*, January 2, 2017. https://www.dn.pt/mundo/entrevista/o-pendulo-de-guterres-5581294.html

Elgie, Robert, Sophie Moestrup, and Yu-Shan Wu. 2011. "Semi-Presidentialism: What Have We Learned?" In *Semi-Presidentialism and Democracy*, edited by Robert Elgie, Sophie Moestrup, and Yu-Shan Wu, 264–274. New York: Palgrave MacMillan.

Elgie, Robert. 1999. "The Politics of Semi-Presidentialism." In *Semi-Presidentialism in Europe*, edited by Robert Elgie, 1–21. Oxford: Oxford University Press.

Feijó, Rui. 2021. *Presidents in Semi-Presidential Regimes: Moderating Power in Portugal and Timor-Leste*. London: Palgrave Macmillan.

Fernandes, Jorge M., and Carlos Jalali. 2017. "A resurgent presidency? Portuguese semi-presidentialism and the 2016 elections." *South European Society and Politics* 22, no. 1: 121–138.

Fernandes, Jorge M., and Pedro C. Magalhães. 2020. "The 2019 Portuguese general elections." *West European Politics* 43, no. 4: 1038–1050.

Fernandes, Jorge M., Pedro C. Magalhães, and José Santana-Pereira. 2018. "Portugal's leftist government: From sick man to poster boy?" *South European Society and Politics* 23, no. 4: 503–524.

Freire, André. 2005. "Eleições de segunda ordem e ciclos eleitorais no Portugal democrático, 1975–2004." *Análise Social* 40, no. 177: 815–846.

Freire, André. 2009. "Mudança do sistema partidário em Portugal, 1974–2009: o papel dos factores políticos, sociais e ideológicos." In *Eleições e sistemas eleitorais: perspectivas históricas e políticas*, edited by Maria Antonieta Cruz, 215–261. Porto: Universidade do Porto Editorial.

Goes, Eunice, and Cristina Leston-Bandeira. 2023. "The Role of the Portuguese Parliament." In Oxford Handbook of Portuguese Politics, edited by Jorge M. Fernandes, Pedro C. Magalhães, and António Costa Pinto, 136–148. Oxford: Oxford University Press.

Jalali, Carlos, and Marina Costa Lobo. 2006. "The Trials of a Socialist Government: Right-Wing Victories in Local and Presidential Elections in Portugal, 2005–2006." *South European Society and Politics* 11, no. 2: 287–299.

Jalali, Carlos, João Moniz, and Patrícia Silva. 2020. "In the Shadow of the 'Government of the Left': The 2019 Legislative Elections in Portugal." *South European Society and Politics* 25, no. 2: 229–255.

Jalali, Carlos. 2011. "The president is not a passenger: Portugal's evolving semi-presidentialism." In *Semi-Presidentialism and Democracy*, edited by Robert Elgie, Sophie Moestrup, and Yu-Shan Wu, 156–173. New York: Palgrave MacMillan.

Jalali, Carlos. 2014. "For whom the bailout tolls? The implications of the 2013 local elections for the Portuguese party system." *South European Society and Politics* 19, no. 2: 235–255.

Jalali, Carlos. 2015. *Partidos e Democracia em Portugal: 1974–2005: da revolução ao bipartidarismo* (2nd edition). Lisbon: Imprensa de Ciências Sociais.

Lijphart, Arend, Thomas C. Bruneau, P. Nikiforos Diamandouros, and Richard Gunther. 1988. "A Mediterranean Model of Democracy: The Southern European Democracies in Comparative Perspective." *West European Politics* 11, no. 1: 8-25.

Magalhães, Pedro C. 2008. "What are (semi)presidential elections about? A case study of the Portuguese 2006 Elections." *Journal of Elections, Public Opinion and Parties* 17, no. 3: 263–291.

Mair, Peter. 1997. *Party System Change: Approaches and Interpretations*. Oxford: Clarendon Press.

Mata, Maria Eugénia. 1991. "A actividade revolucionária no Portugal contemporâneo—uma perspectiva de longa duração." *Análise Social* 26, no. 112/113: 755–769.

OECD. 2022. "Subnational governments in OECD countries: key data – SNG expenditures". https://stats.oecd.org/Index.aspx?DataSetCode=RFD

PCP. 2022. "Pela paz! Não à instrumentalização da Assembleia da República e à instigação da guerra." April 20, 2022. https://www.pcp.pt/pela-paz-nao-instrumentalizacao-da-assembleia-da-republica-instigacao-da-guerra

RTP. 2019. "Sondagem da Católica. Nova geringonça é cenário preferido dos inquiridos." RTP, October 1, 2019. https://www.rtp.pt/noticias/politica/sondagem-da-catolica-nova-geringonca-e-cenario-preferido-dos-inquiridos_v1176336

Sartori, Giovanni. 1997. *Comparative Constitutional Engineering: An Inquiry into Structures, Incentives, and Outcomes*, 2nd edn. Basingstoke: Macmillan.

Sartori, Giovanni. 2005. *Parties and Party Systems: A Framework for Analysis*. Colchester: ECPR Press.

Shugart, Matthew S. 2005. "Semi-presidential systems: Dual executive and mixed authority patterns." *French Politics* 3, no. 3: 323–351.

Silva, Rodrigo Quintas da. 2018. "A Portuguese exception to right-wing populism." *Palgrave Communications* 4, no. 7.

Silveira, Pedro, and Patrícia Silva. 2023. "Executive Politics." In *Oxford Handbook of Portuguese Politics*, edited by Jorge M. Fernandes, Pedro C. Magalhães, and António Costa Pinto, 149–163. Oxford: Oxford University Press.

Tavits, Margit. 2008. *Presidents with Prime Ministers: Do Direct Elections Matter?* Oxford: Oxford University Press.

Wu, Yu-Shan. 2011. "Clustering of Semi-Presidentialism: A First Cut." In *Semi-presidentialism and Democracy*, edited by Robert Elgie, Sophie Moestrup, and Yu-Shan Wu, 21–41. New York: Palgrave MacMillan.

5 The economy

Susana Peralta

5.1 Portugal, a small open economy by the sea

With its surface of 92,226 square metres and its population of around 10 million people, Portugal accounts for little over 2% of the European Union's total surface and population. The EU is a club of a few very big countries and several quite small ones. Portugal, despite its small weight, both surface and population-wise, stands at the middle of the rank of the club in both size indicators. What about the Portuguese economy? The following plot shows the recent evolution of the Portuguese GDP. The choice of the initial year (1981) is rather arbitrary – it has the advantage of putting the turn of the millennium approximately in the middle of the period. It is also five years before Portugal joined the European Union (actually, European Community at the time), which sets the stage for the record that was to come (Figure 5.1).

The Portuguese GDP accounted for 1.4% of the EU-27 GDP in 1995; it reached a maximum of 1.67% in the beginning of the century (2002 and 2003); in 2022, it was 1.52%. The total EU GDP considered here takes into account all the EU-27 countries, some of which were not part of the Union in 1995, and excludes the one which was part of the Union and is no longer (the United Kingdom). Therefore, Portugal represents an even smaller share of the EU economy than of its surface or total population. It is, by all accounts, a small country.

As a small open economy, Portugal trades a lot with the rest of the world, in particular with its EU partners. The combined weight of imports and exports on GDP amounted to 53% in 2005 and reached 65% in 2019. It decreased in 2020 to 61%, a natural consequence of the pandemic that collapsed the main exporting industry of the country – tourism. In 2022, it reached a peak of 78%.

What about trade deficits? Between 2012 and 2019, the value of exports was just slightly above that of imports, with a maximum foreign trade coverage ratio of 104.4% in 2016. Other than that, Portugal has consistently imported more than it exports. There is, however, a stark contrast between goods and services. The value of Portuguese goods imports has always been higher than that of its exports. By contrast, service exports are much more valuable than imports; in fact, just before the strong pandemic shock on the tourism sector, the coverage ratio of service imports had reached more than 200%.

Due to its reliance on the rest of the world, the Portuguese economy accumulated external deficits throughout the decades. This is reflected in the high level of external indebtedness of the country, which led to a demanding conditional bailout by the IMF,

DOI: 10.4324/9781003488033-5

This chapter has been made available under a CC-BY-NC-ND license.

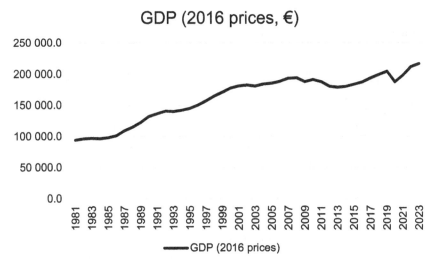

Figure 5.1 The Portuguese GDP

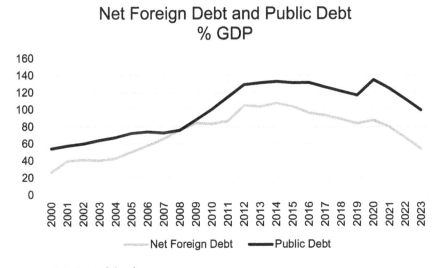

Figure 5.2 An indebted country.

the European Commission, and the European Central Bank in 2011. Portugal officially graduated from the programme in 2014, after three years of a deep social and economic crisis, that saw unemployment reach 17.1% in 2013, after a spectacular and rapid increase from 10.8% in 2010.

Public debt, shown in Figure 5.2, stood at 54% of the GDP at the turn of the century, first surpassed the 100% threshold in 2010, and grew to reach a peak of 133% of the

64   *Susana Peralta*

GDP in 2014. In 2019, just before the pandemic hit, Portugal had a public debt of 117%. In 2023, the public debt reached 99,1% of GDP, an important milestone after 13 years in which it remained above the 100% threshold.

Portugal has started to overcome the chronic dependence on the rest of the world following the great recession of 2008–2011, through a boom on the export of tourism services. In the graph above, this corresponds to a period in which external indebtedness and public debt remain fairly constant as a share of GDP, and start to decrease steadily as of 2014–15. The net foreign debt stands at 54% of GDP in 2023. Indeed, the pre-pandemic period coincided with a very sizeable peak in the export of tourism services. The weight of tourism on GDP increased from around 4% in the beginning of the century to 8.5% in 2019. While the tourism export growth has contributed to attenuate the external deficit of the country, it left the economy in a vulnerable situation during the pandemic years. The Portuguese economy was among the four hardest hit ones (together with Spain, Italy, and Greece), and saw its GDP shrink by 8.4%.

It is not a coincidence that these four economies share a geography which is prone to the export of tourism services. A simple and telling way to illustrate how the reliance on tourism explains part of the pandemic crisis is to zoom into Portuguese regions. In 2019, more than one-third of the overnight stays in hotels and similar establishments by non-residents were concentrated in the southern region of Algarve. The analysis of electronic transactions shows that Algarve (together with the archipelago of Madeira) saw the largest contraction in the Spring of 2020. In addition, in August 2020, these were the only regions whose volume of electronic transactions was significantly lower than the average of the previous years. All remaining regions were back on track, and Lisbon was just slightly below (Carvalho et al. 2022).

Unemployment records (more precisely, the number of individuals registered in local employment offices, a necessary condition to be eligible for the benefits) paint the same picture. Due to data unavailability, we cannot include the archipelagos of Madeira and Azores in this comparison. Still, there were only two regions in mainland Portugal with a consistently higher number of registered individuals throughout the pandemic crisis than in the same month of 2019. These two regions are Lisbon and the Algarve. However, while the number of unemployed in Lisbon is just between 10 and 15% above the 2019 figures, the one in Algarve reaches a height of more than twice as many unemployed in the summer months of 2020 and 2021 than in the equivalent months of 2019 (Peralta et al. 2022).

This raises the question of whether Portugal bears too high a risk due to its reliance on the tourism sector. While a thorough discussion of this concern is out of the scope of this chapter, I would highlight that, on the one hand, a more diversified economy is always better insulated against shocks. On the other hand, it is possible that tourism export is particularly vulnerable to large shocks, given that it entails cross-border movement of people, likely to come to a halt in the face of disruptive events such as a disease outbreak, natural disasters due to extreme climate phenomena, or political risks (e.g., terrorism). Therefore, it is conceivable that a small open economy that relies disproportionately on tourism services for its exports is exposed to higher risks than another with a similar concentration on another sector.

5.2 The 21st century: a mixed record

In 2000, the Portuguese GDP per capita was just below 12,500 euros. In 2019, it amounted to a little less than 21,000 euros (at 2016 constant prices); by 2023, it had fully recovered from the pandemic shock, at constant prices. The 21st century was, therefore, a period of economic growth. However, compared to the last 20 years of the 20th century, growth failed to deliver a similar convergence with the European Union living standards.

Indeed, in 1981 the GDP per capita was just above 1,000 euros, also at 2016 constant prices. The conclusion is obvious: the Portuguese standard of living, as measured by the GDP per capita, increased (roughly) 12-fold in the last 20 years of the 20th century, and did not even double in the first 20 years of the 21st century. Lower growth rates are a natural consequence of the higher level of economic development. Nevertheless, convergence with the European Union slowed down, implying that other countries with similar levels of development converged more rapidly. In 2000, the Portuguese GDP per capita was 85% of the European Union (EU-27) average. As of 2022, it amounts to 79%. The lower growth rates of the 21st century put Portugal on a diverging path with its EU counterparts.

The pandemic was the second crisis that hit the Portuguese economy in the century. The GDP per capita grew every year since 1960, except in 2003, in 2009, between 2011 and 2013, and then in 2020. The GDP contraction triggered by the global financial crisis, followed by the sovereign debt crisis in the Eurozone countries, was a fierce one: it was only in 2015 that the GDP per capita recovered its pre-crisis level. Unemployment, in turn, increased from 5% in 2002 to 17.1% in 2013. For this reason, the period roughly coinciding with 2003–2013 is sometimes named "the lost decade" of the Portuguese economy. It ended with the official date of termination of the financial and economic assistance programme of 2011–2014, during which Portugal was bailed out by the European Commission, the IMF, and the European Central Bank. About five years later, the pandemic caused the greatest shock in several decades. Public debt, which amounted to 117% of the GDP just before the pandemic, hampered the country's ability to accommodate the shock. Still, given the massive amount of public spending implemented to face the crisis and the GDP contraction, public debt jumped to more than 135% of the GDP level in 2020.

GDP per capita tells us a lot about the average economic situation of the people that live in the small open economy by the sea, but it hides considerable heterogeneity among individuals. When these asymmetries are considered, the picture that emerges is somewhat different: the Portuguese economy has been making modest progress both in absolute and relative terms.

Since 2004 we have a representative survey that allows for EU-wide comparability of income poverty, material deprivation, and inequality: the Survey on Income and Living Conditions (EU-SILC). It is a standardized representative survey collected by all the EU countries (and some other European countries, on a voluntary basis), and it was created with the purpose of being used as a tool of social monitoring in the EU. The poverty rate, that is, the share of individuals who live in households with equivalized disposable income (including social transfers) below the poverty line, decreased just slightly, from 20.4% to 18.4%, between 2004 and 2021. It had, however, reached an all-time low of 16.2% just before the pandemic. When compared to the remaining EU countries, Portugal is faring better in recent years than it was at the beginning of the century. In 2004, only Ireland had a higher poverty rate than Portugal. In 2022 the poverty rate in Portugal is slightly below the the EU-27 average, and there are 11 countries with higher rates. While there is still a lot of progress to be made, poverty decreased, in absolute terms, and the country also improved its relative position with regard to the EU average.

However, the drawback of measuring economic fragility through the poverty rate is that the poverty thresholds depend on the median income of each country. A person is poor in the European Union if she lives with less than 60% of the median equivalized disposable income of her country of residence. Therefore, even discounting purchasing power differences, it is conceivable that a poor person in a richer country would be among the relatively well-off in a poorer one. For instance, the poverty threshold in Austria in 2019 was 15,437 euros, while in Portugal it was 6,014 per year. A more direct comparison of living conditions can be achieved by analysing deprivation indicators. According to Eurostat, a person lives with severe material deprivation if her household cannot afford four or more items among a list of nine that are considered desirable or necessary to experience an adequate standard of living. These include (absence of) arrears on utility or mortgage, ownership of durable goods such as a car or washing machine, affording a week-long holiday away from home, or eating proteins every second day. The share of severely material deprived households in Portugal more than halved since 2004, from 9.9% to 4.6% in 2020. As of 2004, only Greece had a higher share of severe material deprivation; in 2020, there are 14 countries with more deprivation. Not surprisingly, Portugal is now below the EU average.

Income inequality, as measured by the Gini index of the equivalized disposable income, also decreased, from 37.8% to 33%. In 2004, Portugal was the most unequal country of the EU-15 countries; it kept this position in 2005, with the ten enlargement countries already included in the data. In 2019, with a Gini of 31.2%, Portugal ranked eighth in the EU-27 and moved to fifth in 2021 due to the pandemic shock.

To conclude, what to say of the 21st century's record? On the one hand, the Portuguese economy made progress, both in absolute and in relative terms, in terms of poverty, deprivation, and inequality. Therefore, welfare transfers have improved as means to smooth out the differences across people in the economy. On the other hand, it was disappointing, in that Portugal fell behind the convergence path with the EU average that it had started when joining the then European Community.

There were two major crises, but these hit the other European (and world) economies as well. Therefore, the crises per se cannot explain the path of divergence. There must be idiosyncratic reasons behind the Portuguese lag. Any list of reasons for this divergence is subjective and the one presented here is no exception to this rule. As a microeconomist, I will focus on bottlenecks faced by economic agents: households and firms. A macroeconomist would likely point out macroeconomic imbalances, such as the level of public debt and overseas trade, and the impact of the common currency, which certainly play an important role. One may argue that the bottlenecks that I am about to discuss were stronger in the last two decades of the 20th century, in which Portugal was catching up more rapidly with the EU average. I take this criticism on board. Let me note, however, that convergence is a non-linear process, and that the challenges of the knowledge-based and digitalized economy of the 21st century may be more demanding. Moreover, I am not implying causality between the bottlenecks, and even less assigning any magnitude to the importance of each in the relative slowing down of the Portuguese economy. More modestly, I will just document the bottlenecks and hopefully convince my readers that they do play a role. To the extent possible, in the figures given below, I plan to provide an account of the structural characteristics of the economy. I will therefore refrain from underlining the pandemic years, due to their many specificities, and the high degree of uncertainty revolving around the day after.

5.3 A (subjective) list of bottlenecks

5.3.1 (Child) Poverty

One of the achievements of the 21st century is the poverty decline. However, the poverty rate in Portugal is still higher than the EU average and so is the Gini index of income inequality. Moreover, the poverty rate before social transfers and pensions remained fairly stable throughout the century and, if anything, it even increased, from 40.8% in 2004 to 42.4% in 2020. These two figures suggest that income transfers became more effective at alleviating poverty. However, they also make clear that neither the system of income transfers nor the broader social state has eliminated the pervasive poverty traps of the Portuguese economy. These poverty traps get the poor people stuck in bad economic outcomes – this lost talent is a lost growth potential for the Portuguese economy.

Poverty is also a consequence of the disappointing record of Portuguese growth. While growth does not always bring about a reduction of poverty (let alone inequality), it is certainly easier to design good anti-poverty policies in a more resourceful economy. The extent to which it arises depends on good institutions, able to deliver sound, evidence-based policies. While this is a valid viewpoint, I will instead discuss why excessive poverty hampers growth, because it generates poverty traps.

Since discussing them all is outside the scope of this essay, I will highlight a particularly costly one: growing up in poverty. There is by now an extended body of research establishing causal links between growing up in poverty and children's educational and health outcomes, but also lasting impacts through adulthood in income levels and risky behaviours (National Academy of Sciences, Engineering, and Medicine, 2019). The fact that child poverty has medium to long-run consequences implies that, by and large, the Portuguese economy is now suffering the consequences of the pervasive child poverty of the last century. However, the 21st century will fail to deliver unless the current levels of child poverty are tackled.

More than 19% of the Portuguese children was poor in 2019. When it comes to material deprivation, 26% lived in dwellings with humidity problems, 13% in households who cannot afford to keep the house adequately warm, and 16% in overcrowded houses. A special module on food security from the 2018 wave of the Survey on Income and Living Conditions concluded that 9% live in households that cannot afford to buy nutritious and healthy food and that 3% felt hungry, but could not eat for lack of financial resources of the household (Esteves et al. 2021). In 2022, 6% of the children lived in households who could not afford an healthy diet, and 2% felt hungry and could not be fed due to financial constraints.

These children lag behind their peers in learning outcomes. Using results of standardized national tests between 2007 and 2018, for the fourth, sixth, and ninth grades, we found that children from households who qualify for means-tested transfers and free or subsidized school meals are 15 to 20 percentage points more likely to obtain a negative grade. Results from the OECD PISA tests show that 15-year-olds from the bottom income quartile obtain, on average, 80% of the grade of those in the top quartile (Esteves et al. 2021).

Poverty and lack of opportunity are more pervasive in some groups of the population. While it is illegal in Portugal to collect ethnicity data, the fact that non-EU immigrants face a poverty rate of 25%, compared with 10% for EU origin ones, and 17% for nationals, signals the difficulties faced by these minorities in the labour market. Immigrant students obtain lower grades in standardized 9th grade national exams, particularly in mathematics. African-born students face the highest achievement gap. The achievement gap is lower for second-generation immigrants, i.e., students born in Portugal to two immigrant parents. Moreover, students of foreign origin are more likely to repeat grades, again with a particularly striking difference for those of African origin. These identity-based gaps are bound to create aspiration failures for the individuals, who have less incentive to invest in the future (Almeida and Nunes 2021).

The achievement gaps in the education system stemming from socio-economic class and immigrant origin are more worrisome given the need for Portugal to catch up with its EU peers in the skills of the population, an issue I discuss below.

5.3.2 Human capital

Portugal lacks human capital. A striking figure shows how badly Portugal was at the turn of the century: in 2000, the Portuguese population had less than eight years of formal education, on average. This is equivalent to Germany in 1930 (Figueiredo et al. 2017). Only 11% of the population older than 15 had graduated from secondary education, and 7% had a higher education degree. In 2020, those figures attained 24% and 21%. Therefore, nowadays, almost half of the population has completed at least secondary education.

The generation gap is considerable: younger generations are more educated, hence time runs in Portugal's favour. As of 2020, only 6% of the residents older than 65 had finished secondary education, which compares to 30% of the ones in the 15 to 64 age interval. When it comes to higher education, the shares are, respectively, 9%, and more than one-fourth. This stems from a monumental effort of investment into higher education: in the last decade of the 20th century, the number of higher education students in Portugal increased from around 150,000 to almost 400,000 (Figueiredo et al. 2017).

However, the convergence pace has been too slow, and Portugal has not yet caught up with its EU peers. Only 55% of those older than 25 years have graduated from either secondary or higher education in Portugal, compared to 79% in the EU. This lack of human capital is particularly damaging at a time when the EU economy wants to embrace the digital transition. Not surprisingly, with a population which is less educated, on average, Portugal also lacks digital skills. According to Eurostat, only half of the Portuguese population had at least basic digital skills in 2019. This figure is slightly below the EU average of 56%, but far from the most skilled countries, such as the Netherlands or Sweden. In any case, this indicator measures basic skills such as copying files, sending emails, installing applications, making online purchases, or producing documents.

One can also look at measures of higher-level digital skills compiled by the European Commission for the Digital Economy and Society Index.[1] The share of Information and Communication Technologies (ICT) specialists in employment, as a share of the population aged 15–74, was 3.6% in 2019, while the share of ICT graduates was 2.2% in 2018. These compare with EU averages of 4.3% and 3.9%, respectively. Gender imbalances in ICT skills remain pervasive: women represent 18% of the ICT specialists' employment.

One of the consequences of the comparatively low level of education of the Portuguese workforce is that wages are low. Sluggish productivity growth of firms also explains the low wage problem. A thorough analysis of the productivity challenge of Portuguese firms is out of the scope of this chapter, but some clues are given below. For now, let me point out that low wages turn into high levels of in-work poverty. As of 2019, even before the effect of the pandemic, almost one in every 10 workers lived below the poverty line.

These 10% of workers are poor even after receiving income transfers such as, e.g., family allowances (which are means tested in Portugal).

Despite being more educated, young generations lack access to the more protected segment of the labour market with long-term contracts, higher salaries, and also the highest level of employment protection of the OECD. Portugal ranks third in the share of temporary contracts across OECD countries, with 22% of the total, twice the OECD average (Nunes et al. 2023). For workers aged less than 25 years old, the share of temporary contracts in 2019 was almost 60%, four times as much as the share for workers who are older than 35. For those in the 25–34 years bracket, temporary contracts are almost one-third of the total. Irrespective of our views on the desirability of the large protection given to long-term contracts in Portugal, it is hard to come up with a good justification for the more qualified generation to fail to qualify for the more formal and protected segment of the market.

One cannot discuss the scarcity of human capital in the Portuguese economy without acknowledging that emigration may contribute to that scarcity. This concern is often referred to in the public debate. The yearly flow of emigrants increased from 2010 until 2014, and it started to decrease thereafter. Still, according to the United Nations estimates, there were 2.6 million Portuguese citizens residing abroad in 2019, which ranks Portugal in 26th place of the total number of emigrants and eighth in terms of the migration rate (i.e., as a percentage of the population). Little is known about the skill or age composition of these emigrants. However, an analysis of census data done by the OECD (therefore limited to emigrants residing in OECD countries) suggests that they may be getting more educated. In the first census of this century (2000/2001), the share of emigrants in OECD countries with higher education was 6%, and it increased to 11% in the second census (2010/11); this is still a fairly small share of total migration, but more recent data is needed to understand if the increasing trend has continued. Note, however, that little is known about the impacts of (recent) emigration on the Portuguese economy, and that the literature points to several positive impacts of out-migration for origin countries. Therefore, while migration may be a driving part of the skill scarcity, I refrain from making claims about the magnitude or nature of its more general impact on the Portuguese economy.

As it turns out, the scarcity of skills and the generational gap in attaining well-rewarded positions in the labour market is reflected in the management of firms. This is just one of the bottlenecks faced by Portuguese firms, to which I now turn.

5.3.3 Financial and managerial capital

The combined effect of the lack of human capital and the generational gap has an unexpected negative consequence for firm management. The average years of education of firm managers have increased less rapidly than that of the remaining population of workers. They are, nevertheless, more educated than workers, on average. As of 2016, almost one-half of CEOs had at most a secondary school diploma. The share with higher education was just above one-fourth (Sazedj 2019). There is a lot of heterogeneity depending on the size of the firm: in medium and large firms, more than half of the CEOs have a higher education degree. However, these represent less than 1% of the total. The lack of human capital in top positions of Portuguese firms limits their performance, and one estimate suggests that if the distribution of manager education in Portugal was similar to the US, aggregate productivity would rise by 20% (Queiró 2022).

Portuguese firms are very small, compared to their European Union counterparts. Micro firms, that is, those with less than 10 employees and less than 2 million euros of annual turnover, represent 96% of the total. Another 3.3% are small firms, that is, with 10 to 49 employees and 2 to 10 million euros of annual turnover. If one includes medium firms as well, one gets to 99.9% of the total. Micro, small, and medium enterprises absorb 77% of the workforce. The share of micro, small, and medium firms is just slightly above that of the European Union (98%), but the share of employment that they represent is substantially higher than the EU average of two-thirds. For that reason, the average firm in Portugal has a little more than three employees, while the Spanish ones have four, and the German ones have 11.

The size of Portuguese firms is a challenge for the Portuguese economy. There is a large body of research showing that micro, small, and medium firms are more likely to face credit constraints and are more exposed to fluctuations. Indeed, they were particularly hit during the sovereign debt crisis. Estimates suggest that 15% of the Portuguese micro, small, and medium firms faced funding restrictions between 2010 and 2012, with consequences for their investment levels (Félix 2018). This creates barriers to firm growth. Moreover, these firms are less productive than their large counterparts, and the difference is greater in the Portuguese economy (Bank of Portugal 2019). Portugal has the second lowest labour productivity of micro and small firms in the European Union, after Greece.

Due to the crisis and financial frictions, Portuguese firms lack financial resources. At the peak of the financial and sovereign debt crisis in 2012, 42% of the firms were making losses. The figure went down to 37% in 2019, which is still more than one third. As a consequence, the ratio of debt over assets of Portuguese firms is sizeable: from 68% at the peak of the crisis in 2012, it went down to 61% in 2019. Moreover, Portuguese firms rely a lot on the banking sector for funding. Following the financial crisis, the banking sector went through a transition aiming at improving the balance sheets, resulting in a deleveraging process that increased the funding barriers of the firms.

This is not necessarily bad. The combined effect of these changes in the banking sector, the reform of the bankruptcy laws, and possibly some cleansing effect of the recession, led to a decrease in the prevalence of zombie firms in the economy, from a maximum of 12% in 2009 to around 2% more recently. There are several definitions of zombie firms; the one used for these figures includes firms older than 10 years old that for at least three consecutive years cannot cover total interest payments with operating income. The death of zombie firms liberates productive factors (capital and labour) which were previously sunk in these inefficient and unproductive firms. As such, it has the potential to foster growth (Gouveia and Osterhold, 2018). On a cautionary note, it is important that the phasing out of public support given to firms during the pandemic crisis avoids the inversion of this tendency.

5.3.4 Institutional capital

The term institutional capital is somewhat vague and is meant to encompass several drawbacks of the legal, judicial, and cultural set-up of the Portuguese economy, which one could also label as context costs.

International comparisons of perception-based indices of corruption systematically put Portugal on the most corrupt half of its European Union counterparts. In the Corruption Perception Index compiled by Transparency International, Portugal obtains a score of 61, below the Western Europe average of 66, and very far from the top scorers of 88 for Denmark or 85 for Finland (higher values, less corruption). It is also worrisome that 63% of the people consider that the government is controlled by private interests, 10 percentage points above the EU average. Actually, Portugal ranks 8th in the EU regarding this negative record. A red flag involves the public procurement reforms related to the pandemic, as 41% of the respondents consider that corruption increased in the previous year, according to the 2021 edition of the index.

A study by the European Parliament estimates the costs of corruption by using a battery of indicators from the Quality of Government dataset of the University of Gothenburg, for 28 EU countries in the period 1995 to 2014. It relies on regression analysis to estimate the impact of the level of corruption, controlling for important variables such as the level of human capital of the countries. The study has technical limitations, despite its use of instrumental variables to mitigate the endogeneity of the corruption indices. Technical limitations notwithstanding, the study estimates that if the Portuguese level of corruption were to match the least corrupt countries in the European Union, its GDP could witness a one-off increase of between 6 and 10% (Hafner et al. 2016).

While one may question the extent to which perception indices reflect actual institutional shortcomings, these are confirmed by the concerns raised by international institutions such as the Group of States Against Corruption, an initiative of the Council of Europe that has been benchmarking and advising countries on anti-corruption policies since 1999. The 2020 edition of the GRECO highlights the fact that Portugal had failed to implement 40% of the reforms recommended in the 2014 round of the assessment.

I now turn to the regulatory framework of business activity. In 2014 and 2017, Statistics Portugal conducted a survey to infer the costs of context faced by Portuguese firms and their impacts. It covered a wide range of costs, from licencing processes to access to funding, several instances of red tape, and the judicial system. The most important barriers to their activity pinpointed by the firms are the judicial system and licencing processes (Amador et al. 2019).

The Small and Medium Enterprises Performance Review by the European Commission compiles several indicators about the institutional set-up in which these firms operate.[2] Portugal scores below the EU average in several indicators that corroborate the findings of the costs of context surveys. For instance, the time to resolve insolvency is almost one year above the EU average. The burden of government regulations is also higher (although less than one standard deviation).

The set of indicators where Portugal scores the worst with regards to its European counterparts is in state aid and public procurement, more precisely in the percentages of businesses participating in public tenders, small and medium enterprises in the total value of public contracts awarded, and bids and contracts awarded to these firms. While the low competitiveness of public procurement may result from thin markets, it is also suggestive of a lack of openness of the tenders. The average delay in payment from public authorities is 24 months in Portugal and 16 in the EU, i.e., one-third lower. There are also dimensions in which Portugal fares better than the average EU country, including the time and cost to start a business, and the strength of the insolvency framework index, reflecting the improvement in the aftermath of the crisis, as discussed above.

The negative consequences of corruption and the regulatory environment in which the firms operate could in principle be mitigated by an efficient judicial system. However, that system in Portugal is known precisely for its inefficiency, long delays, and incapacity to recover assets. The judicial process involving the bankruptcy of *Banco Espírito Santo*, which revolves around major accusations of money laundering and fraudulent funding of the real estate company of the same group, had seized, as of 2020, only 120 million euros out of the estimated 12 billion that were diverted. Seizing assets is the first step in the process of recovering them. This process started in 2014 and is yet to be fully resolved. Actually, the number of days to resolve litigious civil and commercial cases in Portugal (in first instance courts) was slightly below 300 days in 2020; the most efficient judicial systems in the EU resolve cases in just above 100 days. While speed may hide bad decision making, it is fair to assume that these discrepancies in the average length imply that enforcement of private contracts in Portugal is a costly process, which puts a strain on economic activity.

Another institutional bottleneck is the country's public policy design and implementation, which has several problems related to the utilization of sound evidence and the availability of information for policy evaluation and scrutiny. The budgetary process is at the core of the design and implementation of public policies, and it is a telling illustration of these problems. In the aftermath of the sovereign debt crisis, faced with the need to implement a budgetary framework that would allow for sound public finances and effective public policies, the parliament voted a new budgetary law in 2015 that was to be progressively implemented until 2018. The law introduced reforms aligned with best practices, such as programme-based budgeting and the adoption of international accounting standards to improve the quality of the information provided by the public sector. However, as of 2022, the law had not yet been thoroughly implemented.

Programme-based budgeting requires, in short, that the budgetary process be split into programmes, broadly corresponding to categories of public policies, accompanied by sufficient financial information about spending, on the one hand, and the outputs and outcomes related to that policy, on the other hand. Moreover, public institutions in charge of specific parts of a budgetary programme should have autonomy to implement it and be accountable in the delivery of the programme objectives. Such an arrangement requires a vast amount of credible information, but it improves both the capacity of the governmental unit in charge of the programme to monitor its implementation and that of the public and budgetary watchdogs to scrutinize the spending and the results it produces.

The limitations of the Portuguese budgetary process are best illustrated through an example. In November 2022, the Court of Accounts published a report about the implementation of the policies aimed at assisting distressed firms due to the pandemic crisis. According to the Court, the government announced 24 such measures, including credit lines and guarantees. There are five government agencies in charge of 22 of these measures, with different overlaps. In addition, two policies had no agency in charge. More worrisome is the fact that the Court reports that 15 out of the 24 policies reported no spending as of the end of 2020. Therefore, only nine policies existed *de facto*.

For this type of policy, important outputs to consider would be the number of distressed firms, or their importance in the universe of distressed firms, for instance, in terms of employment or turnover. The outcomes, in turn, would be the number of firms (or jobs) that were saved due to the policies. These pieces of information, together with the spending involved, would be an important tool for the agencies in charge of implementation to evaluate the effectiveness of the policies, which could then be abandoned, or finetuned, to improve delivery. Nevertheless, the Court of Accounts signals that the initial situation of the economy that each of the 22 measures wanted to address is not reported systematically, nor are there output and outcome indicators to assess their efficacy. The Court rightly points out the inability to assess the impact of these policies, some for lack of financial execution, others for lack of indicators related to their objectives, and yet others for lack of information about the initial situation. This is just an example of the problems that are repeatedly underlined by the Court of Accounts, the Council of Public Finances, and the Parliament unit that is responsible for the analysis of budgetary information. This lack of transparency (which is just a reflection of the lack of relevant and timely information) impedes both the effective implementation and the accountability of the system.

Budget transparency is not necessarily related to corruption, but it does give an account of the possibility of the citizens to scrutinize the application of public funds. As such, it is, at the very least, an important measure of institutional quality. The Open Budget Index is compiled every year by the International Budget Partnership in several countries, taking into account the quality of the information underlying the budgetary process of the countries and the possibilities for the citizens to participate in its various stages. In 2019, Portugal ranked 23rd in the OECD, with a score of 66, implying that it provides "substantial" information. On a positive note, transparency has been increasing steadily since the index was first compiled for Portugal in 2010.

The lack of transparency of the budgetary law is illustrative of a general incapacity or reluctance of the public authorities to curate and share data for the purpose of evaluating public policy with state-of-the-art statistical methodologies. For instance, in the Inequality Transparency Index computed by the World Inequality Database, Portugal scores low relative to other EU countries due to the unavailability of anonymized tax records to analyse taxable income and wealth. A recent effort by Statistics Portugal is moving in this direction, but Portugal is still lagging behind by more than one decade in the availability of administrative data for research (and policy evaluation) purposes. While the availability of high-quality administrative data on households is still a challenge, firm-level data (excluding tax related) is widely available for research purposes. This is important because it has the potential to create a virtuous circle between academia and evidence-based public policies.

5.3.5 Public capital

The country's high level of public debt and the collective trauma of the international bailout of 2011 have tied the successive governments' hands when it comes to investing in infrastructures. Of course, this ultimately results from political choices – governments can increase tax revenue or opt for a different spending mix between current and capital expenditures. This discussion is out of the scope of this chapter. For our purposes, it suffices to acknowledge that the spending constraint imposed by external debt increases the marginal cost of public funds, which leads governments to spend less than they otherwise would.

In the last decade, public investment has absorbed the bulk of the adjustment of public spending. It is conceivable that part of this phenomenon results from insufficient institutional capacity to plan, budget, and implement investment plans, besides the budget constraint. The poor institutional capacity illustrated by the example of the financial aid to firms during the pandemic also obstructs other parts of the budget implementation. Indeed, between 2015 and 2020, public investment amounted to 85% of the value forecasted in the respective State Budgets. As a share of GDP, public investment has been steadily decreasing from around 5% in the beginning of the century, with the exception of the 2008–10 period. Public investment reached a low of 1% of GDP in 2016, and never reached 2% after that.

74 *Susana Peralta*

Estimates by the Portuguese economist Miguel Faria e Castro (2021) show that the stock of public capital, as a share of GDP, decreased between 2012 and 2019; actually, in 2019, it was back to its 2002 level of around 65% of GDP.[3] Therefore, when it comes to public capital, the Portuguese economy travelled in time back to the beginning of the 21st century. This lack of public capital is reflected in the several weaknesses of the transportation, health, and education infrastructures and technology. These limitations create context costs that make the life of citizens and firms more costly (time and money-wise) to run.

The aftermath of the pandemic created a unique opportunity to catch up, as Portugal will receive 16.6 billion euros from the EU Recovery and Resilience facility, adding to around 30 billion from the Multiannual Financial Framework for the period 2021–2027. For Portuguese standards, this is a substantial amount: it is higher than the total public investment undertaken in Portugal in the ten years between 2010 and 2019. The Recovery and Resilience funding alone is higher than the accumulated public investment between 2016 and 2019. But will it deliver?

Firstly, at this stage, we have planned spending and, as already discussed, there are challenges in implementation. Second, the European Commission puts forward several classifications of spending, which sometimes hampers the clarity of the comparisons. Third, and perhaps more importantly, how spending generates outputs and outcomes depends on the details of the policies and their implementation, which are thus far not known. Finally, at the time of this writing, there is no information regarding the additionality of the plan, that is, the extent to which it just crowds out spending that was otherwise planned.

The Recovery and Resilience Facility is structured around six pillars: (i) **the green transition**, (ii) **digital transformation**, (iii) **economic cohesion, productivity, and competitiveness**, (iv) **social and territorial cohesion**, (v) **health, economic, social, and institutional resilience**, and, finally, (vi) **policies for the next generation**. Since some projects span several pillars, I will rely on the pillar assignment made by the Brussels-based think tank Bruegel, which keeps up-to-date information on the Recovery and Resilience Plans submitted by member states to the European Commission.[4] The Portuguese plan allocates 22% of the fund to the green pillar, 16% to the digital one, 23% to the third one, 5% to the social and territorial cohesion, 24% to the resilience pillar, and finally, 9% to the last one.

On average, EU countries allocate almost half of the funding to the green transition (43%), often combined with other pillars, in particular economic cohesion. Portugal lags behind its European peers in the green pillar, for which it allocates almost 20 percentage points less, compared to the average. Another pillar in which Portugal plans to invest less is the digital transition pillar, which receives 24% of the funding in other EU countries, on average, with particular weight given to combinations with economic cohesion and social and territorial cohesion. By contrast, Portugal plans to spend relatively more under the fifth pillar, i.e., the resilience one. While the EU average stands at 14%, even after accounting for 5% spent in projects under the digital transformation pillar combined with the resilience one, Portugal will spend 24% of the total under this pillar.

Another interesting comparison relies on the so-called seven flagship areas for investment and reforms defined by the European Union, which are the following: (i) clean technology and renewables, (ii) energy efficiency of buildings, (iii) sustainable transport and charging stations, (iv) roll-out of rapid broadband services, (v) digitalization of public administration, (vi) data cloud capacities and sustainable processors, (vii) education and training to support digital skills. This classification is more focused, and overlaps are rare. Unfortunately, some of the spending under the green and digital transition goals of the Recovery and Resilience Facility are not classified under the flagship classification.

The Portuguese plan is the one with the highest share of uncategorized spending (44%), which includes the categories of spending related, e.g., to resilience, that do not have an explicit digital or green component. This makes its assessment more difficult. Portugal allocates a total of 31% to the first three flagship areas, together with other green investments, related to the energetic transition. This compares with an EU-wide average of 46%. Education and training to support digital skills account for 11%, while other digital investments amount to 8% of the total. These figures are aligned with the EU averages. The digitalization of public administration receives 5% of the total, below the 9% average. Broadband connection absorbs only 1.7% of the total funds, in contrast with the 7% average.

One of the conclusions that stands out from both categorizations is that Portugal plans to spend less in the green transition than its EU counterparts. The sectoral level analysis is also conducive to this conclusion, for the "Transportation and Storage" sector has a planned spending amounting to 9% of the total, which is half the EU average. This very preliminary analysis suggests that Portugal is graduating into the adulthood of the 21st century lagging behind on infrastructure, again. In very much the same way as it missed the 20th-century wave of investments in railways, it may now be missing the opportunity to invest in the necessary public capital to ensure the climate transition.

Regarding the bottlenecks identified in this essay, spending on the upskilling of the labour force is aligned with the European average. However, given the relative scarcity of skills in the Portuguese population, this may not be sufficient. The higher reliance of the Portuguese plan on the resilience pillar suggests that poverty traps may have motivated some of the projected spending. This is further confirmed by the fact that, when comparing planned spending by sectors of activity, Portugal allocates 24% of the total to the "Human health and Social Work Activities" sector, which is double the EU average. Finally, the relatively low planned spending on the modernization of public administration may point to limitations regarding the necessary capacity building for the public sector to deliver more effective, transparent, and evidence-based policy.

5.4 Conclusion

Where is the 21st-century Portuguese economy leading? I conclude this chapter with a visualization of where it stands, compared to its EU partners. The two graphs below – Figures 5.3 and 5.4 – exclude Luxembourg (a clear outlier, in terms of GDP per capita), and they also exclude Bulgaria, Croatia, and Romania, due to data availability in 2005. I am using 2005 as the starting point because of the availability of the Survey on Income and Living Conditions. Note that the data from the 2020 wave pertains to the households' situation in 2019, that is, before the pandemic.

The graphs plot where the countries stand in terms of real GDP per capita (measured in 2010 euros), the shares of the population living in poverty (after social transfers and pensions) and severe material deprivation, and also the Gini index (of disposable income). The countries are ranked in the circle in terms of their GDP per capita in 2005. Therefore, non-monotonicities in the real GDP per capita line of 2020 indicate that the countries changed their position in this ranking. From the picture, it is clear that Slovakia, Estonia,

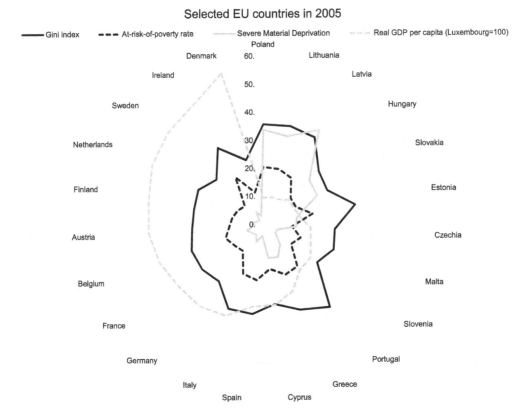

Figure 5.3 Selected EU countries in 2005: inequality, poverty, deprivation, and GDP per capita

Czechia, and Slovenia, all of which had lower income levels than Portugal in 2005, have similar (or higher) levels in 2020.

The graphs show a spectacular decrease in material deprivation, which was pervasive in Eastern and Baltic countries in 2005. All the countries on the right-hand half of the radar (i.e., the poorest ones) improved a lot in this indicator, including Portugal. However, it had lower levels of this indicator to begin with.

The countries that had a Gini index close to 40% in 2005 were Poland, Lithuania, Latvia, and Portugal. Contrary to Poland and Portugal, the two Baltic countries did not change their level of inequality, as measured by the Gini index. It is also clear that there is a set of countries with poverty rates reaching 20% in 2005, which included Portugal. Of this, little noticeable progress was made in Poland, Lithuania, Latvia, and Estonia. As with the Gini, Portugal got to 2019 with a lower poverty rate.

Some countries, like Slovakia and Slovenia, managed to converge faster in terms of GDP per capita, while also improving the remaining indicators. Importantly, the initial conditions of these economies are very different from the Portuguese one, not the least in terms of human capital. Notwithstanding, the picture that emerges does not suggest that Portugal improved its social cohesion indicators at the expense of real GDP growth. They are more suggestive of a story of a country that managed to reach these improvements by

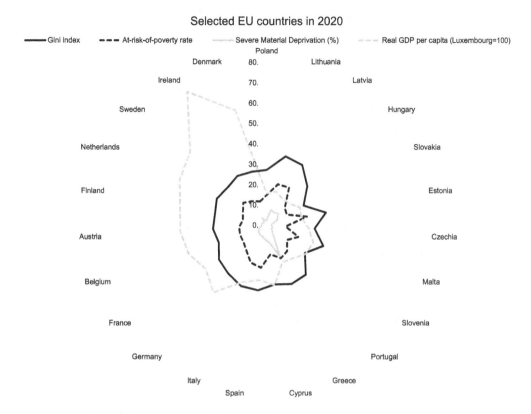

Figure 5.4 Selected EU countries in 2020: inequality, poverty, deprivation, and GDP per capita

means of income transfers but has failed to resolve the bottlenecks that would deliver a more inclusive and thorough growth of its 21st-century economy.

Acknowledgements

I am indebted to Nuno Monteiro for having included me in the list of contributors for this volume. While we never met personally, I was lucky to interact with him over the phone and by email on a few occasions thanks to this book. I hope that my small contribution is up to his expectations. I thank Pedro Magalhães and Patrícia Silva for the coordination and Carlos Jalali for very careful remarks on an earlier manuscript. I also acknowledge José Pedro Sousa's help with the benchmarking of the EU Recovery and Resilience Plans.

Notes

1 https://digital-strategy.ec.europa.eu/en/policies/countries-digitisation-performance
2 The figures reported here are taken from the 2021 edition of the review and refer to the situation in 2019.
3 https://eco.sapo.pt/especiais/a-erosao-do-capital-publico-em-portugal/
4 https://www.bruegel.org/publications/datasets/european-union-countries-recovery-and-resilience-plans/

References

Almeida, Sílvia and Luís C. Nunes (coord.). 2021. *Inclusão ou discriminação? Da análise dos resultados escolares às estratégias para o sucesso dos alunos com origem imigrante.* Lisbon: EPIS – Empresários pela Inclusão Social.

Amador, João, Sónia Cabral, and Birgitte Rigstad. 2019. *Custos de Contexto e desempenho das empresas portuguesas.* Lisbon: Banco de Portugal.

Bank of Portugal. 2019. "Produtividade aparente do trabalho em Portugal na última década: uma abordagem ao nível da empresa". In *Boletim Económico Banco de Portugal "A economia portuguesa em 2018.* Lisbon: Banco de Portugal.

Carvalho, Bruno P., Susana Peralta, and João Pereira dos Santos. 2022. "Regional and sectorial impacts of the Covid-19 crisis: Evidence from electronic payments." *Journal of regional science* 63, no. 3: 757-798.

Esteves, Mariana, Pedro Freitas, Miguel Herdade, Bruno P. Carvalho and Susana Peralta. 2021. "Crianças em Portugal e ensino a distância: um retrato". Accessed May 1, 2023. https://www.researchgate.net/profile/Miguel-Herdade-2/publication/360344626_Criancas_em_Portugal_e_ensino_a_distancia_um_retrato/links/627545562f9ccf58eb32e061/Criancas-em-Portugal-e-ensino-a-distancia-um-retrato.pdf.

Faria e Castro, Miguel. 2021. "A erosão do capital público em Portugal." *Eco,* February 1, 2021 https://eco.sapo.pt/especiais/a-erosao-do-capital-publico-em-portugal/

Félix, Sónia. 2018. *Restrições de financiamento e dinâmica de mercado das empresas.* Lisbon: Bank of Portugal.

Hafner, Marco, Jirka Taylor, Emma Disley, Sonja Thebes, Matteo Barberi, Martin Stepanek, and Mike Levi. 2016. *The Cost of Non-Europe in the area of Organised Crime and Corruption: Annex II - Corruption.* Santa Monica, CA: RAND Corporation.

Hugo Figueiredo, Miguel Portela, Carla Sá, João Cerejeira Silva, André Almeida, Diogo Lourenço. 2017. *Benefícios do Ensino Superior.* Lisbon: Fundação Francisco Manuel dos Santos.

Francisco Queiró. 2022. "Entrepreneurial Human Capital and Firm Dynamics." *The Review of Economic Studies* 89, no. 4: 2061–2100.

Gouveia, Ana Fontoura, and Christian Osterhold. 2018. "Fear the walking dead: zombie firms, spillovers and exit barriers." *Banco de Portugal Working Papers 11/2018.*

National Academies of Sciences, Engineering, and Medicine 2019. *A Roadmap to Reducing Child Poverty.* Washington, DC: The National Academies Press.

Nunes, Carolina, Carvalho, Bruno P., Pereira dos Santos, João, Peralta, Susana and José Tavares. 2023. "Failing Young and Temporary Workers? The Impact of a Disruptive Crisis on a Dual Labour Market." *The B.E. Journal of Economic Analysis & Policy* 23, no. 2: 349–395.

Peralta, Susana, Carvalho, Bruno P., and Mariana Esteves. 2022. *Portugal, Balanço Social 2021.* Lisbon: Nova School of Business and Economics. https://doi.org/10.34619/g5ko-pz3e.

Sharmin Sazedj. 2019. *What has the crisis shown about Portuguese top managers?.* Lisbon. Bank of Portugal.

6 Society

Alice Ramos

6.1 Introduction

Every year the United Nations Development Program (UNDP) releases a report with a wide range of demographic, economic and social indicators for all countries. Based on some of these statistics, the Human Development Index (HDI) is constructed, which ranks countries according to three indicators: life expectancy at birth; average years of schooling and expected years of schooling; and gross national income. At the beginning of the millennium, Portugal was in 37th position and, after slight ups and downs, it reached 2020 in 38th position (UNDP 1999). The Quality of Democracy Barometer is another available index for evaluating and ranking countries, according to three dimensions of democracy: Freedom, Control and Equality. The most recent version of the index, dated 2017, places Portugal in 21st position, in a set of 53 countries, with the country scoring best in the Equality dimension, being in 17th position.

More recently, *The Economist's Democracy Index 2022* again placed Portugal in the group of 'flawed democracies', where it has been since 2020, after having already been part of the 'full democracies' group. In MIPEX (Migrant Integration Policy Index), Portugal emerges as one of the countries with the best public policies regarding the reception of immigrants (only Sweden and Finland score higher). These indices are useful to a certain extent, conveying the image of a country that, despite showing concern for guaranteeing the freedom and equality of those who live here and that, in theory, designs public policies in accordance with these principles, in reality still has a considerable way to go to become a fair and equal society.

The Constitution of the Portuguese Republic (CPR) has established Equality as a permanent concern in Portuguese society, and has been a guiding principle since 25th April. The principle of Equality (Art. 13) provides that '[n]o one may be favoured, benefited, disadvantaged, deprived of any right or exempted from any duty by reason of ancestry, sex, race, language, territory of origin, religion, political or ideological convictions, education, economic situation, social condition or sexual orientation'. The general law is clear, and we are all equal before it. All citizens have equal rights and duties.

Despite the precision of legal indices and the letter of the law, a significant gap often exists between these abstract concepts and the practical realities of everyday life. The primary objective of this chapter is to offer a comprehensive overview of Portuguese society and its evolution over the past two decades. This portrayal is multifaceted and can be examined from various angles and perspectives. In this context, I have opted to focus on the dynamics of social inequalities and the intricate processes of inclusion and exclusion.

DOI: 10.4324/9781003488033-6

This chapter has been made available under a CC-BY-NC-ND license.

80 *Alice Ramos*

Inclusive societies tend to guarantee the needs of all in terms of, for example, education, work, social protection, access to health, social support, housing and civic participation. Within them, the fight against discrimination is a major concern. Due to their better conditions, they are also societies where people have a greater chance of feeling fulfilled and being happy, with all the advantages that this brings, not only for them but for society in general. In turn, societies that exclude, discriminating against people or social groups because they have their own identities or characteristics, are fertile ground for feelings of injustice and powerlessness that often lead to distancing, or even abandonment, of collective life; again, with all the disadvantages that this brings both for them and society in general.

Discrimination is in itself incompatible with the democratic principles of equality, fairness and freedom. It jeopardizes the functioning of institutions, destroys individual expectations and conditions the future by blocking real access to supposedly universal opportunities and resources (education, health, housing, work, wages and quality of life). And it reproduces itself. Halting the cycle of discrimination necessitates a collaborative endeavour involving both citizens and institutions.

This chapter will examine three social groups– women, immigrants and racialized individuals – that, despite the advancements made, still face discrimination for various reasons. Other groups would, of course, deserve the same attention and there would be much to say about them: LGBTQ+ people; people with disabilities; people at more vulnerable stages of life, such as children or the elderly; among others. The choice of women, immigrants and racialized people is justified because they are groups that continue to be the target of blatant discrimination despite the multiple initiatives to combat this promoted by different institutions and entities. This analysis will be made from three points of view: the legal framework, observed facts and societal perceptions. In other words, what the Portuguese law determines should be the functioning of institutions; the actual behaviour of institutions and people; and finally, what people think about the subject. By way of conclusion, we will look at what unites these three groups, i.e., factors that underlie the processes of exclusion and discrimination against them.

6.2 Gender equality, a battle in progress

The movements for women's rights that followed 25 April 1974 were extremely important, opening up access to all professional careers, the right to vote, the end of the right of the husband to open his wife's mail and to authorize (or not) her departure from the country, or maternity leave. The principle of gender equality had already been mentioned in the United Nations Charter, approved in 1945, but it took 30 years for the Convention on the Elimination of All Forms of Discrimination against Women to be approved, a convention ratified in Portugal in 1983. In Portugal, the regime of equal treatment at work between the sexes in Public Administration was only legislated in 1988. The last 20 years have also been marked by the State producing four National Plans for Equality. Among several measures and recommendations, the III Plan (2007–2010) included a guideline on the balanced representation of men and women in the composition of selection boards and the appointment to all levels of decision-making in Public Administration.

In 2018, the National Strategy for Equality and Non-Discrimination 2018–2030 was approved by the Government. The Strategy comprised three action plans with the following objectives: (1) ensuring equality between men and women; (2) preventing and combating violence against women and domestic violence; and (3) addressing discrimination based on sexual orientation, gender identity, expression and sex characteristics. In 2019, an amendment to the 2006 Parity Law was introduced, increasing from 33% to 40% the mandatory minimum representation of each gender on the lists of candidates for the National Parliament, the European Parliament and the elective bodies of local authorities, as well as on the list of candidates for members of local councils. On the same occasion, the regime of balanced representation in Public Administration was established for the first time. This initiative increased the minimum threshold for senior managers appointed to 40%, encompassing both men and women.

Two other measures significantly contributed to the increased effort for equality from the viewpoint of the law. These were the decriminalization of abortion in 2007, and the division of parental leave in 2019, which brought men and women's rights closer after the birth (or adoption) of a child. These examples represent just some of the many measures that have been implemented in Portugal to promote gender equality.

It is true that the role of women in Portuguese society today is a far cry from what it was 50 years ago. It is also true that there is a global awareness, expressed in numerous laws, plans, guides and guidelines, that the fight for equality is a priority. Nonetheless, it is also true that there is still a long way to go to achieve full equality, whether we are talking about concrete measures, such as the principle of 'equal pay for equal work' or more symbolic issues, such as women's supposed emotional fragility or the constraints of motherhood, which make them less able to fulfil roles that require full dedication and a 'firm hand'.

In 2000, women represented about 52% of the resident population in Portugal; on average, they had their first child before the age of 27, and the fertility rate was close to 46%.[1] At that time, 87% of single-parent households were composed of the mother. Over 20 years, the proportion of women has remained almost the same (53%), but the average age at first childbirth has been delayed (30.7 years), with an impact on the fertility rate, which has decreased to 37%. Another area where there have been major changes is in schooling. In 2000, women accounted for 59% of students enroled in higher education. When we recall that in 1970, only 0.5% of women had completed this level of education, the progress made becomes even more impressive. As shown in Figure 6.1, from a position where women accounted for about a third of men with completed tertiary education, the reversal of this ratio became noticeable in 2001 when 8.4% of women had tertiary education. In the following two decades, this figure has continued to grow, reaching above 22% in 2021. Moreover, if we consider only the population between 25 and 64 years of age, the percentage rises to 36%, equivalent to the European average.

If we narrow our focus from the entire population to specifically the 30 to 34 age group, the transformation becomes even more remarkable. In the year 2000, 13.4% of women had attained higher education (compared to 8.8% of men), a figure that surged to 47.3% by 2020 (in contrast to 31.6% of men). Despite this notably positive trend, Portugal ranked 19th among the 27 European Union countries in this indicator in 2020, with 33% of women aged 25–64 having completed higher education (compared to 35% in the EU27).

This growth in women's educational attainment did not, however, have the effect that might have been expected in terms of employability and pay. In 2021, employment in Portugal continued to have two notable characteristics in terms of gender differences: the female employment rate was lower than that of men and the EU27, but higher than the female employment rate of the EU27 (Figure 6.2).[2] This pattern is not recent and is one of the country's singularities (e.g., Casaca 2012; Torres et al. 2005). However, if we

82 Alice Ramos

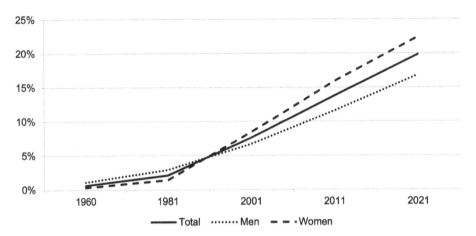

Figure 6.1 Population with completed tertiary education at the time of the censuses, by sex
Source: INE Censos; Pordata

go back to 2002 and look at the progress up to 2020, we see that there have been very marked changes affecting both sexes. In 2002, Portuguese women had an employment rate higher than that of their European counterparts and equal to the EU27 average (50%). This figure was maintained until 2008 and, thereafter, the impact of the economic crisis in Portugal is evident, with employment rates falling to the point where, in 2013, they overlapped with the EU27 average employment rate (in the case of men, it was even lower than the EU27 average).[3]

For Portuguese women, the aftermath of both the economic crisis and the pandemic has resulted in their highest employment rate since 2002. However, for men, there exists a notable divergence of 6 percentage points. In essence, the apparent convergence of male and female employment rates is not a consequence of diminished gender inequality in employment but rather stems from the lack of recovery in male employment.

One of the most challenging battles to overcome pertains to wage disparities. Despite advancements, women persist in earning less than their male counterparts, and this gap amplifies in professions demanding higher qualifications (refer to Figure 6.3). As of 2021, even the most highly qualified Portuguese women earned approximately 25% less than their male counterparts. Remarkably, over 19 years, the gender pay gap has only marginally reduced by 5%. In less qualified occupations, while the gap is smaller, it still persists, ranging between 6% and 8%.

One field that was exclusive to the male world and where women continue to struggle is political representation and leadership positions. In this case, it was even necessary to introduce a quota system, regulating the law on parity and equal representation mentioned above. A strictly quantitative reading shows that important progress has been made, which would not have been possible without the enactment of the parity law in 2006. According to data from the Commission for Citizenship and Gender Equality, in 2005 women represented 21.3% of the Portuguese members of parliament, a figure that rose to 38.7% in 2019 and 37% in 2022. These figures remain below the value stipulated by Organic Law No. 1 of 2019, which set the minimum threshold for representation of each gender at 40%. The participation of women in the different governments has also

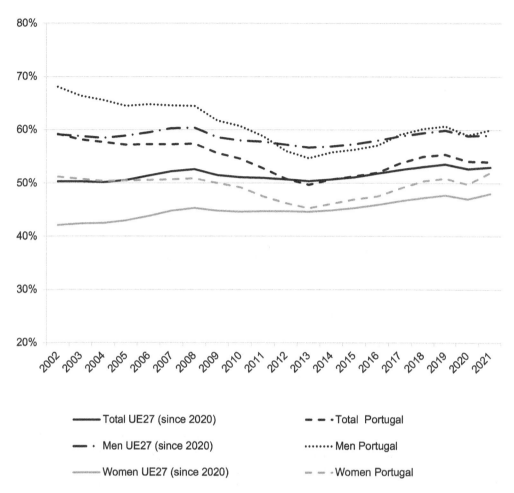

Figure 6.2 Employment rates
Source: Pordata (https://www.pordata.pt/en/home)

shown a positive evolution: in 2005, the percentage of women was 11.3%, rising to 37.5% in 2022.

And what do the Portuguese think about all this? Several national and international surveys have been addressing various issues, such as gender equality, the roles of women and men in different spheres of life, reconciling work and family life. These surveys are a relatively reliable barometer of what has (or has not) changed in the opinions of the Portuguese. Why 'relatively'? Because people are aware of the public debate and do not always want to give their opinion, especially in the presence of an interviewer, and thus stick to what they consider to be the 'right' answer, the same one as the 'experts' who write in the newspapers and appear on television put forward. This phenomenon is all the more frequent the more controversial the topic addressed. The role of women in Portuguese society is one of them. Even so, there has been an important change.

84 *Alice Ramos*

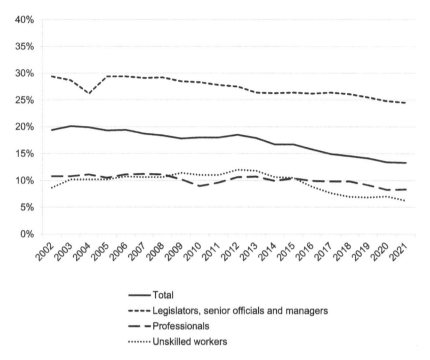

Figure 6.3 Gender pay gap by qualification level
Source: Pordata (https://www.pordata.pt/en/home)

The results of the European Values Study (EVS)[4] carried out in Portugal in 1999, 2008 and 2020 show a considerable change in the last 20 years (Figure 6.4). However, there remains a non-negligible share of the population (46%) who believe that children suffer when their mothers work. Age plays an important role here: in 2020, 25% of respondents aged 18–29 agreed with this view, and 57% of those aged 50 and over. This difference is very similar when we consider the level of education: 55% of respondents with elementary education and 28% with higher education share the idea that maternal work is harmful to children. Equally interesting is the fact that, overall, men and women are equally divided on the negative impact of women's work on their children's lives.

When we analyse the agreement with the statement in all 34 countries that participated in the EVS, we find Portugal in 22nd place. In this ranking, Denmark, Finland and Sweden claim the lowest positions, with agreement percentages falling below 16%. Notably, Georgia and Armenia stand out as the countries where the greatest consensus exists on the negative effects of mothers' professional activity on their children's lives, with agreement values hovering around 70%. The motivations behind these diverse responses may vary, and the available data do not provide sufficient insight. Possible reasons could range from beliefs about a woman's role being primarily at home caring for her children to perceptions that the country does not offer conducive conditions for balancing work and family life.

There are, however, other questions that point more clearly to a view corresponding to stereotypes of a certain social order, where the role of women is closely linked to

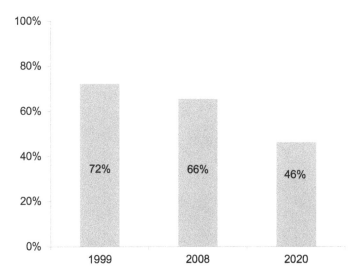

Figure 6.4 'When a mother works for pay, the children suffer' (% agreement in Portugal)
Source: European Values Study

domestic life. This is so with the case presented in Figure 6.5, which refers to the supposed 'nature' of women. In this case, the level of agreement is slightly lower in 2020, but we observe only a difference of 10 percentage points in 20 years.

When we analyse the answers to this question according to the age and education level of the respondents, the trend is the same as that observed in the previous question: the youngest and most educated agree less (35% and 23%, respectively) and the oldest and least educated agree more (52% and 51%, respectively). Here too, men and women share the same opinion. The highest agreement values are found in Georgia and Azerbaijan, with percentages above 70%, and the lowest in Sweden and Denmark, with percentages below 20%.

Let's change the scene. Let's move from the private to the public sphere and start by recalling the percentage of women who held political positions in 2022 (37% in the Portuguese Parliament and 37.5% in the Government) and recording those who held senior management positions[5] (33% on boards of directors and nearly 20% in executive positions). Although women continue to be under-represented in senior management, there has been some progress over the last 20 years: in 2003 women occupied only 3.5% of board positions.

Regarding the public sphere, the Portuguese generally have more positive opinions, mostly disagreeing with the opinion that men are better than women, either as politicians (only 17% agree) or as managers (only 11% agree), which places them among the countries that share more egalitarian gender attitudes.

Overall, Portuguese women live in two worlds. In terms of employment, they are approaching their counterparts in the Nordic countries and moving away from the situation experienced in southern Europe, where female employment rates are among the lowest in the EU (Casaca et al. 2021). Regarding education, the percentage of women with higher education has already exceeded the European average. Nevertheless, the population still has a traditionalist image of the role of women that pushes them into

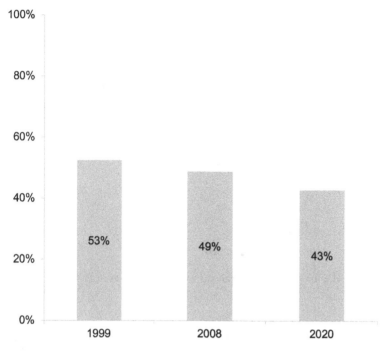

Figure 6.5 'A job is alright but what most women really want is a home and children' (% agreement in Portugal)
Source: European Values Study

the domestic sphere. The wage gap remains, and the representation of women in management positions in the largest companies is still far from 40%, a figure established in 2003 as a minimum parity threshold by the Council of Europe. We need to bridge the gap between these two worlds to reduce the inequalities that persist, using legislation and investing in the education of future generations in a scenario of gender equality.

6.3 The faces of immigration

Two critical aspects of immigration in Portugal shape the foundation for any analysis on the subject. It constitutes a relatively recent phenomenon in Portuguese society and accounts for a modest share of the population. While our focus is on the past 20 years, delving slightly further back provides a more comprehensive context for understanding developments in the recent two decades. Figure 6.6 visually illustrates the expansion of the foreign population with permanent residence in Portugal.

Between 1980 and 2000, immigration grew steadily. The increase in the immigrant population from 2001 onwards was largely due to extraordinary regularization processes and introduction of the residence permits (APs) and long-stay visas (LTVs) in force between 2001 and 2005. At the same time that legislation in the European Union (and in Portugal) became more controlling, criminalizing and penalizing, especially after September 2001, Portugal maintained some flexibility in the measures it implemented, countering criminalization and focusing on the integration and naturalization

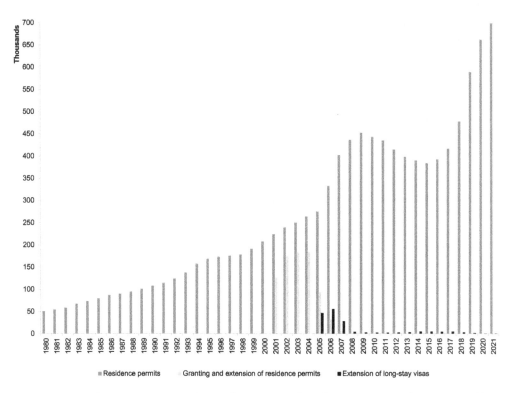

Figure 6.6 Residence permits, granting and extension of residence permits and extension of long-stay visas (1980–2021)

Source: SEF (https://www.sef.pt/en/)

of immigrants (Padilla and Ortiz 2012). In the last 20 years, 11 amendments have been made to Law No. 37/81, of 3rd October (Nationality Law), in order to adapt the attribution of Portuguese nationality to immigrants and their descendants to emerging needs. In 2018, for example, the time required for one of the parents to legally stay in the national territory for Portuguese nationality to be granted to their children was reduced from five to two years. The most recent change dates from November 2020, and nationality will be automatically granted as long as one of the parents has their situation legalized, or has lived in Portugal for at least one year, regardless of their legal situation.

These permanent changes to the naturalization law, in particular, and the implementation of public policies in the field of immigration, in general, are more the result of a reaction process, and not so much of a planned action (Padilla and Thais 2020).[6] In any case, the country's immigration policies are reflected in Portugal's position in MIPEX, as we mentioned at the beginning of this chapter, and in international recognition, namely by the UN.

The major drawback here is that the advanced Portuguese immigration policies are legal tools. In practice, in their implementation and application, the scenario is quite different: one of the most flagrant examples being the accusations of discrimination and racial hatred, which continue to occur in Portugal and of which immigrants are a frequent target. Before we move on to this point, however, let's look at the profile of immigrants in Portugal.

Migratory movements are primarily a response to a combination of socio-economic conditions in their original and host countries, including the legal framework, informal migratory networks and the labour market. However, the latter has played a leading role, absorbing immigrants into the formal and informal labour market (Peixoto 2013, 2009). Until the 1990s, immigrants were mostly from Brazil and the former Portuguese colonies. From then on, and in response to the increased need for labour (Expo 98 and public works), immigrants from Eastern Europe began to arrive.

From 2000 onwards, migratory flows intensified and the diversity of immigrant origins increased, now also coming from China, India, Pakistan, Bangladesh, among other Asian countries. The economic crisis marked a new change in migratory movements: between 2009 and 2015, immigration systematically decreased, even being lower than emigration (in 2013, for example, 18,000 immigrants entered the country and 54,000 Portuguese left). From 2016 onwards, the number of permanent immigrants increased again and, in 2020, there were close to 662,000 foreigners living in Portugal, close to 70% of them in Lisbon, Faro and Setúbal.[7]

Many of these immigrants have brought different customs and cultural practices. Some profess religions the Portuguese are not used to living with, others speak unfamiliar languages. Diversity has never been greater in Portugal and these people are quickly categorized into an 'ethnic' or 'racial' group different from the majority. For those who, for various reasons, do not see diversity as a benefit, 'different' immigrants become scapegoats, blamed for the ills affecting the Portuguese. Moreover, and regardless of how good the laws are that regulate their integration, inequality and injustice continue to be part of their daily lives, just as they did when they decided to leave their countries. The most blatant cases are highlighted in the media, either for their violence or for their continued injustice, but the majority remain silent.

The various cases of immigrants in the Alentejo are an example of what happens when the social fragility of some and the economic interests of others, combined with hatred or simple indifference, intersect. In May 2021, an outbreak of COVID in the town of Odemira, in the south of Portugal, uncovered a Dantesque scenario, years' old but kept silent: thousands of Asian immigrants captured and enslaved by criminal networks, working in agriculture and living in inhumane conditions, with the silence and complacency of agricultural companies. The case led to statements by Prime Minister António Costa vehemently condemning 'the blatant violation of human rights' and by the President of the Republic, Marcelo Rebelo de Sousa, who referred to the importance of immigrants for the Portuguese economy and society. In December 2021, seven GNR agents were convicted of abuse of violence, racist insults and humiliation perpetrated against immigrants between September 2018 and March 2019, in the municipality of Odemira. Faced with the violence of the evidence (videos filmed by the agents themselves), the Prime Minister and the President of the Republic once again expressed their repudiation and the urgency of taking measures. In November 2022, immigrants from Odemira were again in the news, for the same reasons: exploited by trafficking networks, working in agriculture for miserable wages and living in inhuman conditions. In January 2023, the court in Beja passed sentence: six of the defendants saw their sentence suspended, while one was sentenced to six years in prison, since he had already been convicted in a similar case, also involving immigrants.

This reality, much broader than the particular case of immigrants in Odemira, coexists with the idea, still shared by a significant portion of Portuguese, that immigrants bring more problems than benefits. We often hear in Portugal, but also in other countries, that the entry of immigrants should be 'controlled' for economic reasons (because they take jobs away from nationals, because they lower wages, because they abuse the social security system), for 'cultural' reasons (because they have different values from 'ours', because they weaken 'our' culture), or because they contribute to the increase in crime.

The need for 'control' is a message that can be presented in a number of different ways. Some can even be 'well-intentioned', aiming at the well-being of immigrants; but the meaning tends to be the same: to exclude difference and promote cultural assimilation. Here are two very recent examples (February 2023). In the Mouraria neighbourhood of Lisbon, following a fire that broke out on the first floor of an old building, it was learned that 22 immigrants had been living there. The mayor, Carlos Moedas, quickly went to the scene and, of course, was outraged by the situation. As for the residents, there was no outrage, as this was not a unique case and everyone who lived there had been aware of the situation and other similar cases. A few days later, Carlos Moedas declared that economic migrants were welcome, but that the law had to be changed to require them to present a work contract when applying for a residence visa. In other words, solving the problem did not involve guaranteeing dignity and creating housing conditions for those who wanted to live here. It involved creating selection criteria for immigrants that restricted their entry. Still on the subject of immigrants, Luís Montenegro, president of the PSD (the Social Democratic Party), argued that the country should 'look around the world for communities that can interact better with us, that can integrate better into our culture, into our identity'.[8]

Data from the European Social Survey[9] allow us to know some opinions of the Portuguese in this regard and see to what extent they have changed in the last 20 years, in comparison with some European countries. First of all, there was a remarkably sudden and greater openness to immigration observed from 2012 onwards, regardless of its origin. This was despite the significant difference between immigrants considered more similar to Portuguese from an ethnic/'racial' point of view[10] and the other two groups corresponding to the profile of most immigrants in Portugal (Figure 6.7). It is clear how the change of attitudes in other countries is much more gradual and stable. Until 2012, Portugal was clearly below the average of the other countries. In 2014, however, it shows values equal to the average and, since then, it has remained above that average, even in 2021/22.

This growing trend, since 2012, of openness to immigration registered a reversal in 2021/22, affecting all groups of immigrants considered. It is important to notice that data was collected between August 2021 and March 2022, i.e., still in the aftermath of the COVID-19 pandemic, which had disastrous consequences on the financial and employment situation of many families (Susana Peralta's chapter in this book). The economic context has been identified in several studies as a shaper of attitudes towards immigration, and moments of economic crisis have been associated with less openness to immigration (Quillian 1995; Vala et al. 1999; Ramos et al. 2016). It could be contended that the conditions precipitated by the pandemic played a significant role in altering the overall attitude of the Portuguese towards immigrants. However, this argument proves inadequate as Portugal wasn't the sole nation affected by the pandemic. That being acknowledged, among the eight European countries that we can presently compare retrospectively, Portugal stands out as the sole country where openness to immigration diminished in comparison to 2018.

When individuals assert that immigrants snatch jobs from locals, pose a threat to the economy, or introduce cultural practices that undermine 'our' culture, these statements

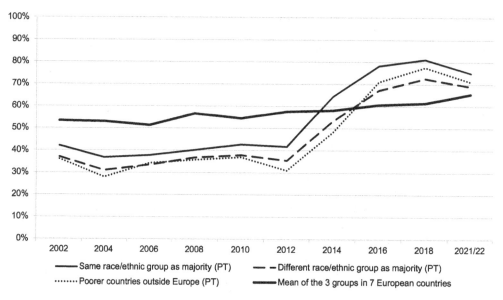

Figure 6.7 Openness to immigration in Portugal and Europe.[11] (% of responses saying 'many' + 'some' should be allowed to come and live here.)

Source: European Social Survey

are not merely viewpoints. In the majority of instances, they serve as justifications employed by people to alleviate the discomfort associated with expressing negative opinions (Pereira et al. 2010). Respondents were asked to express their opinion on a scale from 0 to 10 where 0 meant the least favourable opinion and 10 the most favourable. Figure 6.8 shows the average responses over the years in Portugal and in the set of seven European countries. The similarity between the three responses, and the way they evolve synchronously, is striking, suggesting that they reflect an overall opinion on immigration, rather than specific ones, on the impact of immigration on the economy, culture or ways of life. In fact, these views are in line with the attitude towards openness to immigration, with Portuguese evaluations currently more positive than the average in the European countries under analysis.

The perception that immigrants 'take jobs away from the Portuguese', or that they 'contribute to the increase in crime', has also changed. In 2002, 60% of respondents in Portugal thought that immigrants were a threat in the labour market, a percentage that dropped to 40% in 2014. Compared to the other 20 participating countries, in 2014, Portugal was aligned with Belgium, Austria and the United Kingdom, between the most positive positions, shared by Sweden and Norway (with percentages of perceived threat below 15%) and the most negative positions, registered in Hungary and the Czechia (with values around 65%). In the case of the impact on crime, and for the same years, the results showed that these opinions were shared in Portugal in 2002 by 76% and in 2014 by 59% of respondents, a figure close to the average of the other countries (57%). There was, however, one aspect that did not evolve in the same direction. When the tax contribution of immigrants was compared to the benefits in terms of access to health and social security, the answers showed a tendency towards the belief that immigrants

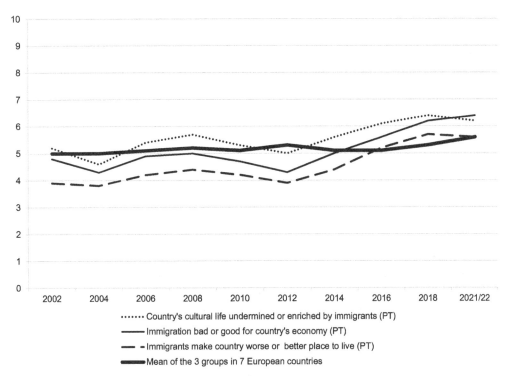

Figure 6.8 Opinions on the impact of immigration in Portugal and Europe (averages)
Source: European Social Survey

benefited more than they contributed (in Portugal it was an opinion shared by 29% of respondents in 2002, that increased to 41% in 2014).[12]

These assessments of the impact of immigration on society are reflected in the desired profile of immigrants. The importance attributed to six criteria in the admission of immigrants in the country was also measured in the 2014 survey. On a scale from not at all important (0) to extremely important (10), the Portuguese considered the professional qualifications that the country needed the most important factor (average of 7.1). This was followed by the willingness of immigrants to adapt to the Portuguese way of life (average of 6.8); with knowing how to speak Portuguese very close in third (average of 6.5). It is very interesting to see how these results relate to the markers of nationality, namely the importance given to language, a widespread marker in all countries, and to 'feeling' Portuguese in order to be considered a true Portuguese (Sobral, this volume).

As mentioned above, these data refer to perceptions, i.e., ways of interpreting reality, which are naturally subjective and highly influenced by external factors. For example, in 2014, data from the ESS indicated that, on average, the Portuguese estimated that 25% of residents in the national territory were not born in Portugal when, in reality, they represented 8.3% of the resident population. This and other distorted views of reality can only be deconstructed through facts based on statistical data.

Portugal is an ageing country: Eurostat data indicate that between 2012 and 2022 Portugal was the country in the European Union where the average age increased the

92   *Alice Ramos*

most (+4.7 years). In 2020 it was the fourth country in the European area with the highest proportion of people over 65 (22%). Portugal is a country with few immigrants: the 18th in number of foreign residents (in 20 years, the foreign population went from 2% to 6.4%). The foreign population continued to be concentrated in the younger age groups, of childbearing and working age. In 2020, women of foreign nationality accounted for 13.5% of total live births, a figure that was particularly significant at a time when the foreign population represented 6.4% of the resident population. In other words, immigrants continued to make a positive contribution to Portuguese demography (Oliveira 2021; Peixoto et al. 2017).

In Portugal, immigrants occupy the least desirable jobs: precarious, poorly paid, riskier and generally in sectors such as construction, hotels, restaurants and domestic service (Oliveira 2021). In addition, as in previous years, and according to the 2019 Staff Tables, the average basic salaries of foreign workers are 8% less than Portuguese workers. Immigrants also continue to be in a disadvantaged position in terms of their employment situation; although the unemployment rates of both immigrants and nationals are getting closer, the former are still at a disadvantage. In 2020, the unemployment rate of non-EU foreigners rose to 14.7%, while that of the total population in Portugal was at 6.8%. Furthermore, schooling brought no advantages to immigrants: the gap between the qualifications obtained and those necessary for the functions they performed was greater among immigrants (+8.7pp) than among Portuguese workers.

In Portugal, immigrants have a positive impact on Social Security: over the last decade, the trend has been the same – a positive and favourable balance for Portugal between contributions and social benefits of the Portuguese Social Security system, with the highest value ever reached in 2019 (+€884.4 million). Moreover, in 2020, foreign taxpayers stood at 64 per 100 residents, while nationals accounted for 45 per 100 residents, i.e., foreigners showed greater contributory capacity than nationals to the Social Security system. On the other hand, that of social benefits, immigrants continued to receive the least: in 2020, the ratio was 52 beneficiaries per 100 taxpayers, while in the case of nationals, the same ratio was 83 to 100. In 2020, social benefits reached unprecedented levels (+55.6% than in 2011) due to the COVID-19 pandemic. It was the contributions of immigrants that kept the social security balance favourable. This situation did not reflect the vulnerability, risk of poverty and material deprivation of immigrants in Portugal, which was still higher than that of nationals.

The information needed to dismantle the negative perceptions that persist in the Portuguese population exists. However, as long as it is not properly disseminated, the sectors of society opposed to immigration will continue to use all available channels to pass on an alarmist message, maintaining the image that immigrants represent a danger to the social, economic, financial and cultural balance of Portuguese society.

6.4 Skin-deep differences

In Portugal, as in all contemporary democratic societies, discrimination against people based on racial or ethnic criteria persists. In fact, there is not a single society that has succeeded in eliminating discrimination against social groups based on these criteria. People everywhere continue to discriminate against others, stripping them of the humanity they claim for themselves. There are institutions that continue to discriminate against people by taking away the rights of citizenship that the law confers on them. This is the case for people who are perceived as belonging to a different race or ethnicity, who continue to be the target of discriminatory attitudes and behaviour, contrary to the fundamental principles of democracy.

'The Portuguese are not racist'. This is a statement that we often hear in different contexts. It is a belief that finds its roots in Gilberto Freyre's lusotropicalist approach, whose foundations were laid in his 1933 work, *Casa-Grande e Sanzala* (translated as *The Masters and the Slaves*), and which emerged as a counterpoint to the social Darwinism and racialism shared by much of the Brazilian intelligentsia of his time (Castelo 1999; Xavier 2008). According to Freyre, the mixed nature of the Portuguese gave them the ability to adapt physically and culturally to tropical contexts. This Lusitanian essence associated with a practically non-existent race consciousness and an impulse towards miscegenation created the conditions for the Portuguese to practice a colonialism different from all other empires. These ideas were used by the *Estado Novo* regime to extol the nation's pluri-racial nature and the denial of racism as distinctive features of Portuguese national identity. At the same time, the same ideas helped to legitimize colonialism on a 'scientific basis' and, remaining alive after the dictatorship, have reached the present day, duly purified.

'The Portuguese are not generally racist'. This was a statement made by Pedro Calado in 2018 when he was High Commissioner for Migration (a strategic position to combat racism) regarding the then-recent assault on a young Portuguese-Colombian woman by a transport company security guard and the assault and kidnapping, in 2015, of six young black residents in Cova da Moura by police officers from the Alfragide police station.[13] According to the High Commissioner, such discriminatory behaviour was also the result of prejudices that the Portuguese had, just like everyone else.

But what are we talking about when we talk about racism? First of all, a belief in the superiority of the white race. A belief built on so-called scientific racism, of which Gobineau was the greatest exponent.[14] Gobineau did not limit himself to dividing humanity into races – the whites (whose expression of perfection is found in the Aryans), the blacks and the yellows – assigning to each race personality traits. Thus, the blacks, the inferior race, possessing little or no intellectual capacity, were driven by desire; the yellows, not very energetic, but less terrible than the blacks; the whites, superior, courageous and ideal, lovers of freedom. It took almost a century to show the scientific unsoundness of biologically based racist classifications.[15] However, racism survives, like a virus in permanent mutation and adaptation to the external environment (Vala 2021) and continues to have its victims. Alcindo Monteiro was 27 years old when, on 10 June 1995, he was assaulted and murdered by a group of skinheads in Lisbon's Bairro Alto neighbourhood.

More recent examples are the cases of Moussa Marega, a player from Futebol Clube do Porto, who walked off the pitch after being loudly insulted by fans of the opposing team who simulated monkey sounds; or the extreme case of Bruno Candé. Candé was shot dead by a former soldier in the colonial war, who was later sentenced to 22 years in prison once racial hatred and the intentionality of the murder had been proven. These cases had wide media visibility and are the tip of an iceberg populated by invisible people who experience such situations in their daily lives, despite the anti-racist and anti-discriminatory norm that is supported by Portuguese law (Henriques 2018).

In Portugal, the anti-discrimination law was first enacted in 1999 and amended in 2017.[16] In addition to the prohibition of discrimination on the basis of 'race', colour, nationality and ethnic origin, new forms of discrimination were added, such as those based on ancestry and territory of origin, multiple discrimination (offence against more than one protected characteristic) and discrimination by association ('by reason of relationship or association with a person or group of persons' holding the protected criteria). Nevertheless, the law is only one (essential) step in the fight against racism. It does not prevent the Portuguese from continuing to believe in the superiority of certain racial or ethnic groups.

In 2014, as part of the European Social Survey, respondents were asked to what extent they subscribed to two ideas that refer to the biological essentialization of differences between groups. These were 'some races or ethnic groups are by nature less intelligent than others' and 'some races or ethnic groups are by nature more hardworking than others'. Figure 6.9 shows how these two ideas remain entrenched in Europe and particularly in Portugal.

Portugal is the second country where the belief in racial or ethnic superiority is highest (41%), only surpassed by Czechia. In the case of the belief related to the innate ability to work, Portugal is even the country with the highest percentage of agreement (68%). This belief is a very powerful legitimizer of inequalities and discrimination against people who are given a lower status because they belong to groups that are considered, in essence, less intelligent and less hardworking (e.g., Ramos et al. 2020). Society is not being unfair. It is not discriminating because, despite the equal opportunities available, some people simply do not have the ability to take advantage of them.

A final word on prejudice: in the social sciences, prejudice defines a negative attitude about people and groups. We say we are not prejudiced, but we choose our companionship. And when we do not choose someone because of the colour of their skin, or because

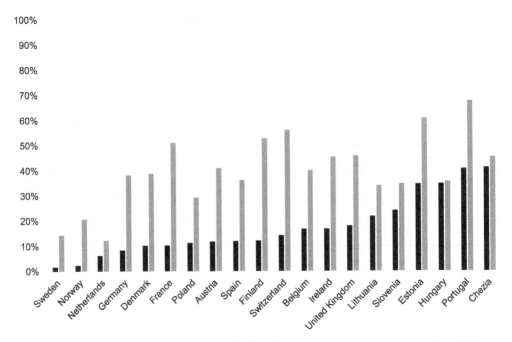

Figure 6.9 Belief in racial or ethnic superiority

Source: European Social Survey, 2014/15

of their religion, or because we consider their behaviour socially or morally reprehensible, what we are doing is regulating the presence of the Other in our environment. Migratory movements, religious and cultural diversity, and the presence of contrasting identities generate situations and scenarios that force individuals to place and replace themselves, in terms of identities and the definition they construct of 'us' and 'the other'. And, in the course of this process, feelings are developed, sometimes more negative, sometimes more positive. Discrimination based on entrenched beliefs, such as those built up over centuries about specific social groups is very difficult to break down or dissolve. It is discrimination based not on what people do, but on what they are, or are supposed to be. It is discrimination based on stereotypes formed on external signs (skin colour, facial features and accent) or social and ancestral characteristics (religion, place of residence and country of origin). All these forms of discrimination, including racism, weaken society and democracy and pose a very serious threat to the equal dignity that everyone deserves.

6.5 Conclusion: an unequal country

We have shown so far how the lives of people belonging to three social groups are limited by two persistent forces: discrimination and the paradox between the openness of the law and the resistance of institutions and people. There is, however, an additional factor that enhances these forces: social inequalities. Portugal, clearly no exception, and despite all progress, remains a country subject to strong social cleavages,[17] which translate into very unequal forms of access to the benefits and advantages of living in a democratic society. Being born into a disadvantaged social class is halfway to being the victim of unequal treatment and discrimination, not least because of the difficulty in using the tools to combat it, such as education, access to information, and a decent standard of living.

In 2004, Portugal was the country with the highest Gini index (which measures income inequalities) in the EU-15. In 2021, it ranked 15th out of the 27 EU countries. During this period, Portugal was hit by two crises, one financial and one pandemic. The financial crisis of 2008–2013 and the intervention of the Troika led to an unprecedented rise in unemployment, lower wages and increased precariousness in labour relations. These conditions aggravated the inequalities already felt by the most vulnerable social classes and affected the middle classes who, until then, had managed a balanced existence. When the pandemic arrived in March 2020, Portugal was still recovering, and the economic indicators showed a relatively encouraging scenario (Caleiras 2022). A new wave of unemployment hit the country, affecting first and foremost the most precarious and vulnerable workers: informal workers, including many immigrants, young people, the less educated and women. Layoffs, teleworking, school and support service closures caused more unemployment, lower wages and thus increased poverty.

At present, poverty in Portugal remains higher than the EU average. In 2019, 9.8% of the population was in persistent poverty, rising to 11.4% among children.[18] In 2020, 18.4% of people were at risk of poverty, an increase of 2.2 percentage points compared to 2019. We do not have data that allow us to know the incidence of poverty in racialized groups, but we know that among immigrants from countries outside Europe the poverty rate is 25%, 10% among immigrants from the EU and 17% among the Portuguese (see the chapter by Susana Peralta in this volume).

As long as inequalities are not understood, first and foremost, as social and class inequalities that are reproduced and perpetuated, the problem will persist. Those who

96 Alice Ramos

are disadvantaged at the outset will continue to be so throughout their lives, save for the rare exceptions serving as examples to meritocratic apologists.

For a long time, Portugal lived closed in on itself as a defence against external threats, in this case the democratic and egalitarian ideals emanating from some European countries. The dictatorship deliberately kept the Portuguese in ignorance. The 25th of April opened the doors to combat the cultural misery (among others) in which the vast majority of the population lived. Schooling and education for citizenship became a priority[19] and the results were extraordinary, with legislation accompanying the integration of other social groups, other ways of life. It is undeniable that Portuguese society in the 2020s is a much more inclusive society than it was half a century ago. However, there are still many people who feel threatened by difference, in addition to those who use these perceptions of threat as a sounding board for xenophobic, racist, misogynistic and other types of discriminatory discourse, deriving political benefit from them. Fortunately, the law exists, as well as a growing awareness among the Portuguese regarding discrimination and inequalities. Nonetheless, 'general policies to reduce social inequalities will not be sufficient and will naturally have to be complemented by proper anti-discrimination policies' (Piketty 2022, 13).

Notes

1 Fertility rate: number of births per 1000 women of childbearing age, i.e., between 15 and 49 years old.
2 Employment rate: number of employed per 100 persons aged 15 and over.
3 More comparative data on gender equality between Portugal and Europe can be found at https://eige.europa.eu/.
4 The European Values Study is a survey that takes place every 10 years on attitudes and values about a wide range of areas of life (work, family, politics, religion and morality, among others). In the most recent wave (2017–20), 34 countries participated. Portugal has been a member since 1990. The data are public and can be downloaded from the Portuguese Social Information Archive (APIS) from the PASSDA infrastructure website (www.passda.pt).
5 According to the meta-information provided by PORDATA, the boards of directors of the largest companies listed on the stock exchange (a maximum of 50) and women occupying senior positions in the two main bodies (the audit committee and board of directors) were considered in these companies.
6 In 1996, the High Commission for Immigration and Ethnic Minorities (ACIME) was created. Later renamed the High Commission for Immigration and Intercultural Dialogue (ACIDI), it is currently known as the High Commission for Migration (ACM), centralizing integration policies in Portugal.
7 The main country of origin was Brazil (28%), followed by the United Kingdom, Cape Verde, Romania, Ukraine, Italy, China, France, India and Angola. These nationalities represented 68% of total immigrants in 2020.
8 Expresso. 2023. 'Montenegro defende que Portugal deve receber imigrantes "de forma regulada"', February 9, 2023 (in https://expresso.pt/politica/2023-02-09-Montenegro-defende-que -Portugal-deve-receber-imigrantes-de-forma-regulada-42533552).
9 The European Social Survey-ERIC (www.europeansocialsurvey.org) is a biennial survey conducted since 2002 among representative samples of populations aged 15 and over living in more than 30 European countries, measuring and monitoring the social attitudes, beliefs and behaviours of people in Europe.
10 The concept of race is part of everyday discourse and it is in this sense that it will be used in this text, as a social construction without any biological foundation. Only the responses of respondents born in and with citizenship of each of the countries were considered.
11 The other countries, besides Portugal, available for comparison between the 10 ESS rounds, were Slovenia, Finland, France, Hungary, Norway, The Netherlands and Switzerland.

12 These questions were part of the ESS-specific module on Attitudes towards Immigration, which was applied only in 2002 and in 2014.
13 Four years after the attack, in 2019, 8 of the 17 accused officers were convicted, one of them with an effective sentence.
14 Between 1853 and 1855, the French diplomat Joseph-Arthur de Gobineau wrote 'An Essay on the Inequality of the Human Races'. It was a work that had an immense political impact on racist ideology as we know it today, as well as on the legitimization of colonial empires and slavery.
15 In 1972, the geneticist, Richard Lewontin, dismantled the concept of biological racism after finding greater genetic diversity within so-called 'racial groups' than between them.
16 See Law 134/99 available at https://data.dre.pt/eli/lei/134/1999/08/28/p/dre/pt/html and 93/2017 at https://data.dre.pt/eli/lei/93/2017/08/23/p/dre/pt/html.
17 For a recent approach on social classes in Portugal, see the 2013 book organized by Renato do Carmo, entitled *Portugal, uma Sociedade de Classes. Polarização Social e Vulnerabilidades.*
18 Source: ICOR, Longitudinal 2017–2020. The 'persistent poverty (Eurostat)' indicator is defined as the proportion of people with equivalized disposable income below the at-risk-of-poverty threshold in the current year (in this case 2019) and in at least two of the previous three years (Peralta, Carvalho and Esteves, 2022).
19 The Profile of Students Leaving Compulsory Schooling, approved by Order No. 6478/2017, 26th July, declares that one of the aims of the education system is to train citizens to reject all forms of discrimination and social exclusion.

References

Caleiras, Jorge. 2022. "Pandemia e desigualdades no emprego: que políticas para uma recuperação sustentável?" In *Que Futuro para a Igualdade? Pensar a Sociedade e o Pós-pandemia*, edited by Renato Miguel do Carmo, Inês Tavares e Ana Filipa Cândido. Lisbon: Observatório das Desigualdades, CIES-ISCTE.
Carmo, Renato Miguel. (Org). 2013. *Portugal, uma Sociedade de Classes. Polarização Social e Vulnerabilidades.* Lisbon: Edições 70.
Casaca, Sara Falcão. 2012. "Mercado de trabalho, flexibilidade e relações de género: tendências recentes". *Mudanças laborais e relações de género, novos vetores de desigualdade*, edited by Sara Falcão Casaca, 9–50. Coimbra: Almedina.
Casaca, Sara Falcão, Maria João Guedes, Susana Ramalho Marques, and Nuno Paço. 2021. "Is a progressive law accelerating the longstanding snail's pace? Women on corporate boards in Portugal." *Revista de Administração de Empresas* 61, no. 2: 1–7.
Castelo, Cláudia. 1999. *O modo português de estar no mundo. O luso-tropicalismo e a ideologia colonial portuguesa (1933–1961).* Lisbon: Edições Afrontamento.
Gobineau, Joseph-Arthur de. 1853/1915. *The Inequality of Human Races.* London: William Heinemann.
Henriques, Joana Gorjão. 2018. *Racismo no país dos brancos costumes.* Lisbon: Tinta-da-China.
Oliveira, Catarina Reis. 2021. *Indicadores de integração de imigrantes: relatório estatístico anual 2021.* 1ª ed. Lisboa: Observatório das Migrações ACM, IP.
Padilla, Beatriz, and Alejandra Ortiz, A. 2012. "Fluxos migratórios em Portugal: do boom migratório à desaceleração no contexto de crise. Balanços e desafios". *REMHU: Revista Interdisciplinar da Mobilidade Humana* 20, no. 39: 159–184.
Padilla, Beatriz., and Thaís França. 2020. "Three decades later… Evolution of immigrant incorporation policies in Portugal: A new reading". *Politica Globalidad y Ciudadanía* 6, no. 11: 171–202.
Peixoto, João. 2009. "New Migrations in Portugal: Labour Markets, Smuggling and Gender Segmentation". *International Migration* 47, no. 3: 185–210.
Peixoto, João. 2013. "Imigração, emprego e o mercado de trabalho em Portugal: os dilemas do crescimento e o impacto da recessão." In *Migrações na Europa e em Portugal: Ensaios de homenagem a Maria Ioannis Baganha,* edited by Maria Ioannis Baganha, Pedro Góis, Jorge Marques, and João Peixoto, 159–184. Coimbra: Almedina.
Peixoto, João, Daniela Craveiro, Jorge Malheiros, and Isabel Tiago de Oliveira, eds. 2017. *Migrações e Sustentabilidade Demográfica: Perspetivas de Evolução da Sociedade e Economia Portuguesas.* Lisbon: Fundação Francisco Manuel dos Santos.

Peralta, Susana, Bruno P. Carvalho, and Mariana Esteves. 2022. *Portugal, Balanço Social 2021.* Lisbon: Nova School of Business and Economics.

Pereira, Cícero, Jorge Vala, and Rui Costa-Lopes. 2010. From prejudice to discrimination: The legitimizing role of perceived threat in discrimination against immigrants. *European Journal of Social Psychology* 40, no. 7: 1231–1250.

Piketty, Thomas. 2022. *Mesurer le racism vaincre les discriminations.* Paris: Éditions du Seuil.

Quillian, Lincoln. 1995. "Prejudice as a response to perceived group threat: population composition and anti-immigrant and racial prejudice in Europe." *American Sociological Review* 60, no. 4: 586–611.

Ramos, Alice, Cícero Pereira, and Jorge Vala. 2020. "The impact of biological and cultural racisms on attitudes towards immigrants and immigration public policies". *Journal of Ethnic and Migration Studies* 46, no. 3: 574–592

Ramos, Alice, Cícero Pereira, and Jorge Vala. 2016. Economic crisis, human values and attitudes towards immigration. In *Values, economic crisis and democracy*, edited by Malina Voicu, Ingvill C. Mochmann, Hermann Dülmer, 104–137. Abingdon: Routledge.

Torres, Anália., Francisco Vieira da Silva, Teresa Líbano Monteiro, and Miguel Cabrita. 2005. *Homens e Mulheres entre Família e Trabalho.* Lisbon: CITE.

United Nations Development Programme. 1999. *Human Development Report: Georgia.* Tbilisi: UNDP

Vala, Jorge. 2021. *Racismo Hoje: Portugal em Contexto Europeu.* Lisbon: Fundação Francisco Manuel dos Santos.

Vala, Jorge, Rodrigo Brito, Diniz Lopes. 1999. *Expressões dos racismos em Portugal.* Lisbon: Imprensa de Ciências Sociais.

Xavier, Ângela Barreto. 2008. "Dissolver a diferença. Mestiçagem e conversão no império português." In *Itinerários. A Investigação nos 25 anos do ICS, edited by* Manuel Villaverde Cabral, Karin Wall, Sofia Aboim, and Filipe Carreira da Silva, 709–727. Lisbon: Imprensa de Ciências Sociais.

7 Science

Joana Gonçalves-Sá

7.1 Introduction

In 2002, the member states of the European Union (EU) identified 3% of GDP as the amount required for a competitive Research and Development (R&D) system, and set out to achieve it by 2010, as part of the "Lisbon Strategy".[1] Even before that, and despite its peripheral position, Portugal had a convergence dynamic with the EU and a series of measures, designed in the last decade of the 20th century, aimed at accelerating this process. However, the expectations created by this combination of circumstances and policies have not been fulfilled for three reasons. Firstly, there is no clear strategy with a long-term vision and objectives. Secondly, the system has been centralized and is too vulnerable to political and economic instability. Finally, the 3% target has been successively postponed. Thus, over the last 20 years, Portugal has been confronted with an expanding scientific system, but in a context of chronic instability and underfunding. These two opposing forces frame the whole ecosystem, making the absence of science policies even more evident.

In the absence of a clear strategy that can be analysed and the rather opaque nature of the system, with missing or poorly comparable data over time, this chapter aims to briefly portray the situation of science in Portugal and to understand some of the decisions taken by successive governments. It begins with a brief description of the convergence context at the turn of the century. This is followed by an incomplete and necessarily skewed view of the landscape, guided by two main questions: (1) How is investment in science decided in Portugal? (2) How is the success of policies evaluated? These questions will be approached from the perspective of three key tensions. The first relates to the structure of the system and whether it should be more or less centralized. The second relates to ambition, including the question of internationalization. The third focuses on the relationship with society and what is expected from science and from scientists. Finally, an attempt is made to present an overall assessment of scientific development in Portugal over the last twenty years.

7.2 Context—late 20th century

It was only in the late 1960s that a concern for Portuguese science began to emerge, accompanied by the creation of public structures able to guarantee some quality and efficiency to it. It was therefore not surprising that Portugal joined the EU with a scientific system that was deeply backward and far from the European average in almost all metrics of investment, scientific production, and number of PhDs (Vieira et al. 2019). In the

DOI: 10.4324/9781003488033-7

This chapter has been made available under a CC-BY-NC-ND license.

last years of the 20th century, a clear desire for convergence emerged and the Portuguese scientific system underwent a profound transformation (Fiolhais 2016). The most significant change was the creation of the Foundation for Science and Technology (FCT), in 1997,[2] which brought together a number of organizations, and which remains the main science funding institution in Portugal. It is the institution responsible for calls for project funding, scientific training and employment, evaluation of institutions, and management of international partnerships. Most of these partnerships were also established at this time, with Portugal joining CERN in 1986, ESFR in 1997, and becoming a member of EMBL in 1998, and of ESO and ESA in 2000.[3]

The FCT launched funding calls for R&D institutions as well as for projects, reinforcing some previous attempts and effectively creating a competitive system for access to funding. In parallel, calls for grants for doctoral students and PhD graduates were systematically reinforced, and a significant percentage of these grants could be done totally or partially abroad. Between 1997 and 2001, these overseas grants accounted for nearly 55% of all doctoral grants and 35% of post-doctoral grants.

From a political point of view, these changes followed the creation of the first Ministry of Science in 1995.[4] Until this date, science had been associated with Culture, Education, or had even been omitted from the name of the ministries. Public funding was mainly managed through FCT's predecessor, the JNICT, under the Ministry of Planning. In 1993, the Agency for Innovation and Technology Transfer (now the National Innovation Agency—ANI) was created, focused on bringing the scientific community and business world closer together, by supporting collaborative technological innovation projects. Given its nature, it was supervised by the Ministries of Economy and Science, in the latter case through the FCT, which currently owns a 50% stake on ANI.[5]

Thus, at the turn of the century, Portugal was still significantly behind, but there was a political will to converge with the European average, expressed in the creation of better institutional conditions and the drive towards internationalization.

7.3 Structure

As the scientific system grew, its management began to be more centralized in order to: (1) facilitate the implementation of a single policy, in articulation with the Government, the scientific community, and companies; and (2) optimize resources, reducing the duplication of tasks and cabinets.

At the end of the 20th century, the newly created Ministry of Science accelerated these efforts, being entrusted with the "coordination and implementation of Science and Technology (S&T) policy and the promotion of scientific and technological development".[6] It became responsible for international cooperation policy (through the ICCTI—Institute for International Scientific and Technological Cooperation, later GRICES—the International Relations in Science and Higher Education Office); for the Observatory of Science and Technology, a support body for planning; for the Lisbon Academy of Sciences, a counterpart of the American National Academy of Sciences; and, almost importantly, the FCT. Between 1996 and 2006, there was also a profound restructuring of the "State Laboratories": institutions under the supervision of the different Ministries, dedicated to providing answers to concrete problems of public interest and to guaranteeing resources and technical advice.[7] This restructuring was coordinated by the Ministry of Science, and the FCT gained evaluation and monitoring powers. Already in 2012, the FCT had absorbed the Knowledge Society Agency, starting to coordinate public

Science   101

policies for the Information Society; and in 2013, it accumulated the attributions of the Foundation for National Scientific Computing (FCCN). In addition, with universities increasingly dependent on competitive funding for project development and maintenance of research infrastructures, the Ministry of Science moved closer to Higher Education, merging relatively steadily from 2002 onwards.[8]

Gradually, through the FCT, the Ministry of Science began to evaluate and finance the vast majority of scientific activity in Portugal, whether carried out in public or private institutions, and whether the funds came from the State Budget (OE) or from the European Union, defining national policies and international cooperation. While in other European counterparts several institutions fund and implement S&T strategies, in Portugal, the FCT has become the sole (*de facto*) funder, over the last 20 years.

The growing importance of the FCT has not been accompanied by political or operational autonomy, and this dependence has had highly negative consequences. With all the bodies relevant to science policy directly under one ministry, with politically appointed Board of Directors, budgets dependent on the annual approval of the State Budget, and priorities redefined by the different overseeing political entities, the attempt at centralization has neither helped to create stability nor allowed the design of medium-term strategies. On the contrary (and also contrary to what is recommended by comparative studies—Aghion et al. 2010), not only is science subject to the political and economic cycles as identified in Chapters 4 and 5 of this volume, but this lack of autonomy and independence extends to universities and research centres, making the whole system inefficient.[9]

Some examples of how this centralization and political dependence impact the whole system should be considered. A particularly serious one is the opening of calls for projects in all scientific fields (PASF, or PTDC in the Portuguese acronym), which represents the main source of funding for research projects developed in Portugal: (1) both the opening of such calls[10] and their allocation and success rate have been erratic, with only the maximum possible funding remaining constant (and not exceeding 250,000€ for three years); (2) between submission and approval (or rejection) of proposals many months can elapse. In the absence of real national funding alternatives, this instability prevents medium-term planning, failing to attract the best scientists and undermining the quality of the system (Figure 7.1).

A small system, heavily dependent on a single body, lacking transparency, with many agents knowing each other and where promotions and appointments are often made for political reasons, is particularly subject to nepotism and can fuel self-censorship by institutions and individuals. In addition, there are no scientific lobby associations, functioning scientific councils, or science promotion institutions in Portugal that could play a role in policy design (unlike the case of the American Association for the Advancement of Science (AAAS) or the National Academy of Sciences (NAS)), as we will see below.

In a situation of instability, strong dependence on a single supervisory body, and chronic underfunding, it becomes even more fundamental that science policy is clear and that there is transparency in decisions and in the allocation of funds. So, what has been the strategy?

7.4 An attempt at convergence

At the turn of the century, the strategy was to seek convergence with Europe, measured by quantitative metrics. The five most common indicators are, on the input side, R&D

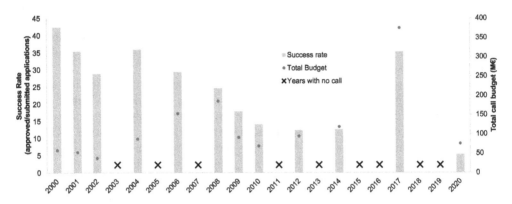

Figure 7.1 Calls for Projects in All Scientific Fields (PASF) between 2001 and 2020. Success rate (Projects approved/Projects submitted): grey bars, left axis; Total call budget in millions of euros (grey dots, right axis). "X" marks the years in which no calls were opened

Source: FCT

investment and the number of researchers, and in terms of output, the number of PhDs, scientific publications, and number of patents. Whenever possible, we will compare Portugal with the USA and with the European average.[11] At first sight, this strategy was successful: in the first decade of the 21st century, there was convergence to the European average, despite this trend being attenuated or even reversed, in the second. However, the use of some of these metrics can create distortions that we will also discuss.

7.4.1 Inputs 1: financial resources

In Portugal, research funding is reported as being done almost equally between the private and the public sector. In the latter case, it is mainly through the State Budget. Being annual, as previously mentioned, it tends to have little predictability, being dependent on the economy and political cycles. This funding thus rose very significantly between 2003 and 2009, decreasing from 2010 to 2014 and remaining almost constant (around 300M€) thereafter. This stagnation was partly offset by European funding, mostly from structural and cohesion funds, mainly through the European Regional Development Fund (ERDF) and the European Social Fund (ESF). These funds are channelled through the FCT, other intermediate bodies, or directly by the Regional Coordination and Development Commissions (CCDR). On average, European funding accounts for around 30% of the FCT total budget, but reached 38% in 2013 (Figure 7.2).[12] The remainder is distributed through other intermediate bodies and the CCDRs and is intended more for innovation and technology than for science.

In the case of companies, there are public incentives to invest in R&D activities and report them as such. These can take different forms, including access to venture capital and support for hiring researchers, with the ANI-managed SifIDe being a particularly important instrument. Through it, companies describe their R&D investment, itemizing spending on personnel, patents, etc. If approved, a substantial part of these expenditures is deducted from corporate income tax. This programme has a very high success rate and little effective control: almost 90% of tax benefit applications are approved, and almost

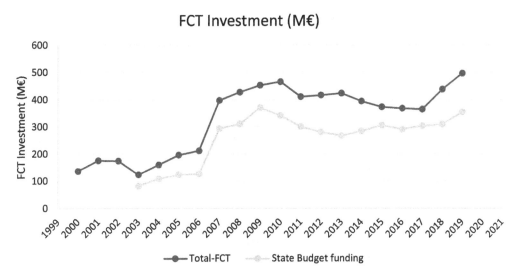

Figure 7.2 FCT Investment. Total: black line; From the State Budget: grey line
Source: FCT

60% of the declared investment is considered eligible.[13] This declared funding, close to 11,000 M€ between 2006 and 2011, is considered as national R&D investment and counts towards the convergence objectives (e.g., to reach the 3% of GDP R&D target). A potential problem then arises: for the companies, there is a strong incentive to declare as much as possible in R&D activities, because this is converted into generous tax benefits; for the state, which controls the SifIDe application, there is an incentive to show that private investment is growing.

However, even accounting for all these figures, R&D investment never reached the European average and even diverged between 2009 and 2015 (Figure 7.3).

7.4.2 Inputs 2: human resources

Research in Portugal has been mainly carried out in Higher Education Institutions (HEIs), such as universities or polytechnics, research institutes, and companies. One of the main convergence targets is the number of PhD graduates per million inhabitants, and this has been approaching the European average, thanks to funding from the FCT (Figure 7.4).

However, this increase has not been matched by an equivalent growth of the scientific system funding, creating an environment conducive to precariousness and brain-drain, for several reasons. Firstly, the FCT has converted postdoctoral grants into contracts (Figure 7.4) without proportionally increasing funding. With significantly higher costs, calls for proposals have become less frequent and have very low success rates: if at the turn of the millennium calls for postdoctoral grants had success rates of 90%, these have not exceeded 10% since 2018 (Figure 7.5). Secondly, the number of faculty in HEIs is almost stagnant (Figure 7.6, dark grey line). Thirdly, although the number of researchers exceeded the European average in 2007 (Figure 7.7) and companies reported hiring a

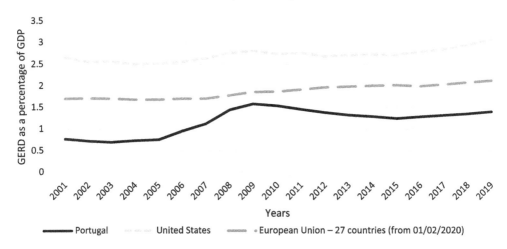

Figure 7.3 R&D expenditure as a percentage of GDP
Source: OECD

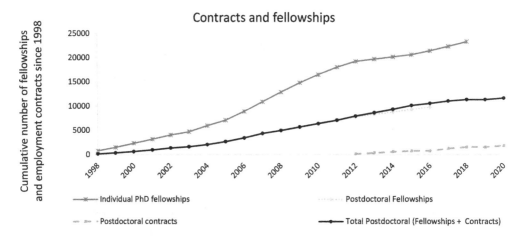

Figure 7.4 Cumulative number of individual fellowships and contracts, since 1998. Individual PhD Fellowships: Grey line; Total number of funded postdoctoral contracts (fellowships and employment contracts): Black line. Individual fellowships for doctoral graduates: light grey, dotted line (superimposed on the black line until 2012). Individual employment contracts for doctoral graduates: dark grey, dashed line

Source: FCT.[14]

large number of researchers (in 2019, 40% of all researchers were reportedly there), only 8% of PhD graduates worked in industry.[15]

Thus, it is not surprising that the proportion of precarious PhD holders is very high,[16] corresponding to more than 30% of the total and reaching 60% of PhD holders under 45

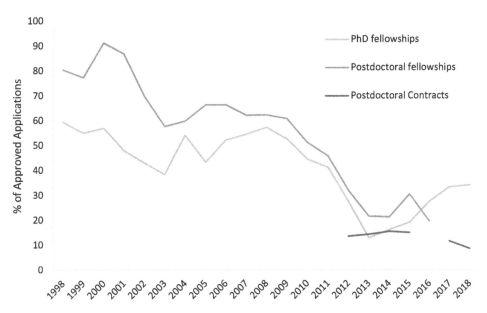

Figure 7.5 Success rate of FCT calls for individual funding. PhD fellowships (light grey) or postdocs (dark grey for fellowships and black for contracts)—individual calls, see footnote 7

Source: FCT.

years old.[17] Precariousness is also higher among female researchers: despite the fact that Portugal has systematically awarded more PhDs to women than men since 2008 and that there is parity in the number of PhDs employed, in 2018, 11% of female researchers had no contract or had contracts with less than one year duration, compared to 8% of men (and around 8.5% of the EU_27 average). Moreover, this equal proportion of women within academia disappears as one moves up the career ladder: women occupy only 26% of the top positions in the academic system (Figure 7.8).[18] However, given that parity in the number of doctoral graduates is recent and that precariousness mainly affects the younger age groups, it is possible that the gender gap will narrow over time.

In short, although Portugal is training highly qualified human resources, mostly women, the system is still not egalitarian and is strongly pyramidal, with PhD graduates having difficulty reaching universities, companies, or research careers.

7.4.3 Outputs

On the output side, we have looked at patents, scientific publications, and the ability to attract competitive European funding.

Besides national calls, researchers and scientific institutions can apply for competitive funding through the European R&D Framework Programmes (FP). In the last two decades, there have been four such programmes with increasing budgets and more or less variable aims. In the case of Horizon 2020, which operated from 2013, there were three

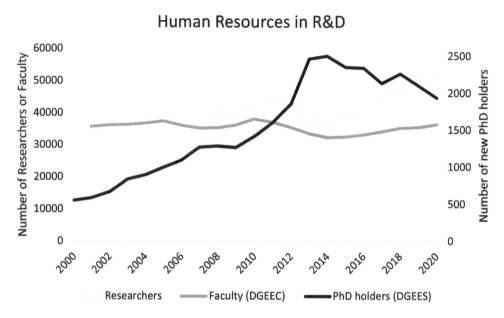

Figure 7.6 Human resources in R&D. Left axis: Number of university professors (dark grey) and number of researchers in R&D (total) (light grey and crosses). Note that yearly data is only available from 2008 onwards. Right axis: New PhD graduates per year (black)

Source: DGEEC and DGEES.

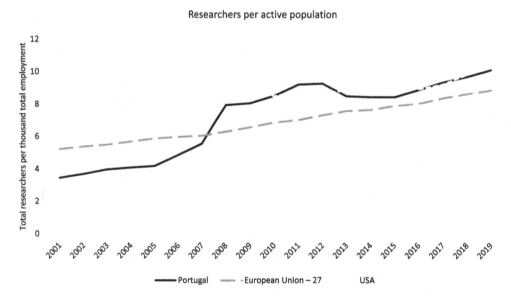

Figure 7.7 Researchers per thousand of the active population
Source: OECD

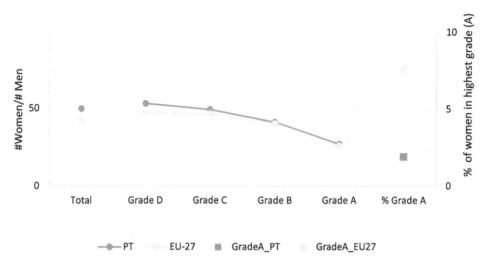

Figure 7.8 Proportion of women by academic level in Portugal (dark grey) and EU-27 (light grey). Grade D corresponds to postdoctoral researchers, Grade C corresponds to assistant professors or similar, Grade B corresponds to associate professors or equivalent, and Grade A corresponds to full professors or equivalent. "Total" shows weighted averages per grade. The values of "%Grade A" (squares) indicate the percentage of all employed researchers/professors at Level A (right axis). Data from 2018[19]

Source: European Commission.

pillars (accounting for 42% of total funding): Pillar 1, "Scientific Excellence", mainly supporting basic research; Pillar 2, "Industrial Leadership", focusing on the modernization of European industry; and Pillar 3, aimed at mitigating "Societal Challenges". Instruments were also created to support areas of strategic interest or specific industries. On average, the success of Portuguese rates has been comparable or even higher than its percentage contribution to the EU budget (Figure 7.9) and has been particularly successful in securing funds from the "Widening" programme, designed to reduce scientific imbalances within the European Research Area.[20]

In total, between 2014 and 2020, Portugal attracted close to 2,258M€, a similar amount to the SB investment in the FCT during the same period. Most of this funding was achieved through Pillar 1 (14% of the total) and by HEIs and Research Centres (RCs) (Figure 7.10).

On the scientific publications side, the number of articles per million inhabitants and their impact have been considered, measured in the form of citations, i.e., the number of other articles that refer to them. In absolute terms, the number of articles grew and, measured per million inhabitants, exceeded the European average in 2009 and the US average in 2012. This growth has been slowing down, although productivity is not low (Figure 7.11).

However, in terms of citations per paper, Portugal's position in the world ranking remained virtually unchanged between 2000 and 2012 and then started to decline.[21] This was not necessarily due to a drop in the quality of Portuguese science, but to a huge

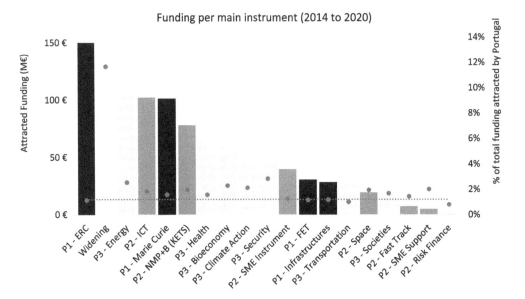

Figure 7.9 Funding by main instrument of Horizon 2020 in millions of euros. Left axis: Pillar 1: black; Pillar 2: dark grey; Pillar 3: light grey; Widening; white. Right axis: Percentage of total funding secured by Portugal per instrument: grey dots. Portugal's contribution to the EU budget (1.2%): grey dotted line

Source: ANI

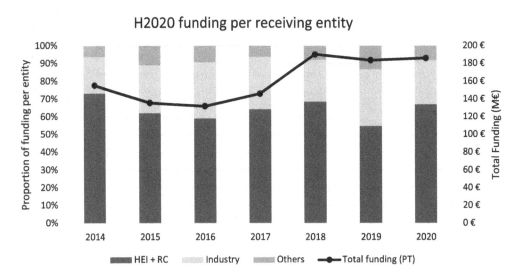

Figure 7.10 Horizon 2020 funding attracted by Portugal by type of entity. Left axis: proportion by entities: Higher Education Institutions and Research Centres (HEIs-RCs); Industry; Others. Right axis: Total funding per year in millions of euros

Source: ANI

Science   109

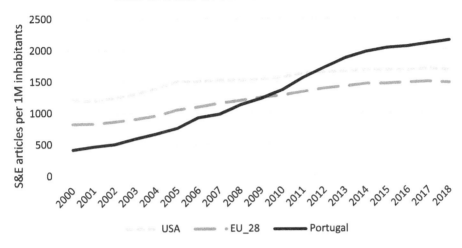

Figure 7.11 Articles in all scientific and engineering areas per million inhabitants
Source: SCImago

growth in the quality of other countries, mainly Asian and European. Figure 7.12 also shows a drop in the citation ratio of indexed scientific articles, which is also reflected in the positions of the USA (which went down) and the European average of 28 (which went up).

On the other hand, the proportion of publications in the group of the 1% most cited, considered here to be those with the highest impact, exceeded the European average in 2004, varying little since 2007 (Figure 7.13).

Finally, the number of patents per million inhabitants is not significant (Figure 7.14). The fact that companies report high amounts of R&D investment despite hiring few PhDs and producing almost no patents begs the question of how R&D investment in industry should be accounted for and evaluated.

7.4.4 Summary

In general, there was an approximation to the European average in the first decade of the 21st century, a trend that was attenuated or even reversed in the second. Investment in R&D has remained very low and is far from reaching the target of 3% of GDP. Despite this underfunding, Portuguese science has grown, which implies that investment per doctoral researcher is decreasing. The production of scientific articles has increased both in quantity and in quality. However, given the enormous growth of the global scientific system,[22] this effort has been insufficient to make Portugal a truly competitive country. Indeed, in terms of citations per paper, Portugal has been losing ground when compared to the rest of the OECD or the EU. On the other hand, the (a) large difference between the average number of citations of papers, (b) the proportion of papers in the top of the most cited, and (c) the ability to attract European funding indicate that we may have a scientific system on two different speeds: one that produces poor quality research and another that competes with the best in the world.

110 *Joana Gonçalves-Sá*

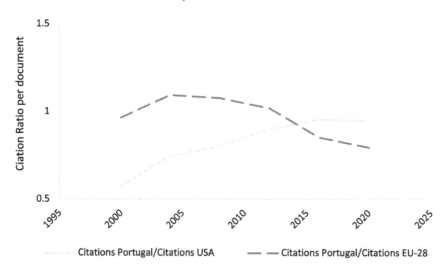

Figure 7.12 Ratio of citations per indexed document between Portugal and the USA, and between Portugal and the EU-28 average

Source: SCImago

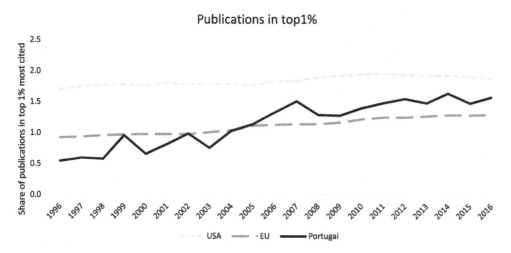

Figure 7.13 Proportion of all indexed publications by country reaching the top 1% of the most cited

Source: SCImago

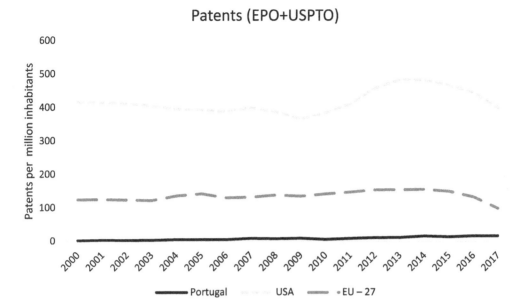

Figure 7.14 Patents granted by European (EPO) and US (USPTO) patent offices per million inhabitants

Source: OECD

This poses interesting questions about the best strategies to distribute scarce funding and how to evaluate the success of policies. Both will be discussed in the next section.

7.5 Strategy

At the invitation of the Portuguese government, the OECD conducted an assessment of the national higher education, science, and innovation system,[23] published in 2019. This highly critical report followed other independent assessments with similar findings[24] and was aligned with several documents produced by the scientific community[25] (with this chapter also reaching very similar conclusions). Firstly, and contrary to what is found in other OECD countries, the report highlights that in Portugal there is no clear strategic vision to guide policies, and it recommends the creation of a National Strategy for Knowledge and Innovation. It notes that funding remains below the targets set by the government itself and expresses some scepticism about the real capacity to increase it and the effect that this increase would have if not accompanied by the necessary reforms. It also recommends decentralization of funding and more autonomy for both the FCT and R&D institutions, particularly HEIs. Thus, it is clear that the lack of strategy, the institutions' lack of autonomy, and the system's lack of predictability and funding are widely known and diagnosed problems.

A scientific system with these characteristics is expected to be particularly sensitive to political changes, whether great or small. We have therefore chosen to try to understand what choices have been made along three axes: (1) Ambition, referring to what is expected of Portuguese science, and on what time perspective, (2) Internationalization,

112 *Joana Gonçalves-Sá*

using the training of doctoral graduates as a case study, and (3) Society, both in terms of science communication and the presence of science in political decision-making. Once again, due to the absence of documents outlining clear visions and indicators (such as strategic areas for doctoral studies), it becomes challenging to assess Portuguese science policy within these frameworks. As a result, our discussion is confined to illustrative examples.

7.5.1 Ambition

In what we described as a "two-speed" scientific fabric, has Portugal particularly supported institutions that appear to be lagging behind, helping them to catch up? Or, alternatively, has its support been primarily distributed among the institutions that appear more competitive?

The FCT has a number of instruments to fund individuals, projects, and institutions, with these changing over time. For example, the definition of "Research and Development Units (R&DUs)" has varied, generally corresponding to structures mainly dedicated to scientific research, which may or may not be linked to universities and whose number of associated researchers can vary from fewer than 10 to more than 400.[26] Between 2001 and 2020, there were 4 R&DU evaluation rounds, with no predefined periodicity. These were carried out by international panels, typically including the submission of a report by the institutions, followed by visits and face-to-face interviews. Only the two most recent ones (published in 2013 and 2018) made public the funding approved per R&DU, but in all four cases there was an evaluation on a five-value scale.[27] There is little information on funding and the names of the R&DUs themselves have varied over time, which frustrates attempts of quantitative analysis. However, three simple comparisons can be made: how many and which units are classified in the two highest categories and what is the correlation between funding and this classification?

In three of these assessments, half or more than half of the institutions were rated with the two highest scores. In contrast, the two worst scores were typically only awarded to around 20% of R&DUs. The exception was in the assessment published in 2013, which followed a more statistically normal distribution, with the majority being assessed with intermediate ratings and only 6% with the highest rating[28] (Figure 7.15).

It is interesting to note that, in general, fundamental science institutions, i.e., institutions that mostly use curiosity as a guide for their research, studying problems without short-term application, tend to have very good evaluations and greater ability to attract international funding (Vieira et al. 2019 and author's analysis, see below).

For the last two evaluations we also correlated the ratings with the funding allocated to each institution. In both cases, the correlation was low, but almost non-existent in 2018. In that year, the factor that seems to have been decisive was the number of researchers integrated into the R&DU. One interpretation is that, in 2013, the policy was to selectively fund better-rated institutions, with the amount distributed per researcher increasing slightly with the rating. However, in 2017/18, it was decided to distribute the funding per researcher almost equally, as long as institutions were rated with at least "Good—3" (corresponding to 89% of the total number of institutions evaluated), as shown in Figure 7.16.

Similarly, 2017 saw the first PASF call in 3 years—as noted earlier in Figure 7.1—with a much higher than average funding and success rate. Thus, in general, the funding distribution strategy in this axis has varied, with policies that either fund the system as a

Science 113

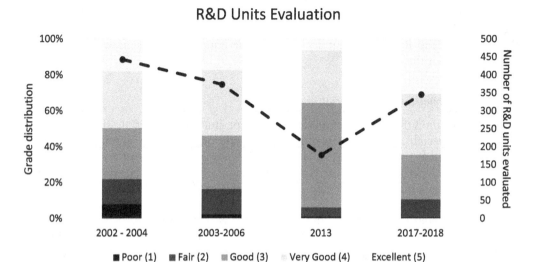

Figure 7.15 Results of the evaluations of R&D Units. Left axis: proportion of R&D Units scoring each rating/grade (from 1 to 5), with 5 corresponding to the highest rating (darkest grey) and 1 to the lowest rating (lightest grey). Right axis: number of units evaluated in each round—date of publication of results (black dotted line)

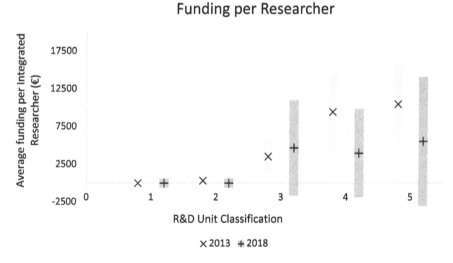

Figure 7.16 Average amount funded per integrated researcher by R&DU classification. Crosses mark the average value and bars the standard deviation for the 2013 (light grey) and 2018 (dark grey) classification

Source: FCT

114 *Joana Gonçalves-Sá*

whole, or aimed at selecting the better evaluated institutions. These policy swings coincide with different political cycles and are visible in other areas, such as the preference for individual doctoral fellowships (FCT-centralized) versus doctoral programmes (managed through HEIs and R&RUs). That such structuring issues can be partisan has increased the instability of the system.

7.5.2 *Internationalization and specialization*

According to the OECD report and another recent study (Vieira et al. 2019), the level of scientific specialization in Portugal is low. In addition to calls for funding projects in all scientific fields (PASF—Figure 7.1), the FCT has thematic calls in areas considered strategic. The trend has been towards a greater weight of specific calls, especially in some engineering areas, but PASFs still account for the largest share of the budget for research projects.

It is interesting to note that fundamental science institutions tend to have higher impact publications (Vieira et al. 2019) and greater ability to attract international funding than their applied counterparts (Figure 7.7 and author's analysis in the next section). This is surprising for three reasons: (1) the number of patents produced or impact on society are among the evaluation metrics; (2) projects that promise solutions to concrete problems or technological innovations are more likely to be funded (and the articles arising from them to be published); and (3) in Portugal, investment in basic science is very low, never having reached 0.4% of GDP (Vieira et al. 2019), hindering leveraging attempts.

If there is a will to specialize, the question of how to choose and evaluate priority areas arises and possible options have been discussed. Should Portugal (a) focus on areas of national interest, dictated by geographical issues, such as maritime research; (b) support areas in which the country has been stronger in the past; (c) adjust to externally defined priorities, for example to the availability of European funding, or (d) equally support all areas hoping that the most competitive ones will emerge naturally and secure international funding? We do not think there is a long-term decision, and the international doctoral programmes serve as an example.

The training of scientists through international doctoral grants was a late 20th-century priority and during the late 1990s, as many grants were awarded for doctoral theses in Portugal as abroad. This movement followed similar attempts by many other countries to train staff mainly in other European countries and in the USA. However, contrary to what happened in Brazil, for example, there was no obligation for those trained abroad to return to Portugal, nor were specific programmes designed to reverse the brain drain (as happened, for example, in France, mainly with post-doctorates). At the turn of the century, and despite Portugal still being far from most convergence targets, the proportion of grants abroad started to fall sharply and went from approximately half in 2001 to less than 5% in 2015 (Figure 7.17).

At the beginning of the 1990s, the concept of doctoral programmes also began to emerge in Portugal. Still uncommon in Europe then, they consisted of a first phase of coursework followed by 3 to 4 years of funding to develop PhD theses, mostly abroad. From 1993 onwards, three of these international programmes in life or health sciences (LHS) emerged, with similar models, no clear counterparts in the other sciences, and associated more with research institutes than with universities. These programmes were gradually converted into PhD grant programmes at national institutions. However, in

Figure 7.17 PhD grants awarded by the FCT by the type of competition between 1994 and 2015. Lines mark grants to be carried out exclusively in Portugal (black), abroad (light grey), or mixed (between Portugal and abroad, dark grey)

Source: FCT

total and up to 2005, they are estimated to have funded some 340 overseas or mixed grants.

To the best of our knowledge, there has never been an evaluation of the different training strategies that would justify a preference for doctoral programmes vs. individual grants or the choice of a certain ratio of national vs. foreign doctoral grants, nor could we find information that would allow us to do so.[29] We have therefore tried to assess their success with the FP7 and H2020 pillar of excellence, particularly in projects funded by the European Research Council (ERC).[30] This analysis shows that (1) in Portugal, the LHS area received half of all ERC grants, when the European average was 35%; (2) of the 108 grants obtained by Portugal from 2007 onwards,[31] in all scientific areas, almost 25% went to scientists involved in these three doctoral programmes (although they represented only 3.5% of all doctoral grants funded in Portugal between 1994 and 2005, and 7% of all grants abroad or mixed, in the same period[32]); (3) if we consider only the life sciences' panel, 43% of these grants went to former students of these programmes.

Of course, it is not possible to tell whether the programmes were responsible for helping to train particularly successful scientists; whether they merely had the merit of knowing how to select them; whether these scientists were better supported on their return, or whether their success was due to a combination of these or other factors.[33] Moreover, these programmes did not emerge as a result of a centralized and deliberate strategy to support LHS, although they may have played that role in the medium term: from 2002 onwards, when many of the students in the doctoral programmes started to return and publish from Portugal, the LHS area started to grow consistently, becoming the area with the highest number of publications in the top 1% and with the highest proportion of international collaborations (Vieira et al. 2019).

116 *Joana Gonçalves-Sá*

Despite its apparent success, the FCT opted to fund almost exclusively individual grants from 2016 onwards, to the detriment of structured international programmes,[34] and continued to reduce international grant funding. Exceptions were found mainly in engineering and technological innovation, with continued support for three programmes that emerged between 2006 and 2007. In these, fellowships were generally mixed between Portugal and three partner institutions in the USA: Carnegie Mellon University, the Massachusetts Institute of Technology, and the University of Texas-Austin. In addition to more than 500 fellowships, these collaborations included funding for projects, mobility of researchers, and support for innovation. There has been insufficient time to assess the impact of these programmes, but their more applied nature and frequent link to business suggests that they aim at shorter-term results, possibly shown in patents and business creation, and their ability to attract funding could be measured in pillars 2 and 3 of H2020, Europe 2030 (or future equivalents).

It should also be noted that after 2016, the area of Space was identified as strategic and the alleged success of these programmes was almost always the justification for this choice. Two new structures were created, the AIR Centre and the Portuguese Space Agency, with access to grants and specialized research projects. We were unable to find financial and activity reports from these institutions that could allow us to gauge the volume of investment and outputs, but their political importance is evident in recent reports and in the "Portugal Space 2030" strategy,[35] published in 2018 and one of the only political documents that advocates an intense specialization strategy.

In the coming years, it will be important to analyse these programmes and the level of differentiation achieved, compared to other countries.

7.5.3 *Science and society*

With the increase of investment in the scientific system and in the "production of science", the late 20th century also brought a greater concern with the connection between science and society. There was an attempt, on the one hand, to seek social support for that same investment and, on the other, to increase the scientific literacy of the population in general. Thus, with an increasing visibility of science and its applications in society, in this section we seek to summarize (1) the relationship of the Portuguese with science; (2) the way it is used in political decision-making; and (3) the role of society and of different scientific organizations in the definition of science policies.

According to data from the 2001 Eurobarometer on Science and Technology,[36] the Portuguese were among the least knowledgeable, the least interested in science (38% of the population said they had little or no interest), and the least likely to visit science museums or spaces (only 9% said they had done so in the previous year). However, these numbers have been almost reversed and, in 2021, Portugal became the European country with the highest number of people declaring themselves very interested in medical (70%) or scientific and technological discoveries (62%) and with almost 60% of the population saying they visited science and technology museums regularly (11%) or occasionally (48%).[37] The level of general knowledge of the population also increased very significantly, with Portugal now above the European average in virtually all knowledge items in these surveys. This progression is similar to that observed in the PISA tests, with Portuguese students (in the case of mathematics) having been consistently above or (in the case of science) very close to the OECD average since 2009.[38]

Certainly, this progression is due to a large number of factors and, during recent decades, there have been several initiatives with the deliberate aim of promoting science and increasing the literacy of the population, from both the State and the citizens. This has included the reinforcement of school laboratories, computers and Internet access, science sections in leading newspapers, and even the launch of a collection of science books that became extremely popular during the 1990s (Granado and Malheiros 2015).

Science funding agencies (national and international) started to allow and even encourage the allocation of funds specifically for dissemination of results, public consultations, outreach to schools, or the development of easily accessible resources aimed at the non-specialist public. Thus, in the early 2000s, research institutions also started to create dedicated science communication and outreach offices, building bridges with the media and promoting both science in general and the research done at the institutions.

In institutional terms, the Associação Ciência Viva—National Agency for Scientific and Technological Culture (NASTC) was created in 1998 to promote science education in schools, through a network of "Ciência Viva Centres", of the interactive museum type.[39] It also designs promotional campaigns to disseminate science, as well as integrating international initiatives (such as the European Researchers' Night). This network's central institution is the Knowledge Pavilion, in Lisbon, which holds its own activities and imports or commissions international exhibitions. In line with what has been discussed above, the NASTC offers an almost perfect example of the politicization of these structures. Its director was appointed in 1996,[40] apparently for life, and its budget has varied greatly according to political cycles. Although it had average annual budget allocations of €14M between 2007 and 2011, these fell under €600,000/year between 2012 and 2015, then increasing again to average values close to €2M between 2016 and 2019. However, and despite the fact that it is almost exclusively funded by public money, either through the State Budget or through European funds channelled through the FCT, its reports are not freely available, making it difficult to assess the impact of these variations on budget allocation on its activities.[41]

It is also important to note that the COVID-19 pandemic sharply increased the visibility of science around the world, with Portugal being no exception. There was an almost daily presence of researchers and scientists in the mainstream media, as well as in public sessions and social media, explaining and discussing scientific publications and experimental results with interested citizens. The impact of this visibility can only be analysed in the future, but Portugal had one of the highest vaccination rates against SARS-CoV-2 in the world and, along with Ireland, was the European country that most supported the intervention of scientists in the political debate.[42]

However, the importance of science in decision-making remains unappreciated. In 2021, a study coordinated by the European Joint Research Council (JRC) identified a paradoxical situation: on the one hand, there is broad recognition of the quality and dynamics of the Portuguese scientific community, but, on the other, there is no awareness of the advantages of scientific advice, especially outside of crisis situations (Simões 2022). Thus, in Portugal, there is no structure dedicated to policy advice, and the creation of advisory councils or similar bodies is done on an *ad hoc* basis, depending on the will of the Government, and changing with political cycles. There are also no formal mechanisms that define the quality of this advice, such as rules for the selection of "advisors", instructions on how and when such advice should be sought, or reports summarizing such advice, when it exists. This lack of framework raises important issues regarding the lack of transparency, independence, and even potential conflicts of interest. Indeed, the

118 *Joana Gonçalves-Sá*

instrumentalization of science by political power has been identified by several scholars in the relationship between science and society (Gonçalves and Delicado 2009), along with a certain lack of interest of the scientific community in participating in public discussions.

There are also no structures for science lobbying or actively participating in the design of science policies. For example, the Science Law, published by the government in 2019,[43] was in public consultation for approximately one month, but the results of that consultation were not known, and the final document, published more than a year later, was substantially different from what had been presented to the community. Similarly, the studies or consultations that led to the definition of the "Portugal Space 2030" strategy, mentioned above, remain unknown.

In addition to universities and other higher education institutions or structures, including the Council of Rectors, five structures could play this role of scientific lobbying and reflection on S&T: the main union of higher education workers (SNESUP, created in 1990); the association of scientific research fellows (ABIC, founded in 2003); the National Association of Researchers in Science and Technology (ANICT, founded in 2010); the Lisbon Academy of Sciences (ACL), a counterpart of the US National Academy of Science (NAS), founded in 1779; and the Council of Associated Laboratories (CLA, created in 2003). SNESUP and ABIC have played an important role but typically more focused on labour issues. ACL has among its missions "to contribute to the development of science and cultural progress of the country" and "to provide the Portuguese Government with advice on linguistic and scientific matters of national interest". It is, however, financially dependent on the FCT and, unlike NAS, which publishes "policy reports" with its members publicly announcing their positions on issues, we did not find any position on science policy in any document published by ACL in recent years. CLA brings together the Associated Laboratories, created in 1999 as institutions or consortia of institutions with joint scientific projects. The "Associate Laboratory" status offers a seal of quality and specific funding, and the main aim for creating the Council was to help build critical mass, in particular areas, through scientific cooperation. However, while CLA has had some position papers and joint document production, these initiatives are rare and unsystematic. Moreover, as the LAs compete directly with each other for FCT funding, the incentive for joint positions and opposition to political authorities (Ministry, FCT) and public policies is potentially low. The more recent ANICT has produced documents with a medium-term vision and taken relevant positions but holds very limited political leverage. Individual scientists have also publicly demonstrated in support of science and worked on the production of Manifestos, Whitepapers, and Open Letters, with varying success.

Overall, there is an urgent need for the creation of stable institutions that can design strategies or take on long-term commitments. However, it is fundamental that they are financially independent from the FCT or that any dependence occurs in long life-time cycles, to allow for autonomy and long-term vision.

There is, thus, a broad consensus on the importance of science, with the Portuguese population showing interest in and support for the scientific system. Nevertheless, the link between science and society has room for improvement, especially in its connection to political power and technical advice.

7.6 Concluding remarks

The analysis presented in this chapter has a number of serious weaknesses: not only does it ignore central problems, such as the very high level of "inbreeding" in Portuguese HEIs

Science 119

or links to smart specialization areas, but it is also limited by the difficulty in finding structured and good quality public information. The lack of transparency of institutions is a transversal problem and data sharing does not seem to be a priority. However, few conclusions are possible:

1) In Portugal, the importance of science is politically consensual,[44] but it is more rhetorical than real and the country has never invested seriously in science or integrated science in the decision-making process;
2) Possibly as a consequence of science's lack of centrality (and excessive centralization of its governing structure), there is no culture of transparency or the definition of objective indicators;
3) With no long-term commitment, no autonomous institutions, and no strategic plan, political alternation is often synonymous with discontinuity and instability in R&D investment and planning;
4) Despite an improvement (reflected in doctorates or in the attraction of international funds), Portugal has been falling in several rankings, such as that of publications: science is growing at a much faster rate in emerging economies and in other European countries;
5) The scientific community participates little (or only informally) in the decision-making process and there are no effective structures dedicated to reflecting on the scientific system or monitoring its policies.
Despite this and Portugal's peripheral role:
6) Some institutions in the different areas have managed to adapt and compete at an international level;
7) There is a highly trained scientific fabric, capable of attracting funding and guaranteeing the system's quality;
8) Both politicians and the general population express interest in and support for science.

On these bases and with a thorough overhaul of structures, it should be possible to achieve a sustained and competitive development of the Portuguese scientific system.

Acknowledgements

The author wishes to thank the editors and other authors of this book for comments on the text. She also thanks Ana Aranda da Silva, António Coutinho, Ana Ferreira, Carlos Fiolhais, José Antão, Leonor Parreira, Mário Pimenta, Cláudio Sunkel, and members for the Social Physics and Complexity Lab for conversations, comments, and sharing data.

Notes

1 *More research for Europe—Towards 3% of GDP*. [ebook] Brussels: communication from the commission. Available at: https://ec.europa.eu/invest-in-research/pdf/499/en.pdf [Accessed in January 2022].
2 Decree-Law 188/97, 28th July. *Diário da República* n. ° 172/1997, Série I-A, 28-07-1997.

3 CERN—Conseil Européen pour la Recherche Nucléaire, now known as the European Organization of Nuclear Research; ESFR—the European Synchrotron Radiation Facility; EMBL—the European Molecular Biology Laboratory; ESO—the European Southern Observatory; ESA: the European Space Agency.

4 Decree-Law 144/96, 26th August. *Diário da República* n. º 197/1996, Série I-A, 26-08-1996.

5 Like other public structures ANI received unstable political attention, but its mandate and structure have remained broadly constant since 2014.

6 Decree-Law 144/96, 26th August. *Diário da República* n. º 197/1996, Série I-A, 26-08-1996.

7 In 2006, these laboratories were supervised by the Ministry of Agriculture, Health, Defense, Public Works, Economy, Foreign Affairs and Science.

8 The name of the Ministry has undergone various changes to include Technology or Innovation and, later, Higher Education. As of 2002, it's been most frequently known as the Ministry of Science, Technology and Higher Education.

9 Evaluation of the Portuguese Foundation for Science and Technology—Report of the Evaluation Panel. [online] Fundação para Ciência e a Tecnologia (FCT). Available at: https://www.fct.pt/docs/Evaluation_of_FCT_Report_EP.pdf [Accessed in January 2022].

10 Between 2001 and 2020, there were no calls in 2003, 2005, 2007, 2011, 2013, 2015, 2016, 2018, and 2019.

11 The comparison will be made including the United Kingdom (EU-28), unless data is not available, in which case the EU-27 will be considered.

12 2020. *Estatísticas da Fundação para a Ciência e a Tecnologia (FCT)—Investimento no Sistema Científico e Tecnológico Nacional*. [online] Available at: https://fct.pt/estatisticas/global.phtml .pt [Accessed in December 2021]. According to official figures, FCT public funding corresponds to only 38% of all State funding in R&D but, as the remainder is most likely distributed through other intermediate bodies and the CCDRs, with more being earmarked for innovation and technology than science, we do not discuss it here.

13 *SIFIDE—Tax Incentive System for Business R&D 2006-2020*. [online] Available at: https://www.ani.pt/en/funding/fiscal-incentives/sifide/ [Accessed in January 2022].

14 These figures do not include: (a) grants or contracts awarded through projects because they represent a choice made by researchers and not a political decision; (b) grants offered through doctoral programmes; (c) contracts for post-doctoral researchers through the Science 2007, Science 2008, and Welcome II programmes, due to unavailability of data or because they were distributed institutionally and not individually. However, the available information indicates that the number of doctoral grants offered through doctoral programmes is much higher than the number of post-doctoral contracts not accounted for here, so that per year, there are at least two to three times more salaried opportunities for PhD students than for PhDs.

15 2021. *Inquérito aos doutorados - CDH20 principais resultados - provisórios*. Direcção Geral de Estatísticas da Educação e Ciência, Available at: https://www.dgeec.mec.pt/np4/208/%7Bc lientServletPath%7D/?newsId=114&fileName=DGEEC_CDH20_SumariosEstatisticos.xlsx.

16 Defined as having no contract or having a fixed-term contract.

17 2021. *Inquérito aos doutorados - CDH20 principais resultados - provisórios*. Direcção Geral de Estatísticas da Educação e Ciência, Available at: https://www.dgeec.mec.pt/np4/208/%7Bc lientServletPath%7D/?newsId=114&fileName=DGEEC_CDH20_SumariosEstatisticos.xlsx.

18 European Commission, Directorate-General for Research and Innovation, *She figures 2021. Gender in research and innovation: statistics and indicators*, Publications Office, 2021, available at https://data.europa.eu/doi/10.2777/06090.

19 European Commission, Directorate-General for Research and Innovation, She figures 2021: gender in research and innovation: statistics and indicators, Publications Office, 2021. Available at https://data.europa.eu/doi/10.2777/06090.

20 Targeted at member states with the lowest success rates in FP7, namely: Bulgaria, Croatia, Cyprus, Czechia, Estonia, Hungary, Latvia, Lithuania, Luxembourg, Malta, Poland, Portugal, Romania, Slovakia, and Slovenia.

21 SCImago, (n.d.). SJR—SCImago Journal & Country Rank [online]. Available at: http://www.scimagojr.com_[Accessed in January 2022].

22 According to Scimago, in 2001, 1,309,244 citable documents were published; 28.5% of which was in the USA. By 2020, this number had more than tripled to 4,236,262, with "only" 18% originating in the USA.

23 OECD, 2019. OECD Review of Higher Education, Research and Innovation-Portugal. Available at https://www.cnedu.pt/content/OECD_Review_-_Portugal_2018_26_2_019.pdf.

24 See *Evaluation of the Portuguese Foundation for Science and Technology—Report of the Evaluation Panel*. [online] Fundação para Ciência e a Tecnologia (FCT). Available at: https://www.fct.pt/docs/Evaluation_of_FCT_Report_EP.pdf and 2007. *Reviews of National Policies for Education: Tertiary Education in Portugal - OECD*. [online] Available at https://www.oecd-ilibrary.org/education/reviews-of-national-policies-for-education-tertiary-education-in-portugal-2007/executive-summary_9789264009769-2-en.

25 See, for example, http://cienciaportugal.org/ and https://anict.wordpress.com/.

26 A 2019 decree-law identified them without defining them, by opposition, i.e., those that were not State Laboratories, etc. In 2013, these also included the Associated Laboratories, a distinction created by the Ministry of Science in 1999, to create critical mass and promote collaboration between institutions or consortia of institutions with joint scientific projects.

27 Between evaluations the name given to each category could change. For example, the maximum category was "exceptional" in some and "excellent" in others.

28 This assessment was heavily criticized by the community for several reasons: for greatly reducing the number of units (from an average of 400 to under 200); including Associate Laboratories; and imposing on assessors quotas for the highest levels.

29 A recent thesis focused on one of these programmes financed by the FCT and with the support of the Calouste Gulbenkian Foundation (PGDBM), reports that 78% of these former students remain in the academic world, mostly as principal researchers and group leaders. Despite seeming a high number, there was no comparison with other programmes or grantees.

30 It is not possible to obtain nominal information from recipients of Marie Curie grants.

31 Just considering Starting, Consolidator, and Advanced for three reasons: (1) they are the vast majority (108 out of 126); (2) it can be argued that the "Proof of Concept" grants are more applied than fundamental and (3) the "Synergy" (only 2) grants are not individual nor necessarily from a single country.

32 It was not possible to find the number of grants awarded in 1993 nor to confirm whether the total number of grants reported by the FCT in this period included grants awarded through the programmes or not. Therefore, it is possible that this estimate is wrong.

33 Another possibility would be that the LHS area grew very significantly during this period all over the world. This being true, when we look at the average number of citations per article, Portugal's position in the OECD ranking increased between 2001 and 2020 (having dropped in areas such as Physics and Chemistry.

34 Although the recommendation of the FCT evaluation panel was the opposite.

35 Council of Ministers' Resolution No. 30/2018. *Diário da República* n. ° 50/2018, Series I-A of 12-08-2018. Available at https://www.portugal.gov.pt/pt/gc21/comunicacao/documento?i=estrategia-portugal-espaco-2030.

36 European Commission. "Europeans, science and technology". Eurobarometer 55.2 (2001).

37 European Commission. "European citizens' knowledge and attitudes towards science and technology". Special Eurobarometer 516 (2021).

38 OECD (2019), PISA 2018 Results (Volume I): What Students Know and Can Do, PISA, OECD Publishing, Paris, https://doi.org/10.1787/5f07c754-en.

39 In 2020, there were 21 of these centres, the largest being the Knowledge Pavilion, in Lisbon.

40 According to the Director's LinkedIn page, consulted in June 2022.

41 When I asked the ANCCT for access to these reports, I received no reply; and the way in which the FCT reports present investment in Promotion and Dissemination varies. In some years, we only find this information through the State Budget and, in other years, it also includes European funds or co-financing. In any case, it is clear that ANCCT received the vast majority of funds and that these were greatly reduced after 2012, only to exceed €1.4M again (or a tenth of the previous average funding) in 2018.

42 The question was actually phrased in the negative: 72% of Portuguese people disagreed or strongly disagreed with the statement "Scientists should not intervene in the political debate when decisions ignore scientific evidence". The European average was 37%.

43 Decree-law 63/2019, 16th May. *Diário da República* n. ° 94/2019, Série I-A de 16-05-2019.

44 2010. *A Ciência em Portugal*. [online] Lisbon: Comissão de Educação e Ciência da Assembleia da República. Available at: https://ciencias.ulisboa.pt/sites/default/files/fcul/investigacao/RelatorioCienciaPortugal%2C%202010.pdf.

References

Aghion, Philippe, Dewatripont, Mathias, Hoxby, Caroline, Mas-Colell, Andreu and André Sapir. 2010. "The governance and performance of universities: Evidence from Europe and the US." *Economic policy* 25, no. 61: 7–59.

Fiolhais, Carlos, 2016. *A ciência em Portugal*. Lisbon: Fundação Francisco Manuel dos Santos.

Gonçalves, Maria Eduarda and Delicado, Ana, 2009. "The politics of risk in contemporary Portugal: tensions in the consolidation of science–policy relations". *Science and Public Policy* 36, no. 3: 229–239.

Granado, António and Malheiros, José Vítor, 2015. *Cultura científica em Portugal: Ferramentas para perceber o mundo e aprender a mudá-lo*. Lisbon: Fundação Francisco Manuel dos Santos.

Simões, Vítor Coroado, 2022. "Science for policy in Portugal." In *EUR 31023 EN,* edited by Lorenzo Melchor and Kristian Krieger. Luxembourg: Publications Office of the European Union.

Vieira, Elizabeth, Mesquita, João; Silva, Jorge, Vasconcelos, Raquel, Torres, Joana, Bugla, Sylwia, Silva, Fernando, Serrão, Ester, and Nuno Ferrand. 2019. *A evolução da ciência em Portugal*. Lisbon: Fundação Francisco Manuel dos Santos.

8 The arts

António Pinto Ribeiro

8.1 Introduction

Portugal entered the 21st century having lived through a long dictatorship. Until the second half of the previous century, the country had been cut off from the world, particularly from the major cultural changes and artistic and international movements. Since the revolution of 1974, and the years of democracy that have followed it, the cultural system has been established through various phases. The arts have gone from a revolutionary period – "the song is a weapon" – to the Europeanization of learning models for cultural and artistic practices in which the urgency of internationalizing the system's protagonists and artists in particular has been keenly felt; especially since the second half of the 1980s.

Having entered the third decade of the 21st century, it is possible to say that there have been continuities in the field, particularly in the greater professionalization of the sector, as well as discontinuities regarding investment. At the same time, Portuguese society has become clearly multicultural, particularly in the larger cities, where the construction and use of a range of large-scale facilities, a network of galleries, music organizations, arts research centres, professional training in various areas of artistic production and dissemination and participation in multiple international artistic forums have changed substantially. However, a fragile arts system, given Portugal's peripheral status, and a late recovery from what it lost in the "leaden years", suffered immediately, and with particular intensity, during the economic and social crises that occurred, causing the greatest harm to a desired intense and diversified cultural life in everyday life. Even so, the protagonists of this cultural system, which includes the arts, have often found an effective way of producing and exhibiting art in the face of the country's limitations. In the various disciplines, artists should be recognized for producing individual and richly differentiated works, which have contributed to the important international standing of their works and consequent investment in artistic activity, both in Portugal and in the diaspora. From music to cinema, from dance to theatre, there are already many works and artists from Portugal who are firmly established on the international art scene.

We have been witnessing the creation of cosmopolitan exchanges, where highly promising dynamics are being established for the integration and presence of Portuguese art at the forefront of European cosmopolitanism, albeit with minority representations. There have, for example, been multiple presences at film and theatre festivals, and other international exhibitions (the Avignon Festival, Kunstenfestivaldesarts, Berlinale, the Cannes Festival and the Venice, S. Paulo, Istanbul and Gwangju Biennales, Sonar, Manifesta, the Rotterdam Film Festival, etc.).

DOI: 10.4324/9781003488033-8

This chapter has been made available under a CC-BY-NC-ND license.

124   *António Pinto Ribeiro*

Social changes, which include artistic and cultural changes in permanent interaction, are not linear. They are complex, difficult to understand in the short term, depend on multiple dynamics, and often occur suddenly, as is clear in changes in the arts system, where the decision-making centres and their players are diverse and do not necessarily coincide in their thinking, objectives and actions. On the other hand, cultural life, especially artistic life, is the result of a combination of the planned and the accidental, and only historical rationality, a posteriori, can make sense of the succession of events. Finally, it should be added that although there are aspects common to the various arts, they also have many more unusual and unique aspects for both their producers and audiences (Pinto Ribeiro 2009, Pais, Magalhães, and Antunes 2020).

Even so, it is possible to determine today the determining factors that have brought us to where we are at the start of the 2020s. Demographic change, an increase in the circulation of works on national and international territory, some inventiveness in production methods and sustainability, always under very limited conditions, defined artistic culture in Portugal in the first two decades of this century.

8.2 Demographic change

In 1980, the foreign population living regularly in Portugal corresponded to 0.5% of the general population, a figure that increased in 2000 to 2.1% and in 2020 to 6.4%. A substantial part of this population comes from European countries, followed by African countries, mostly former colonies of Portugal, and Brazil. Initially, from the 1960s onwards, this migration was mainly made up of construction and domestic service workers, but in this century, it has included other professionals, including artists of various kinds. This demographic change has led to a substantial increase in cultural and artistic activity in terms of the contribution of popular cultural practices emerging from the various diasporas. There has also been an increase in artistic creation from artists originating in these diasporas; as well as in the treatment of themes previously exogenous to Portuguese society. Finally, new audiences have been created for the most diverse activities. The emergence on this continent of new artist profiles and new genres – facilitated by new communication technologies lowering production costs and, above all, causing an exponential increase in the circulation of information – has been decisive in changing Portugal's artistic landscape.

If we just consider immigration at the beginning of this century, there are some particularities worth noting. There was a significant demographic change between 2010 and 2020. In 2000, there were 207,587 foreigners living in Portugal. In 2020, the number rose to 509,348, with citizens between the ages of 25 and 54 accounting for 58.3% of this population. In terms of national representation, those from European countries represented 174,200 inhabitants, or 29.5% of the immigrant population, followed by Brazilians with 151,304 (25.6% of the immigrant population), followed by those from former Portuguese colonies with 92,755, or 15.6% of the immigrant population. There were then other less represented and residual nationalities.

In the mid-2000s, European immigration associated with the arts was mainly represented by young men from Europe who integrated more easily into the fields of dance and music. According to the study, *Licença para criar – Imigrantes nas Artes em Portugal* (Licence to Create –Immigrants in the Arts in Portugal) (Nico et al. 2007), which aimed to profile immigrant artists and identify their contribution to Portuguese society, women of predominantly European origin were a minority among immigrant artists. Among the

The arts   125

study's various conclusions, it was Europeans – with their various nationalities –, who tended to be more self-employed and live outside the Lisbon Metropolitan Area, with the exception of Spanish self-employed workers. The British and Germans stood out in the areas of sculpture and painting; and the research also showed that artists from Europe arrived in Portugal when their career was already well-established. However, those from Africa, for example, came mainly in search of training with, according to the study, Angolans being the most numerous and most qualified; while Cape Verdeans were notable for their youth- almost 70% being under 34. Music was the area with the highest concentration of immigrant artists, but theatre, dance and cinema also attracted a significant number of foreigners.

Nonetheless, Portugal was not an attractive country from the viewpoint of artistic development for the majority of those interviewed. It appeared more as a gateway to Europe or an opportunity to work in a less competitive market when compared to other countries, especially for those from Eastern Europe and Brazil. With regard to new organizations and alternative spaces to institutions, Marisa Falcón's thesis in 2008 stated that, in Lisbon, the vast majority of these spaces had arisen on the initiative of foreigners living in Portugal or Portuguese people returning after years of living outside Portugal: a trend that an empirical assessment can confirm.

8.3 The cinema

In the 1980s and 1990s, recognition for Portuguese culture abroad was largely due to the works of Fernando Pessoa, António Lobo Antunes, José Saramago and Agustina Bessa Luís, and the cinema of Manoel de Oliveira and João César Monteiro. The first two decades of this century added the writings of Lídia Jorge and Gonçalo M. Tavares, as well as the cinema of Pedro Costa, João Salaviza, Miguel Gomes and Gabriel Abrantes to this list. This came about because the themes dealt with now dared to deconstruct the taboo of Portuguese colonialism. These filmmakers introduced a new realism in which life on the outskirts of big cities, the condition of immigrants and the normalization of all sexualities became central and recurring themes. Moreover, the inventiveness of the production mechanisms, often referred to as Portuguese craftsmanship, allowed it.

In this field, documentary cinema, as a genre, its fundamental role of deconstructing the world fully recognized, also played a decisive part, as confirmed by the massive attendance of film festivals such as Doc-Lisboa, Porto/Post/Doc, IndieLisboa and other regional festivals.

However, to give a brief history of these two decades of cinema, it could be said that the century began with three films: *Branca de Neve* (Snow White) (2000), one of the last irreverent films by João César Monteiro (1939–2003), in which he used no images; *No Quarto da Vanda* (In Vanda's Room) (2000), a new incursion into Pedro Costa's colonial memories; and *O Fantasma* (The Ghost) (2000), the first feature by João Pedro Rodrigues, a radical filmmaker and quite cruel in his vision of male homoerotic relationships, or the relationships of power and rationalization in *Fogo-Fátuo* (Will-o'-the-Wisp) (2022).

Another kind of filmmaking, moving away from *auteur* cinema, and aiming to make a profit at the box office has emerged as a result of the participation of private television companies, which are demanding Portuguese productions in the style of soap operas or series. In this commercial cinema, the television aesthetic and the use of dubious humour led to the fleeting box-office success of films like *O Crime do Padre Amaro* (The Sin of

126 *António Pinto Ribeiro*

Father Amaro) (2005) by Carlos Coelho da Silva, and *O Filme da Treta* (which could be roughly translated as the 'Blah-Blah Film') (2006) by José Sacramento. However, *auteur* cinema survives because of the quality and inventiveness of its themes and languages: a daughter lost in the city of Lisbon – *Alice* (2005), Marco Martins' first film, presented at Cannes; and the dramatic death, in the same troubled city, of a young man with ambiguous sexuality and the false pregnancy of a betrayed girlfriend – *Odete* (2005), another João Pedro Rodrigues film, also presented at Cannes. Ten years after it was filmed, Joaquim Sapinho's documentary, *Diários da Bósnia* (Bosnia Diaries) (2005) premiered, illustrating a serious international conflict at the time. With a penchant for the theatrical and for parody, João Botelho used *O Fatalista* (The Fatalist) (2005) to illustrate the power of destiny in his own particular way, with the film marking his return to the limelight at the Venice Film Festival.

In the field of the documentary, Serge Tréfaut has emerged with an urban record exploring multiculturalism in Portugal, along with the conflicts of war that, for the genre, and as visual anthropology, had a considerable audience. His films, such as *Lisboetas* (Lisboners) (2004), *A Cidade dos Mortos* (The City of the Dead) (2009), *Viagem a Portugal* (Journey to Portugal) (2011), *Alentejo, Alentejo* (2014) *A Noiva* (The Bride) (2022), always deal with communities in society at large.

Since becoming established, Pedro Costa has frequently been featured in the international press and, besides cinemas, his work has also been shown in museums, university cinemas, competitions and cinematheques. With an identical path, through universities and cinematheques, as well as through countless festivals, Miguel Gomes has also come to prominence. His *Aquele Querido Mês de Agosto* (That Dear Month of August) (2008) combines fiction and documentary, using ordinary people cinematically within a fictionalized narrative.

During the more than 30 years since the democratic revolution of 25th April, the dictatorial regime, the colonial wars and their consequences – the deaths and traumas of the ex-combatants, the returnees, the decolonization process – have been forbidden topics, even though we could say that they stem from the collective unconscious. This taboo was broken by the films *Casa de Lava* (Down to Earth) (1994) by Pedro Costa, which continues this theme of Cape Verdean immigration in Portugal, and *Natal de 71* (Christmas 71) (1999) by Margarida Cardoso. In making documentaries and fiction, Cardoso has been acknowledged as the protagonist of Portuguese post-colonial cinema with a solid filmography and an unmistakable language in works such as *A Costa dos Murmúrios* (The Murmuring Coast) (2004), *Yvone Kane* (2014), *Understory* (2019) and *Sita* (2020). These two groundbreaking filmmakers who "brush history against the grain", in Walter Benjamin's beautiful expression, can be joined by a group of other major figures, such as Miguel Gomes with *Tabu* (2012), Ivo Ferreira with *Cartas de Guerra* (Letters from War) (2016) and Hugo Vieira da Silva with *Posto Avançado de Progresso* (An Outpost of Progress) (2015). To these names should be added Ariel de Bigault, a French director who has been working in Portugal for many years. In *Fantasmas do Império* (Ghosts of an Empire) (2020), Bigault takes a journey through cinematographic images from the colonial regime to the most recent works by the aforementioned directors.

In the meantime, two new generations of filmmakers have been emerging in this cinematic landscape. Having trained in alternative schools, had foreign experiences, attended cinematheques as well as film festivals and schools of the visual arts, they have mixed cinema with video and the visual arts, producing work in a collaborative system between director and technicians. Always dependent on production conditions, these films are mostly short or medium-length. Today, at the world's biggest film festivals, such as Cannes, Venice, Berlin, Locarno and Rotterdam, they have become a regular presence and received awards.

Diversity is not limited to formats. There has been a clear increase in the number of women directors and the themes dealt with are increasingly inclusive, both in terms of characters and narratives, whether the scale is large or small. The focus on foreigners living among us is not just about Africans but also includes Roma communities, internal migrations and people from the East. *Balada de um Batráquio* (Batrachian's Ballad) by Leonor Teles (2016), Golden Bear for short film in Berlin, focuses on prejudice towards the Roma community, on xenophobic behaviour. In contrast, foreign directors are filming in Portugal from an external viewpoint. *A Volta ao Mundo Quando Tinhas 30 Anos* (Around the World When You Were 30) (2011), by Aya Koretzky, is the director's portrait of her father based on the diary he kept in the 1970s about a trip around the world from Japan. Silas Tiny, a director from São Tomé and Príncipe working in his home country, Angola and Portugal, brought the vulnerabilities of former European colonies to the international stage with *Bafatá Filme Clube* (Bafatá Film Club) (2013), *O Canto de Ossobó* (The Song of Ossobó) (2018) and *Constelações do Equador* (Equatorial Constellations) (2021).

Following in the footsteps of João Salaviza and his films with heroes from the outskirts of Lisbon – *Arena* (2009, Palme d'Or for short films at Cannes), *Rafa* (2012) and *Cerro Negro* "Black Hill" (2012) – and from the Amazon – (*Chuva é Cantoria na Aldeia dos Mortos* (The Dead and Others) (2018)) – David Pinheiro Vicente made the short films *Onde o Verão Vai: Episódios da* Juventude "Where the Summer goes: Chapters on Youth") (2018) and *O Cordeiro de Deus* (The Lamb of God) (2020) that portray a particular time of youth, through the awakening of desire amid the heat and humidity of summer. Gabriel Abrantes, a filmmaker and visual artist with an unusual production capacity, has made 14 films in 12 years, as well as script collaborations, sound works and holding exhibitions. His cinematic highlights include *A History of Mutual Respect* (2010), *Taprobana* (2014), *Diamantino* (2018) and *Quatro Contos* (Four Stories) (2020), films in which all sexualities have permanent inclusion and expression.

André Gil Mata and Catarina Vasconcelos are also political but less manifestly so. The former's feature debut, *The Tree* (2018), shot during a harsh winter in Bosnia in long sequence shots on 16mm film, tells the story of a man and a child who meet under a tree by a river, sharing the same memory and a secret. Catarina Vasconcelos uses archives as well as family and autobiographical memories to make the short film, *Metáfora ou a Tristeza Virada do Avesso* (Metaphor or Sadness Inside Out) (2013) and the feature film, *A Metamorfose dos Pássaros* (The Metamorphosis of Birds) (2020). This working process and methodology is common to visual artists who politically seek alternative narratives about facts from the past relating to their family and country. On the other hand, Ana Rocha de Sousa, after many short films, presented her first feature, *Listen* in Venice in 2020, which won the Lion of the Future and the Horizons special jury prize.

Salomé Lamas stands out among all those who began directing at the turn of the decade, both for the quantity of her work and for the multiplicity of media she uses, as witnessed by *Jotta: a Minha Maladresse é uma Forma de Délicatesse* (Jotta: My Maladresse is a Way of Délicatesse) (2009). From cinema to video, together with installation and writing, Lamas has produced dozens of works marked by an approach to the most diverse social, political and artistic themes. She is one of the Portuguese directors who is a major presence in national and international festivals and museums, and if one of her

128   António Pinto Ribeiro

films had to be singled out, it would probably be the dantesque *El Dorado* (2016). Made high in the Bolivian mountains, it tells the story of thousands of people working deep in the mines, extracting precious metals

8.4 The performing arts

The 21st-century Portuguese performing arts are marked by an urgency to intervene, using the most sophisticated communication technologies, reinventing the process of "performance" in its most fundamental aspects: unpredictability, taking place in outdoor and unconventional spaces, employing other ways of using traditional performance spaces, and the ability to summon unexpected audiences. This updating of performance brings with it the novelty of being more organized, more produced, repeatable and spreading part of its legitimizing assumptions to dance, theatre and some music. Hence the emergence of the term "performing arts", most often associated with the arts of the body and replacing "stage arts" in production vocabulary. Festivals, programmes and performance artists have emerged and moved, with some effectiveness, into the space of critical discourse and questioning (Ciclo Serralves 2023).

This turn of the century in the performing arts was marked by two highly uncommon events that were decisive in the following two decades. In 2000, the Directorate General for the Arts was created, the result of the transformation of the now-defunct "Arts Institute". This was the public reference structure for the state's artistic activity, responsible for contemporary arts policy. However, its instability and limited budget did not contribute to creating the necessary platform to fulfil its mission with the appropriate consequences for the production, dissemination, promotion and maintenance of Portuguese creations. In statistical terms, this institution's support for the eleven artistic areas amounted to 237 projects in 2010 and 463 in 2020. Although this difference corresponded to a 95% increase in the number of projects supported over a ten-year period, there was little growth in financial terms.

The other notable event was the performance *António Miguel* (2000) by Miguel Pereira, with Antonio Tagliarini, seen as the first explicitly queer piece in the Portuguese repertoire. In performance and dance during this period, performers and choreographers from the New Portuguese Dance of the 1990s coexisted with the dance of *expressionismo branco* (white expressionism). Among them, Margarida Bettencourt, Vera Mantero, Miguel Pereira, Madalena Victorino, João Fiadeiro and Paulo Ribeiro who, in 1999, set up his company in a theatre in the interior of the country. The same happened with other choreographers, such as José Laginha, with DeVIR/CAPa – an association of cultural activities in Faro – and Rui Horta, with Espaço do Tempo, in Montemor-o-Novo. Ballet-Teatro, in Porto, welcomed a new generation of creators and performers from both more academic and more informal backgrounds, particularly from Fórum Dança. Meanwhile, producer Miguel Abreu's ongoing work as an organizer of large performance platforms, particularly multicultural ones, such as the TODOS Festival – Caminhada de Culturas, invests in the presentation of mostly solo shows, duets, short plays with mobile and inexpensive scenography, and restricted circulation.

The network is fragile, discontinuity is more common than continuity, and the companies are ad hoc. This whole situation denounces the enormous limitations on production and dissemination conditions, despite the existence of centres for presentation, some of which are responsible for continuous productions, the emergence of new festivals, dance exhibitions, television programmes and dance publications. Many artists are unable to survive this precarious situation and stop performing, even though some of Portugal's leading cultural institutions have been involved in the continuous programming and promotion of new contemporary dance and performance productions, such as Culturgest, Centro Cultural de Belém, Teatro Municipal Maria Matos, São Luiz Teatro Municipal, Teatro Municipal Rivoli, Fundação Calouste Gulbenkian, Danças na Cidade/Alkantara and Materiais Diversos.

As a response to this situation, REDE – Associação de Estruturas para a Dança Contemporânea (Association of Structures for Contemporary Dance), founded in 2004, mobilizes and boosts the participation of this community, representing it in discussions with the Ministry of Culture on the Arts Support Model and the implementation of a cultural policy that acknowledges the importance of contemporary dance. At the same time, choreographers and performers' consecutive response to the system of financial dependence, mostly on the state, for the development of productions, has been to follow in the footsteps of previous generations, creating associative projects with a view to artistic creation and production of a tendentially collective nature. New production companies such as CEM – Centro em Movimento (1997), Bomba Suicida (1997), Companhia Instável (1998), Rumo do Fumo (1999), Materiais Diversos (2003), CasaBranca (2006), [PI] Produções Independentes (2009), Nome Próprio (2010), Parasita (2014), Apneia Colectiva (2019) have emerged and autonomized dancers, choreographers and artists, who independently manage their cultural associations, and their production and circulation processes, nationally and internationally. Marlene Monteiro Freitas, for example, is one of the only choreographers with her own structure (P.O.R.K.), managing her creations and circulating nationally and internationally.

This framework is paradigmatic. On the one hand, artistic creation in the field of performance and contemporary Portuguese dance has been enriched by the eclecticism of projects and the dynamism of productions, ensuring the international recognition and visibility of Portuguese artists. On the other hand, it demonstrates the continued precariousness of the sector, which depends on temporary funding programmes limited to projects, never guaranteeing the medium and long-term subsistence of these structures and artists.

There are therefore new structures and more creation, but the cultural policy models are still deficient. We should also add the lack of criticism in the public sphere to these factors, which goes hand in hand with a crisis in the country's own media with specialization almost non-existent. Although there are cultural facilities, such as theatres and cultural centres, spread throughout the country, the development and study of audiences is still a work in progress. Taken together, these factors represent an unbalanced panorama between creation, production, circulation and reception.

There are artists and works whose unusualness bears witness to these times ensuring they will be remembered in the future: one example being Tânia Carvalho. Sónia Baptista is another, with her *Haikus* (2001), the first in a long series of pieces from a luxuriant repertoire dealing with the question of gender and gesture. João dos Santos Martins and Joclécio de Azevedo are other outstanding figures. There is also Cláudia Dias and her cycle of seven pieces for seven years; Luís Guerra; Vitor Roriz & Sofia Dias. *Comer coração* (Eating heart), by Vera Mantero in co-creation with sculptor Rui Chafes, presented at the S. Paulo Biennial in 2005; Vítor Hugo Pontes as a choreographer and theatre director. Marco da Silva Ferreira; and Marlene Monteiro de Freitas, who received the Silver Lion at the Venice Dance Biennale in 2018 for her work as a whole.

A final important note is that, as of 2018, dancers have benefited from a new social security scheme. This recognizes the rapid "wear and tear" of classical and contemporary

130 *António Pinto Ribeiro*

dancers, guaranteeing them protection and support during their activity and the stability they need throughout their lives.

8.5 The theatre

On 18th September 1995, the play *António, um rapaz de Lisboa* (António, a Lisbon Boy) premiered at the Gulbenkian Foundation's Grand Auditorium (Encontros ACARTE). This date, the play and its creators were decisive for all the theatre that would be produced in the following decades in Portugal. Jorge Silva Melo, in particular, contributed greatly to this. After co-creating a theatre company during the Portuguese dictatorship, Cornucópia, he travelled to various European cities and returned to Portugal as an actor, director, playwright and film director, venturing into a new life where theatre was fundamental. With this play, he began a process of collective writing with the actors – most of them very young –, who became co-authors. Silva Melo encouraged improvization as a method of composition in Artistas Unidos, the name given to the theatre group that emerged following the production of *António, um rapaz de Lisboa*. He also changed the rules of production and circulation of works to more minimal, but no less effective models; increased the number of performance days; and established theatre as an interventional art based on multiple experiences. The other "independent theatre" companies that appeared in the 70s and 80s – Novo Grupo, TEP, A Comuna, O Bando – continued their journeys based on the figure of the resident director, the published repertoire and established venues, creating a ballast of repertoires and aesthetics for audiences to get to know. Artistas Unidos, however, as well as the new theatre companies, began to operate in a minimal but often highly significant way.

It could be said that in 21st-century Portugal, a Theatre of the Ideal has come to coexist with a Theatre of the Real. Two new aspects have been decisive for the multiple aesthetics, artistic qualities and performances of the latter to happen. Firstly, the texts were often written by the collective and the playwrights – directors and non-directors. Secondly, they were texts coming *from* the theatre, not written *for* the theatre, even when they were published later. The most representative writers of these texts were Jorge Silva Melo, José Maria Vieira Mendes, Luísa Costa Gomes, Tiago Rodrigues, Carlos Pessoa, Joana Craveiro and the collectives "As Boas raparigas vão para o Céu, as Más para todo o lado" (Good Girls Go to Heaven, Bad Girls Go Everywhere), Teatro Griot, Primeiros Sintomas (First Symptoms), Teatro Praga, Visões Úteis (Useful Visions) and Cão Solteiro (Lone Dog), among others.

Theatre and performance have, along with cinema, been the arts in which various innovations, such as the creation of new production methods, managed to overcome the limited state support. Innovations emerged in terms of themes considering the various perspectives and approaches to dictatorship, colonialism, the colonial war and immigration. Diverse groups, actors and playwrights have created alternative narratives to the colonial one and, to this end, they have researched, interviewed and compared testimonies to produce works. Joana Craveiro, the mentor of Teatro do Vestido, has done exemplary and continuous work, in works such as *Retornos, Exílios e Alguns que Ficaram* (The Returnees, the Exiled and Some Who Remained) (2014); *Um Museu Vivo de Memórias Pequenas e Esquecidas* (A Living Museum of Small and Forgotten Memories) (2016); and *Elas Também Estaram Lá* (They were There Too) (2018). Other groups and actors have added works to this type of repertoire, such as *Hotel Europa*, directed by André Amálio and Tereza Havllícková. In line with this theme, the emergence of groups of black actors and directors in the early years of this century has definitely contributed to the creation of a decolonizing repertoire by appropriating and rewriting canonical texts or using African authors or works written by collectives. Teatro Griot, directed by director and actress Zia Soares, is, in this respect, the group that has most revolutionized this process with works such as *As Confissões Verdadeiras de um Terrorista Albino* (The True Confessions of an Albino Terrorist) (2014) and *Que Ainda Alguém nos Invente* (May Someone Still Invent Us) (2014).

This theatrical landscape would not be complete without mentioning the investment made by artists and companies in theatre for children. The focus on children has even led to the founding of LU.CA, Teatro Luís de Camões, dedicated exclusively to children and teenagers.

Festivals such as FIMFA and FIMP (puppets and animated forms) and others, such as the Almada Theatre Festival, FITEI, Verão Azul, Materiais Diversos, Festival Internacional Vaudeville Rendez-Vous and Festival A Salto allow audiences, through their persistence and tradition, to experience works by national and international authors, companies and processes. Although there is a continuous presentation of works in more institutional spaces or in the homes of some companies, the problem of most works having very short seasons is one of the major obstacles to the dissemination of theatre and, in part, to its sustainability, particularly financially. We might think that commercial theatre – very much focused on stand-up comedy and using popular actors from soap operas as a marketing resource – would be financially self-sustaining, but it too only survives with commercial sponsorship and a swift tour of its shows.

Even so, theatre has been renewed, and much is due to the presence of playwrights, directors and, in particular, actresses – such as Joana Craveiro, Zia Soares, As Boas Raparigas, Beatriz Batarda, Carla Galvão, Isabel Abreu and Mónica Calle – who have brought another reality to the stage, multiplying other perspectives and other repertoires. Ideally, their work will henceforth tour Portugal and abroad more extensively.

8.6 The visual arts

A fundamental aspect of contemporary art is the semantic and lexical mutation taking place within the field. After the institutionalization of the performing arts as a genre that encompasses the old arts of the stage and spectacle and their innovations, the revolution in aesthetics that shifted the reception and enjoyment of art from the works themselves to the mechanisms of reception with an appreciation of the senses ended up creating the term visual arts. Because they are received by sight, the classic boundaries between the visual arts, video and photography have been broken down, bringing them together under the term visual arts.

On 6 June 1999, the Serralves Foundation Museum of Contemporary Art opened in Porto with the exhibition CIRCA 1968, curated by Vicente Todoli and João Fernandes. At the time, the programmatic line set out by the museum and the exhibition constituted a decisive moment in the decentralization of contemporary art, particularly in the north of the country. It also played a major role in changing tastes, encouraging collecting and the creation of a small gallery market – an obvious example of which was the organization of a street in the city dedicated to galleries, Rua Miguel Bombarda. It also promoted the first attempts to internationalize Portuguese artists, in an unprecedented back and forth between foreign institutions and the city of Porto. Porto's status as European Capital of Culture in 2001 was decisive in boosting culture in the north of the country, just as Lisbon's had been in the previous decade.

132   *António Pinto Ribeiro*

In Lisbon, the creation of the Calouste Gulbenkian Foundation's Modern Art Centre, inaugurated in 1983 with a collection of works mostly by Portuguese artists, gave the city the chance to enjoy this important collection and a range of interdisciplinary activities. New major multidisciplinary cultural centres, such as the Centro Cultural de Belém (1992) and Culturgest (1993), also contributed to the city's dynamism and openness to the world. The Museu do Chiado reopened as a contemporary art museum in 1994. . Twenty-two years later, 2016 saw the Museum of Art, Architecture and Technology (MAAT) open. To these should be added two important centres on the islands: the Centro de Artes-Casa das Mudas (2004), in Calheta, Madeira; and the Centro de Artes Contemporâneas (2015), in S. Miguel, the Azores. With different values, budgets and prominence, as well as exhibition and curatorial programmes – in some cases hosting collections outside the institution – these facilities are the anchors of museum institutions dedicated to contemporary arts (Jürgens 2017). Given their scale, especially their volume, they mostly reproduce Western mainstream taste, as well as the hierarchical structures of the art market and its circulation from financial centres and political power. So, let's say that – bearing in mind their financial and programmatic possibilities – they bring international art as close as they can.

In the meantime, over the course of two decades, regional museums or museums dedicated to artists have increased the rather informal network of national museography. These include the Centro de Artes de Sines; the Museu de Arte Contemporânea Nadir Afonso; the Casa das Histórias – Paula Rego; the Centro de Arte Contemporânea Graça Morais; the Centro Internacional das Artes José de Guimarães; the Centro de Arte Oliva; the Centro de Cultura Contemporânea de Castelo Branco and the Museu do Neo-Realismo. Sometimes more authorial, essayistic and on a minority scale, these spaces have boldly held other types of exhibitions, examples being the Arte Bruta/ Outsider Art – Treger Saint Silvestre Collection, at the Centro de Arte Oliva in São João da Madeira; *Encontros para além da história* (Encounters Beyond History) at the CIAJG in Guimarães; and the COSMO/POLITICS Cycle at Neo-Realism in Vila Franca de Xira.

On another theatrical map of the country, marked by attention to different issues and artists, in alternative circuits, ranging from the iconoclastic to the more submerged or even suburban, multiple projects have emerged with very variable duration. There have been non-profit organizations, with light structures or intense curatorial programmes. These projects, scattered all over the country, have presented the urgency and emergence of contemporaneity in its life-art-work-social dimension. In Lisbon, the pioneers of this alternative approach have been Galeria Zé dos Bois, a cultural centre created in 1994 focused on music, performance and contemporary art. Kunsthalle Lissabon (2009) and Hangar-Centro de Investigação Artística (2015) have been similar pioneers; the latter being a residency and exhibition space promoting transdisciplinary exchanges and public engagement, with a particular emphasis on post-colonialism and the Afro-Portuguese scene. Maumaus (1992) and the Lumiar Cité space have played an important, albeit informal, role in the internationalization of the Portuguese art scene, introducing, for example, a whole generation of artists, filmmakers and theorists to the local public (Harun Farocki, Diedrich Diederichsen and René Green among them). This has shaped the path of a younger generation of artists, such as Pedro Barateiro, Ramiro Guerreiro, Francisco Vidal and Bruno Leitão, whose careers have radically changed the spirit of the city's art scene.

In Porto, this alternative scene has also meant the reach of a broader, more decentralized artistic field, open to experimentation with artistic practices and more differentiated programming. From this group, we can highlight the curatorial activity of more recent spaces, such as Rua do Sol (2013), Sismógrafo (2014) or Rampa (2018), or the historic alternatives that, since the beginning of the millennium, have created a strong local and national cultural dynamic: W. C. Container (1999), Caldeira 213 (2000), Maus Hábitos (2001), IN.TRANSIT (2002), Pêssego Prá Semana (2002), Salão Olímpico (2003), A Sala (2006) and Uma Certata Falta de Coerência (2008).

Towards the end of the 20th century, the art market began to make its presence felt as more dynamic galleries with an international vocation appeared. However, it has been since 2015, with the arrival of foreigners in Portugal, that this market has emerged in a country where family resources reserved for the arts and cultural practices are quite low. The number of collectors has increased. The private collections confirm this, through their presence in existing museums or, in some cases, by creating their own spaces in partnership with Portuguese municipalities or the state: the Colecção Berardo, at the Centro Cultural de Belém; the Colecção António Cachola, at the Museu de Arte Contemporânea de Elvas; the Colecção Norlinda e José Lima, at the Centro de Arte Oliva; and the Colecção Fernando Figueiredo Ribeiro, at the Quartel da Arte Contemporânea de Abrantes. As in other genres, the situation, visibility, internationalization and status of artists in the visual arts are not homogeneous either. The prices of works and their reputation vary between a number of groups. There are the women artists (the most international of all): Vieira da Silva, Paula Rego and Helena Almeida. There is also the group created in the 1980s, from wild painting to site-specific artists, such as Julião Sarmento, Pedro Cabrita Reis, João Penalva, Ana Jotta, Ana Hartherly, José Pedro Croft, Rui Chafes, Ângela Ferreira and Fernanda Fragateiro, with appearances in multiple biennials and international fairs. This was followed by the 90s and turn-of-the-millennium artists, such as Francisco Tropa, João Maria Gusmão + Pedro Paiva, Leonor Antunes, Filipa César, Gabriela Albergaria, Susanne Themelitz, Joana Vasconcelos, João Pedro Vale and Nuno Alexandre. Finally, there are the more recent emerging figures, recognized for their radical positions towards the arts and their histories. These stem, first and foremost, from a pragmatic reading of the situation:

> there will be no other alternative than the unequivocal enunciation of the problem, since not even the most elaborate articulation has managed to solve it. It is assumed that a reflection on a reflection on a reflection will not make a fairer distribution of wealth possible – and will certainly not bring about a revolution.
>
> (Jürgens 2017: 5)

The heterogeneous group comprising, among others, Inês Brites, Tiago Madaleno, Ricardo Passaporte and Horácio Frutuoso are in this situation.

One of the singularities of the visual landscape of the first decades of this century, reflecting what had already begun not only on the international art scene but also in Portugal, with the Coimbra and Braga *Encontros de Fotografia* and the *Colecção de Fotografias do Estado*, was the increased significance at all levels of photography, in its multiple formats and techniques. There are now dozens of photographers who have joined their precursors from the final three decades of the last century – Paulo Nozolino, Jorge Molder, Fernando Lemos, José M. Rodriges, Daniel Blaufuks, Rita Barros – and who have become a decisive presence in the galleries focusing on photography: António Júlio Duarte, José Luís Neto, André Cepeda, Valter Vinagre, Catarina Botelho and Carlos Lobo.

134 *António Pinto Ribeiro*

Finally, we come to video art, this hybrid genre between moving images and painting. This genre claims a more classical history and is presented at FUSO, the only video art festival in the country.

8.7 Music

The inauguration in 2005 of Casa da Música, a project conceived as part of Porto, European Capital of Culture 2001, came like a meteor to Portugal; not only because of the unique architecture designed by Rem Koolhaas, but also because of the shock waves it caused in the country's music scene. With a programme by Pedro Burmester and António Jorge, Casa da Música avoided hierarchies in musical styles, proclaiming itself a project with a repertoire extended to all music and aimed at a more universal audience. In addition, it has created an experimental orchestra – the Remix Ensemble – a choir and has hosted the Porto Symphony Orchestra and the Baroque Orchestra. This project, just as vernacular as erudite, created a new paradigm for musical programming in the country and became an international benchmark. At the same time, the Gulbenkian Foundation's Music Service continued to offer a quantitative and qualitative offer that was decisive for audiences further south, followed by the Lisbon Metropolitan Orchestra and other more recent formations.

At the same time, the impact of the revolution in music teaching, led by the University of Aveiro, began to be felt. This created a degree in music teaching in 1991, which had a boomerang effect on the country. It began to train teachers for the conservatoires with the creation of new teaching models that resulted in a change in the training of musicians, the creation of new conservatoires, each with its own orchestra, choirs and ensembles, all over the country. In all sectors of Portuguese musical life, this dynamic has changed the state of teaching and, consequently, the creation of new audiences and new performers who today are at home with, for example, fado, classical and contemporary erudite music, pop and Afro-music.

The area of composition itself has changed. While commissions for composers born in the last century – António Pinho Vargas, Isabel Soveral, João Pedro Oliveira, António Chagas Rosa, Luís Tinoco, João Madureira, Eurico Carrapatoso, for instance – have continued, the profile of contemporary composers has changed. They are now integrating materials from a wide variety of sources into their compositions, and not just necessarily musical ones. Examples include: João Madureira, Rui Penha, Joana Gama, Henrique Portovedo and Sara Carvalho. The same phenomenon is happening with symphony orchestras which, while growing in number, are now trying to fight against diminishing audiences by establishing dialogues with other types of music, whether performing alongside fado singers, rock musicians or those from different quadrants of popular music. Today, Portugal has eleven national symphony orchestras and numerous ones specializing in, for example, baroque, string and jazz orchestras. In the case of jazz, the increase in specialized schools has also accompanied the professionalization of musicians and the creation of aesthetic movements that seek a kind of language of their own for contemporary Portuguese jazz, such as the Porta Jazz Association in Porto. Jazz is now an important area of musical life in Portugal, visible in the 50 jazz festivals organized in 2022, most of which have been running regularly for more than 10 years.

Fado, which for decades was associated with the authoritarian regime, began to be reinvented in the last century. Its inclusion on UNESCO's list of Intangible World Heritage in 2011 captured the attention of a universal audience. Contributing to this change were the new fado lyrics, a decision taken by the new fado singers, who called on poets and lyricists of enormous literary quality. This renewal was created by the new artistic styles of singers such as Mísia, Camané, Cristina Branco, Marisa, Aldina Duarte; and a proud youth's appropriation of this internationalized musical genre through, for example, Ricardo Ribeiro, Gisela João and Carminho. Os Madredeus (1985–2015), while not exactly a fado group, integrated into their urban band image a musical and visual component combining tradition with innovation. As a result, they were the first Portuguese group to be classified by the British industry as "world music", offering them major opportunities for internationalization. This is probably why they were the Portuguese band that gave the most concerts during their existence.

In the field of popular music, the industry, regardless of its interests, has been instrumental in creating hundreds of festivals, including "mega-events". The industry has been responsible for a substantial part of the national and international circulation of the various groups and artists that have emerged in Portugal in the meantime. In many cases, these groups have created new repertoires and revisited musical traditions that appeal to a kind of "Portuguese sound", even reviving almost extinct instruments from popular culture such as the ten-string guitar, the accordion or the concertina, sometimes modified, electrified or using live loops.

Afro-Portuguese music is the response of African communities to European interculturalism. Its contribution from the 1990s onwards has been fundamental in understanding the process of cultural and spiritual decolonization taking place in Portugal (Belanciano 2020). After the presence of musicians from Portugal's former colonies in the wake of the 1974 revolution, there followed a movement of new musicians from the outskirts of Lisbon, made up of politically committed young people. Through music, General D, Boss AC, Da Weasel and others began their social intervention influenced by Hip Hop and the tapes they heard coming from London or the USA. There is, however, not just one form of Hip Hop. In addition to this genre, the second and third generations of Afro-descendants, most born in Portugal, have come to mark an unmistakable musical territory within the European music scene in the last two decades by taking advantage of the facilities of global information and much greater accessibility to music production technologies. In a more urban situation, black singers, whether or not they were born in Portugal (Sara Tavares, Mayra Andrade, Lura and Aline Frazão) have been an essential presence in new music festival programmes across the country.

For all these artists, no music of African origin is foreign to them, no social scene is indifferent to them, whether it is the Kuduro or Kizomba beat, protesting rallying cries, lyrics sung in Creole or lyrics about distant loves, everything serves as material for composition and work. Buraka Som Sistema was the first band to incorporate and internationalize this new musical spirit and it is common to find other musicians playing on the most remote stages, as well as at festivals in London, New York, São Paulo or Luanda. They are, as they define themselves, Afro-Portuguese musicians, be they Dino d'Santiago, Dj Marfox, Dj Kampire, Scúru Fitchádu or Batida, the artists who produce the sounds of Afro-Europeanization in Portugal.

8.8 Looking for scale

The arts, in their multiple production conditions and functions, constitute a system. The arts' system has two particularities that are crucial to its survival. It is highly porous, and significantly affected by other social, economic, political and psychological systems. Furthermore, it is a very unequal system regarding each genre or artistic practice.

In Portugal, resources to invest in and sustain an arts economy are scarce. This reality can be seen in the low level of funding for production and dissemination and the low level of willingness on the part of citizens to contribute to sustaining this system. The average gross salary in Portugal in 2002 was €879; in 2017, it was €925, and the annual household consumption of culture (including education and leisure activities) in 2019 accounted for €2,019.5.

To these limitations must be added the responsibilities of a dictatorial regime that inhibited the acquisition of knowledge, production and the implementation of innovation in these areas. The ability to adapt to technology can also limit production and dissemination, and technological literacy is crucial for the current arts system in Portugal, both from the point of view of production and reception.

Added to these liabilities is the country's semi-peripheral status, both geographically and in terms of the transportation and communications network. Despite some progress in recent years, the tendency is for the flow of artistic culture to remain anchored in the country and its diasporas, although it is trying to engage in dialogue with the world. Finding the right scale for the country's resources, training and the importance of a place in the dispute over territories of influence has been the great challenge for artistic culture in Portugal. To this must now be added the digitalization of the world and everyday life; the imperative of finding the main networks for the circulation of works and their agents; and the urgent acceleration of the constitution of a critical mass capable of anchoring and disseminating the diverse imaginations within the arts system in Portugal.

Acknowledgements

Ana Barata, Ana Bigotte Vieira, Carlos Nogueira, Cristina Grande, Inês Lampreia, João dos Santos Martins, Mónica Braz Teixeira, Umbigo Magazine (Elsa Garcia and António Néu), Rute Mendes, Sandra Vieira Jürgens and Susana Sardo.

References

Belanciano, Vítor. 2020. *Não Dá Para Ficar Parado, Música Afro-Portuguesa. Celebração, Conflito e Esperança*. Lisboa: Edições Afrontamento.

Ciclo Serralves. "Exposição Para uma Timeline a Haver." Accessed [January 15, 2023]. [https://www.serralves.pt/ciclo-serralves/2104-exposicao-para-uma-timeline-a-haver/].

José Machado Pais, Pedro Magalhães and Miguel Lobo Antunes. 2020. *Inquérito às Práticas Culturais dos Portugueses*. Lisbon: Imprensa de Ciências Sociais.

Jürgens, Sandra Vieira. 2017. "Boas maneiras. Breve curriculum das práticas independentes no contexto artístico do Porto." In *Ao Monte (2015–2017)*, 4–9. Porto: Maus Hábitos.

Nico, Magda, Gomes, Natália, Rosado, Rita and Sara Duarte. 2007. *Licença para criar: imigrantes nas artes em Portugal* (No. 23). Lisbon: Observatório da Imigração.

Pinto Ribeiro, António. 2009. *À Procura da Escala, cinco exercícios disciplinados sobre cultura contemporânea*. Lisbon. Livros Cotovia.

9 Literature

Helena Buescu

9.1 To begin with: the imperfect present

Time in literature is never present time, but a time that brings to the pretence of the present all the times it represents, past and future. This is why the 'pretence' that Fernando Pessoa spoke of is, among other things, a pretence that is as much personal as it is historical and symbolic. This is also why literature is part of culture as a 'memory not inherited from the community' (Lotman and Uspenskij 1975, 66). It is not an inherited memory, but one that is incorporated, directly or indirectly, into discourses, which are always many, the discourses of the community (of the 'tribe', in Mallarmé's words). It is not a strictly individual memory, but a communal one (in other words, greater than the sum of its parts). It is ultimately a cultural memory, a heritage that is textually encrypted in various ways. Most importantly, in my opinion, literature brings to light a memory that is historically discontinuous and fragmentary, and whose past and future are therefore impossible to predict. The holes and discontinuities it weaves integrate fictions, inventions (a word whose nobility should be reintegrated into our vocabulary) and, not least, forgetfulness. This will be one of the driving forces guiding this reflection, as well as the options it supports. While not neglecting the legacies and authors who, in the 21st century, have extended work begun in the previous one, greater emphasis will be placed on those who began creating in the present century, as there is naturally less criticism on them available.

Extended into this century, this situation thus stems from one of the threads inherited from 20th-century Portuguese literary practices: post-colonialism and post-imperial melancholy. In a classic book by Paul Gilroy (2005), the Freudian concept of *trauer* (grief) is the touchstone of a cultural analysis integrating (and therefore not denying) the idea of the internal violence that all post-colonial and post-imperial societies have built up. This form of melancholy is not finished, much less perfect. In the case of Portuguese literature, it is part of a process of continuity which, having established itself in the last quarter of the 20th century, has continued well into the 21st, although it has suffered natural crises of representation. As a result, the concept of post-imperialism here has to be taken in a very broad sense, not limited to the strictly political content of the post-revolutionary period of 25 April 1974 (in particular 1975, when most of the colonies became independent).

Portuguese literature appropriates this post-colonial and post-imperial background in two different ways. From a stricter perspective, we find those that directly relate to the cesura established for the former colonies and the former metropolis (now European Portugal) by decolonization, seen from the viewpoint of what happened, both during the war in the former colonies and/or in Portugal, and in the post-25th April 1974 period in

---

DOI: 10.4324/9781003488033-9

This chapter has been made available under a CC-BY-NC-ND license.

Portugal. This includes, but is not limited to, some of Maria Velho da Costa's greatest novels, in particular *Missa in Albis* (Mass in Albis) – which, in 1988, focuses on 'political and affective passion' (suffering) in East Timor; or at the beginning of the new century, *Irene, ou o Contrato Social* (Irene, or the Social Contract) (2000). Since his initial novels, *Memória de Elefante* (Elephant Memory) (1979) and *Os Cus de Judas* (South of Nowhere) (1979), António Lobo Antunes has steadily built up a body of work on the individual and historical trauma related to the colonial and post-colonial process. His novel *As Naus* (Return of the Caravels) (1988) should be highlighted here for reasons explicitly related to the 16th-century Portuguese expansion and its 19th-century reverse. Lídia Jorge's novels are similarly important, as are more recent works, such as Dulce Maria Cardoso's *O Retorno* (The Return) (2011), whose central plot revolves around that almost supra-historical moment that was, for European Portugal, the sudden and unprepared return of 500,000 returnees (5% of the total Portuguese population) from the former colonies in 1975. In the case of Lídia Jorge, her most recent novel *Misericórdia* (Mercy, 2022) highlights her awareness of vulnerable subjects also in the surprising setting of a nursing home, with a powerful meditation on what is at stake in the human condition. A similar condition stems from the intense lyrical universe of Filipa Leal (*Vem à Quinta-feira*, Come on Thursday, 2016; *Fósforos e metal sobre imitação de ser humano*, 2019), in which the tragic experience of ordinary life in our contemporary world takes into account those 'unseen' inhabitants to which we Europeans are usually blind.

Some of these authors have woven their fictions between the 20th and 21st centuries, while others only began after 2000 (like Dulce Maria Cardoso). However, it is a question of recognizing continuities which, despite being in different forms, are developing without apparent ruptures. Even more recent is the case of the writer, Djaimilia Pereira de Almeida, who in several of her works (published since 2015) has created a set of personal and historical ghosts clearly based on the identity of someone who, born in Angola, is Portuguese and writes and lives in Portugal. If *Luanda, Lisboa, Paraíso* (Luanda, Lisbon, Paradise) (2018) presents the restless crossing of historical and imaginary spaces haunted by the past (but also by the present), the recent *Maremoto* (Tsunami) (2021) aggravates the pain of those who search and ask questions, even though they know they won't find answers. Perhaps they don't exist.

From a broader perspective, and politically less obvious (but no less productive), the post-colonial question is represented by a series of narratives, chronicles, novels, novellas and even essays (of which Eduardo Lourenço is the greatest representative). They seek to reconfigure an idea of a post-imperial Portugal capable of situating itself in a multilateral symbolic, cultural and political relationship with the Portuguese-speaking countries, together with the Europe in which it is geo-symbolically located, and with the world as a whole.

These two perspectives (deriving from the post-colonial and post-imperial ethos) will also help clarify the selection principles that guide me here: what I will call the grand systematic entry of the world into contemporary Portuguese literature. Not that the world hadn't been part of it before. But what the 21st century shows is a change in the relative visibility of the connections between Portugal and the world, the various worlds. This gradual reduction in the weight of self-identity seems to me to be perhaps the greatest symbolic change in the literary production of this century. Therefore, although my choice is bound to be selective, I will include authors and works that are still subject to an identity questioning (namely the post-colonial question), and show that other paths are currently being travelled in the new century's literary production. I will therefore pay special

Literature 139

attention to the way in which a national literature (Portuguese) can also be seen in the context of comparative literature and even world literature, which will involve looking at works that pose cosmopolitanism as a current problem, especially when it offers itself as an inactive or untimely question. Post-colonialism, untimeliness and cosmopolitanism are therefore three of the major thematic vectors guiding this reflection.

The entire works of Maria Velho da Costa, one of the greatest writers and playwrights of the late 20th and early 21st century, must be read in this light, even those that apparently don't strictly relate to the post-colonial moment. In some of them, because the plot takes place before it happened (*Casas Pardas* (Dun-Coloured Houses), 1977); in others, because society itself has changed, and everything has become frayed in its fabric, revealing all the personal, ethnic and class rifts that make it up. This is the case in the abovementioned novel, *Irene, ou o Contrato Social*, in which the existential 'contract' established between Orlando, the mestizo in Lisbon, and Irene is at the centre of the plot. Or in *Myra* (2008), in which immigration, exile and abandonment within a society that seems to have increased its outcasts are allegorized by the pairing of the Russian immigrant child and the abandoned dog.

In the somewhat different case of José Saramago, his novel *A Jangada de Pedra* (The Stone Raft) (1986) fits precisely into this context because it questions the position (geographically, but above all symbolically and culturally) of a Portugal that, precisely because it is post-imperial, 'sails' across the Atlantic, only to become immobilized between Europe, Africa and South America. Saramago here presents the Iberian Peninsula as a platform for readings and multilateral relations not only between countries but between continents.

This marked the beginning of a cosmopolitan aspect to the questioning of Portugal, which I believe is one of the most serious features to consider regarding the present and the future. So, among stories of immigration, miscegenation, questions about Portugal's historical-symbolic place, what we find at the beginning of the 21st century, in fictional terms, is a kind of 'world entrance' through the wide-open door of a 'small' (because post-imperial) Portugal. This feature, as we shall see, has been consolidated in the literary production of the last two decades.

The same is true of António Lobo Antunes' body of work, mainly novels and chronicles, written over a long period. Since the 1980s, Lobo Antunes has addressed the exploded question of what Portugal and the Portuguese 'can be'. His novels and chronicles detail all the mismatches between personal lives, with their emotions and deceptions and illusions, as well as the anti-utopian experiences of the present. Throughout Lobo Antunes' work (as well as Maria Velho da Costa's), there seems to be no release from the Gordian knots in which personal and historical lives are tied. The incongruous metamorphosis between the historical past and the present, the story of the Expansion as a Big Bang that, in the present, has unleashed the violent responses of the Big Crunch, run through all Lobo Antunes' work produced after 2000. The 16 novels and four volumes of chronicles published after 2000 constitute a complex and desperate work by someone who can't seem to find a possible future community.

The post-imperial and post-colonial perspectives mentioned above also enable us to see that the first two decades of the 21st century have seen literary production in Portugal progressively move away from what was, in the last quarter of the 20th century, one of its major themes: Portugal's socio-political and symbolic identity. It has, in fact, been spreading more wildly and bringing a more complex and less self-centred set of issues together. Increasing diversification has broadened the scope of literary production in

140   *Helena Buescu*

Portugal and the directions in which it has developed, giving rise to the awareness that the question of 'who are we' has to be reformulated because historically and symbolically 'we' are always 'other'. In the case of David Machado, his recent novel *A Educação dos Gafanhotos* (The Education of the Locusts) (2020) is set in the aftermath of the fall of the New York Twin Towers in 2001. It is against this background that the main characters, Portuguese, see themselves, at the same time as they see their identity in the context of a cosmopolitanism that, after all, inaugurated the violence of the present century. This is also the case with writer Julieta Monginho, whose novel *Volta ao mundo em vinte dias e meio* (Around the World in Twenty and a Half Days) (2021) contrasts the minimal Alentejo locale with the cosmopolitan metropolis of Amsterdam, weaving a story 'where truth and lies are confused'. There is also Joel Neto's novel *Meridiano 28* (28th Meridian), about the Second World War in the restricted but cosmopolitan environment of the island of Faial (the Azores).

The community and political implications of the literary are particularly evident in one of the greatest poets of the late 20th century and the period we are considering here, the 21st, Manuel Gusmão. Throughout his work, we find the poet personally and politically involved as a witness to his city (which is also his world). Bearing witness means ensuring some form of presence in what happens. In the complex web interwoven between what happens, presence, language and address, the notion of testimony is raised, as an awareness that the idea of responsibility does not constrain the aesthetic idea constructed by poetry. Books such as *A Foz em Delta* (At the Mouth of a Delta) (2018) or *Pequeno Tratado das Figuras* (Short Treatise on Figures) (2013) confirm that poetry, history, politics and philosophy ultimately share what has always been common ground.

This is also the case with the great poet Gastão Cruz, one of the founders of the 'Poesia 61' movement, who has continued to publish over the last few decades. In this movement, it is the idea of the poet's (and poetry's) presence within reality that becomes the foundation. In his 21st-century published works, Cruz revives the feeling of reality as something that affects the subject, in other words, humans. *Fogo* (Fire) (2013) or *Existência* (Existence) (2017) are examples of texts that extend this intensified experience of the real, which has been revived in his poetry in recent decades. We find a similar ethos throughout Luís Filipe Castro Mendes' magnificent poetic output, especially in the recent *Voltar* (Going Back) (2021), where the return to the homeland is tinged with a melancholy bringing the cosmopolitan into the home scene. There is furthermore, the poetry of authors such as João Miguel Fernandes Jorge (whose *Fuck the Polis* came out in 2018); Joaquim Manuel Magalhães (with several 21st-century titles, including the most recent *Canoagem* (Canoeing), 2021); or António Franco Alexandre (who published *Poemas* (Poems) also in 2021, including the earlier unpublished *Carrossel* poems). These are poets whose verbal inventiveness allows for a discursive reconfiguration of the paths they have previously trodden. Yes, they go back a long way, but what's certain is that their output shows poetic material that is constantly being renewed.

9.2 Portuguese literature as possible comparative literature

The idea of Portuguese literature as a possible comparative literature seems to be one of the most interesting features of recent decades. With regard to some of the aforementioned cases, I mentioned a clear trend, which will perhaps intensify in the near future, towards a broader vision of what is literarily configurable, from a personal, historical or aesthetic-symbolic point of view.

One of the examples I find most interesting is that of works that manifest the power of the inactual or untimely. The concept of untimeliness does not in fact represent a true and innocent delay. It implies that the things that happen come 'out of time', have circulated in a historically complex way and have arrived at a moment that manifests a historical mismatch between their happening and their arrival. In the case of literature, this process is intensifying in the 21st century. This is a historical concern, of course, but one that goes beyond the idea of a self-centred community, umbilically closed in on itself. On the contrary, it is through a gradual intensification of the relationship with the 'outside', with what is 'non-Portuguese' and with a complex awareness of the 'not-now', that Portuguese literature has been developing. In connection with the concept of anachrony, I will discuss the different ways in which this 'alterization' of so-called national literature itself brings together stories, themes and motifs dealt with by a contemporaneity that questions various forms of loss.

However, and in what might seem, at first glance, to be a counter-current (but isn't, because it participates in what is thought to be inactual), we are witnessing the encounter of a spirituality of which one of the exponents was the young poet-monk, Daniel Faria, who burst on the literary scene in the 1990s. His posthumous collection *Dos Líquidos* (Of Liquids) was published in 2001 and was followed, in 2021, by *Sétimo Dia* (Seventh Day), an unfinished book of biblically inspired prose poems. Faria's (re)publication, throughout the 2010s, of manuscripts and collected poetry, underlined his status, along with José Tolentino de Mendonça (a poet priest I will also talk about), as the spectator of scintillating simplicity. Moreover, we are witnessing the transformation of apparently lost traditions, the encounter with history, or the confrontation with community differentiation (which is symbolically and politically much more interesting than 'multiculturalism').

These contradictions, which paradoxically combine loss and quasi-epiphany, are visible in much of the most recent Portuguese poetry, in its evolutions and ruptures with previous lyrical traditions. We can evoke here the sense of counter-epic that one of the greatest writers to begin publishing in the 2000s, Gonçalo M. Tavares, took up in 2010 with his surprising work *Viagem à Índia* (Voyage to India), a parodic response to Camões' epic *Os Lusíadas* (The Lusiads) (1572). This same movement of continuity and rupture can also be seen, however, in the greatest lyric poet of the second half of the 20th century, Herberto Helder, who, until his death in 2015, continued to publish a fascinating body of poetic works whose corporeal and material intensity, with an orphic dimension, responded to the cerebralism of Fernando Pessoa, the great poet of the first half of the 20th century in Portugal. And it's interesting to note how, for example, more recent works, such as Andreia C. Faria, *Alegria para o Fim do Mundo* (Joy at the End of the World) (2019), take up precisely the carnal, even visceral vein of Herberto Helder's legacy, especially with *Canina* (Canine) (2022). In another powerful poet, Maria do Rosário Pedreira (*Poesia reunida*, 2012; *O meu corpo humano*, My Human body, 2022), we may be able to read the same kind of material reflection on the way body and time interact and determine the experience of life itself.

It is also possible to link this radical authorial rupture with Joaquim Manuel Magalhães who, in 2010, published *O Toldo Vermelho* (The Red Awning) that, in his words, rewrote, 'annulling and replacing', all of the poet's previous work. What is going on here? A re-reading which, in its radicalness, implodes what was written before, making it illegitimate, so to speak (as Virgil wanted, when he asked Emperor Augustus to make his epic disappear). The controversial interpretations to which this gesture has

142 *Helena Buescu*

given rise can be seen as a rupture with that which had wanted to be the century of all ruptures, the 20th century. A kind of inaugural gesture of another historical moment: a new century that is also a new millennium.

Another (albeit parallel) idea of rupture in poetry is that of the group Manuel de Freitas joined early this century. His perception of the present as an experience, and of the aesthetic experience of the present, is associated with a recognized inability to build homogeneous groups, be they generations or artistic programmes. At the beginning of the 21st century, poetry seemed to favour the idea of intrinsic diversity, which is praised as such. This is Manuel de Freitas' line, who underscores the fact that there is no positive definition that can characterize what has been called the 'new Portuguese poetry'. His movement towards a distinction stems from the notion of *Poetas sem Qualidades* (Poets without Qualities), the title of the anthology of contemporary poetry he prefaced in 2002. What Freitas proposes is the idea that it is above all what 'the poets are not' that can paradoxically bring them together in a kind of disjointed whole that he calls 'homelessness'. This ultimately comes from investing in the Musilian notion of a 'man without qualities'. The poets thus linked seem to shift the notion of a break with the past to the relationship with their own present.

We can, however, find another path in the minimal poetry of the private and the everyday produced by poets such as Pedro Mexia. In the 'minimal' pictures or episodes of life, there is a sometimes surprising, albeit thinly woven, spirituality. Luís Quintais, João Luís Barreto Guimarães and José Tolentino de Mendonça, the latter following on from Daniel Faria, are, like Mexia, poets who can find wonder and, potentially, joy or tragedy in the slightest appearance of the world. In them, noting everyday simplicity brings out the plasticity of life that is common to us all. It could be said that they summon up, albeit in a different way, experiences harking back to metaphysical poetry (especially baroque).

Thus, in Quintais, poetry intersects with anthropology, veiled in melancholy, and develops around an *Angst* (the title of one of his works). Even when it claims to be anti-metaphysical, it is still metaphysical: noting the decomposition of the world, its little undoings, as the concrete and metaphysical Baroque poets did. On the other hand, the tension through which the poet rediscovers poetry as something belonging to the family of epiphany. José Tolentino de Mendonça, for example, further underlines the search for the poetic as the unexpected manifestation of the sublime and even the transcendent in the smallest elements of the world. His poetics is a poetics of faith and of the human, which also, like Daniel Faria's, brings the freedom of thought and the poetry of prayer to the narrowness of the smallest things. Regardless of the genre chosen, however, it is the lyrical voice of dense beauty and sensitivity to the things of the world that we find in him (*O Pequeno Caminho das Grandes Perguntas*, 2017, or *Uma Beleza que nos Pertence*, 2019). Here, the metaphysical question arises in the immanence of the world itself, in a poetic experience similar to that of Tatiana Faia (*Lugano*, 2011, *Um Quarto em Atenas*, A Room in Athens, 2018) and Manuel António Pina, who in 2012, the year of his death, saw the appearance of *Todas as palavras: Poesia reunida*. Pina adds another experience, however, to the experience of the materiality of things: returning home (to childhood) made impossible and, therefore, the awareness of death, which is at the origin of the melancholic and philosophical thought in his poetry.

In other authors, this minor tone appears in a completely different manner. There is, for example, the recognition of the emotional value of everyday life in Ana Luisa Amaral's poetry, but also, and inversely, in the merciless and cynical gaze with which Adília Lopes de-poeticizes reality through, for instance, the parodic representation of eroticism and the kitsch disintegration of everyday life. In Ana Luísa Amaral, it is no longer a question of the momentary epiphany of reality, nor of the sublime nature of the experience, but of an experience of the dissonant (*Ara* (Altar), 2013), or even of a recovery of poetry as an art talking to other arts (*Ágora* (Agora), 2019). In this last title, we find a dialogue between poetry and the arts; but also one between poetry and the traditions underpinning European culture; and, finally, another between a perfect History and a revisited (and, not least, 'rectified') History. It's no coincidence that this writer's last book (*Mundo* (World), 2021) is dedicated to retaining and observing simple objects, small animals, things that populate and fill life.

We can relate this set of issues to the 21st-century consolidation of the female literary voice, with its powerful emotional and historical tensions finding its epitome in Maria Velho da Costa's narrative and dramaturgy. However, and also in line with what was said above about Ana Luísa Amaral, we can't forget all of Hélia Correia's work, always working in a tensional way with various literary genres and bringing into her narratives a history made up of confrontations between times, places and characters (*Lillias Fraser*, 2001). Her work spans drama, narrative and poetry (the powerful lyrics of *Acidentes*, Accidents, 2022), in an experience of alterization fully affirmed in the 21st century. Something similar has happened in Teolinda Gersão's long fictional oeuvre, which has broken away from previously used models to subtly engage in a dialogue between personality and history: *O Regresso de Júlia Mann a Paraty* (Júlia Mann's Return to Paraty) (2021) is a magnificent example of the intersection between biography, fiction, historical notes and displaced intrigue, both in time and space. An untimely story, then, which starts with the figure of Thomas Mann and his 'peer', Freud, moving on to reflect on contemporary links between Germany and Brazil.

Another powerful female voice is that of Dulce Maria Cardoso: we have already talked about *O Retorno* (2011). In 2019, her novel *Eliete – A Vida Normal* (Eliete – Normal Life) develops a fictional poetics in which it is 'normality' that takes the narrative stage, in a kind of almost desolate realization of how much the 'underside' of events subsumes, in the historical framework of the present, much of what can be told. The voice of the great writer Ana Teresa Pereira is not very different in this respect. Her impressive fictional output (more than 30 titles published this century) combines various narrative genres, with particular emphasis on crime fiction, which, in the recent *Atelier da Noite* (Night Studio) (2020), serves as an acute reflection on the status of literature itself. The almost Gothic mysteries on which her work is based are, at heart, mysteries about language and its difficult, if not impossible, relationship with reality. They are mysteries that appear in the guise of detective stories so that the reader is also faced with mystery and the need to interpret (reality, language, life, after all). *A Dança dos Fantasmas* (The Dance of the Ghosts) (2001) is an extraordinary example of this, underlining another dimension of Ana Teresa Pereira's narrative to be highlighted here, because it is one of the traits of Portuguese literary production in recent decades: its cosmopolitanism.

In fact, one of the most interesting directions of recent Portuguese fiction reflects the idea of a historical untimeliness leading to the confrontation of the literary and the historical with 'alternatives' of themselves, often unforeseen. These alternatives seem to be oriented in three main directions. Firstly, there is the concept of literary circulation, which should be taken, on the one hand, in the sense of translation into other languages (and other markets) that, until recently, were not very open to Portuguese literary production and, on the other, in the circulation of themes whose non-identification as 'Portuguese' becomes especially fruitful. Then comes the concept of anachronism, which shapes the

144 *Helena Buescu*

project of 21st-century multiple fictional productions, even in the sudden entry of themes historically 'out of their time' in previously published authors (Rui Nunes), or in authors who have just started publishing in this century (such as Tavares and Gardeazabal). Thirdly, there is the relational concept that runs through the very idea of Portuguese literature as national literature, namely through the awareness that it shares with other literatures, on different continents: a language with different 'worlds' and yet using the same code – Portuguese – in one of its versions.

In the cases already mentioned, literary circulation and the question of translation or reappropriation/rewriting of themes and plots are particularly important. In this regard, we could mention the dramaturgical experience of an author like José Maria Vieira Mendes, built around the concept of the literary as circulation and even, as he says, 'theft' – a concept that Manuel Gusmão also uses in a note on his poetry. In *Dois Homens* (Two Men) (1998), *Aos Peixes* (To the Fish) (2008) and *Ana* (2009), Vieira Mendes shows a path that, although it follows the idea of writing, publication and even volume, does not rule out its contrary emergence as a performance text (a performative text, therefore).

The concept of literary circulation, similar to that discussed regarding Ana Teresa Pereira and Hélia Correia, characterizes 21st-century literary production as something that is being liberated, little by little, from the encapsulation that it seemed to have previously had. In this respect, Djaimilia Pereira de Almeida's *Esse Cabelo* (That Hair) (2015) is particularly interesting, in which a form of autofiction centres on an identity that is, among other things, racist and of colour. This is again the case with *Maremoto* (Tsunami) (2021), by the same author, which crosses generations and races in a contemporary Lisbon, just as Maria Velho da Costa had done.

Another, different case of literary circulation, although it doesn't serve here in reflecting on other Portuguese-language literatures, justifies considering the concept of literary circulation in the paradoxical case of Macau and the production that, in Portuguese, continues to be linked to that region. From this point of view, Macau has a special significance, since it was never, in a political sense, a colonial territory, but a Chinese territory under Portuguese administration for centuries. This does not exempt it from being the target of culturally expressed post-imperial melancholy (which came from the beginning of the 20th century and the great poet, Camilo Pessanha). Certainly, a poet like António Manuel Couto Viana, with his work on Macau, which began in the 20th century and continued into the 21st (*O Velho do Novo* (The Old of the New), 2003), expresses this attitude of attachment and simultaneous detachment from a cultural and symbolic place that seems to exert an even spiritual attraction on several Portuguese poets. The poet and translator António da Graça de Abreu also stands out in relation to Macau and the oriental alteration it evidently produces. In this century, he has continued to publish his own poetry and translations, with a lyrical approach to Chinese poetry. Of particular interest here is the example of writers who continue to write (mainly poetry) in Portuguese, such as Fernanda Dias. Macau, in China, is one of the interesting examples of how Portuguese literature can no longer be considered exclusively Eurocentric.

Various different forms of literary circulation seem to have produced a sense of liberation (and even rupture) from previous traditions in recent decades. Curiously, this has manifested itself around more visible breaks with the various modernist movements, favouring traditions that predate the 20th century (a clear issue in much of the poetry and narrative, as well as dramaturgy, which we have been mentioning). The effect of literary circulation is thus that of a search for historical times and literary traditions that seemed to have been overtaken (such as the poetry of spirituality, for example, the metaphysical dimension, or the epic). The essential thing to remember, however, is that nothing in literature is ever truly closed or complete: what seemed finished can happen again as new (and simultaneously different, of course). It is this quality that I think it is essential to recognize in 21st-century literary production in Portugal.

This is the case, for example, with the return of a certain historical or historicizing novel, whose relationship with biography has been very successful, and with an impressive readership, since the last quarter of the 20th century and in the first two decades of the 21st. However, the works published and the authors who write them are very diverse in quality, ranging from anachronistic kitsch that only has a historical appearance, and which therefore does not deserve a mention; to a group of very fine authors, but with very different approaches to the genre. In this last group, perhaps the most individual is Mário Cláudio, whose works always centre on a historical character (who may even be fictional) from whom historical times of impeccable characterization unfold; not only with great aesthetic and historical rigour, but also with surprising narrative gravitas. A case in point is the fictionalized autobiography (through the quasi-heteronymic figure of Tiago Veiga, recently revisited in *Embora eu seja um velho errante* (Though I'm an Old Wanderer), 2021), as well as the continuation of his Romanesque historical and sometimes ironically counterfactual reflections (*Os Naufrágios de Camões* (Camões' Shipwrecks) 2016 and *Camilo Broca*, 2006). In a less ironic way, but with a picaresque twist, Paulo Moreiras (*Os Dias de Saturno*, The Days of Saturn, 2002; *O Ouro dos corcundas*, The Gold of the hunchback, 2011) revisits historical novels and short fiction, mainly in its popular and rural roots in a world past.

Mário de Carvalho is another author with a particular profile in Portuguese narrative. In his case, it is for the parodic, historical and even sarcastic way in which he looks at the Portuguese past and present. As there is no strong (or continuous) satirical tradition in Portuguese literature, Carvalho revisits the now distant surrealism in order to imbue his narratives with a simultaneously realistic and unrealistic character. The fusion of these two environments gives his narratives an unexpected and somewhat dislocated tone, in which it becomes impossible not to see the absurd as the driving force behind the story.

Different instances of historical inadequacy and greater breadth, already mentioned in relation to Ana Teresa Pereira and Hélia Correia, are also explored by a less continuously published but equally unique fiction writer, Paulo José Miranda. In his latest work, *Aaron Klein* (2020), we find an imaginary space that could curiously be thought of in terms of Claudio Magris' concept, *Mitteleuropa* – that central Europe of complex and troubled historical crossings. This leads the author to choose a Jew as his main character who, coming from Israel, returns to Lisbon, on a kind of small odyssey across the seas in the middle of lands by which Europe is defined (the Mediterranean and Dead Sea). Paulo José Miranda's previous work was already characterized by an awareness of nonconformity, manifested both in his production in different genres and in the way in which there seems to be a light that, coming from other authors, illuminates his own production – hence his relationship with biographical writing. Manoel de Oliveira, the great 20th-century filmmaker (Miranda's biography of him being, *A Morte Não É Prioritária* (Death is Not a Priority)); Domingos Bomtempo, the romantic composer; Cesário Verde and Antero de Quental, two of the greatest names in 19th-century poetry, are historical characters who have given rise to fictions related to literary biography, the last three of which are brought together in the work, published in 2019, *Um Prego no Coração. Natureza Morta. Vício* (A Nail in the Heart. Still Life. Addiction).

146 *Helena Buescu*

Rui Nunes is another writer who, having begun his career in the last two decades of the 20th century, continues to publish fiction regularly. Starting with *O Choro é um Lugar Incerto* (Crying Is an Uncertain Place) (2005), he re-encounters the ghosts of Europe's Nazi past and fictionalizes them. In a recent interview, Rui Nunes reflected in particular on the apparent strangeness of the fact that, not being Jewish, never having lived in Germany, and having been separated from this historical memory by a significant lapse of time, he realized that this theme should have a special place in the contemporary narrative, which opens up to a set of themes and stories that had only touched it laterally until then (*Os Olhos de Himmler* (Himmler's Eyes), 2009). Some of the authors with whom Rui Nunes has close affinities also deal with this issue, and underline the transversal importance of figures such as Tolstoy or Kafka (*Nocturno Europeu* (European Night), 2014). Similar types of cosmopolitanism, highlighting the inadequacies of contemporary society, also run through the works of other authors, such as Alexandre Andrade and his dominant relationship with history (*O Leão de Belfort* (The Lion of Belfort), 2016; *As Não-Metamorfoses* (The Non-Metamorphoses), 2004). Or there is the unprecedented appearance of a novel in which the setting and the whole atmosphere are centred on a region of the Alentejo linked to the proximity of the Spanish Civil War, in *O Gesto que Fazemos para Proteger a Cabeça* (The Gesture We Make to Protect Our Head) (2020), by Ana Margarida de Carvalho. This author had already set *Não se Pode Morar nos Olhos de Um Gato* (You Can't Live in the Eyes of a Cat) (2016) on a dystopian Brazilian beach, from which no one can leave, a harsh reflection on the borders that surround us. The novel was based on the shipwreck, at the end of the 19th century, of a clandestine slave ship and the few characters who are rescued from this shipwreck, only to be imprisoned on the beach where they land.

In recent Portuguese literature, therefore, there has been a form of liberation produced and amplified by the effects of dissonance and disparity. Human events can be perceived as untimely for the simple reason that one of the forms that historicity takes is, as in the cases mentioned above, anachronism. In this respect, the work of Gonçalo M. Tavares, which began in 2001, is such an expanding world that it is almost impossible to take into account everything he publishes in its various forms (although he favours narrative fiction). The voracity of this writing, always haunted by the idea of evil, represents the essence of what can be considered a between-text, such is the laborious dependence of each title on the overall body of Tavares' work. To date, he has published more than 30 titles, predominantly (but not exclusively) narrative fiction, and is most probably the Portuguese author today who, having emerged in the 21st century, has achieved the greatest international recognition.

His writing is defined by an intertextuality and culture that looks to the centre of Europe (and *Mitteleuropa* once again) as a place where Portuguese literature undoubtedly seeks and finds roots in the cosmopolitan 'outside of itself'. Gonçalo M. Tavares' work is the epitome of the cosmopolitanism that seems to be one of the most important characteristics of Portuguese literature today. Not that the question of 'what is Portugal' or the post-colonial and post-imperial melancholy have disappeared. But because, with the authors we have been mentioning, and in particular Gonçalo M. Tavares, it is unexpectedly with an 'other' Europe and its alternative history that Portuguese literature confronts itself. Curiously, this is done (as with the authors already mentioned, and José Gardeazabal), in my opinion, almost as a response to the old myth and accusation of Eurocentrism – a myth because, in reality, supposed Eurocentrism is only European. Thus, Gonçalo M. Tavares' gaze is the gaze of anachronism in Portuguese literature and of the greatest European dislocation, questioning within what can be national everything that precisely isn't.

Two of Tavares' greatest novels, *Jerusalém* (2005) and *Aprender a Rezar na Era da Técnica* (Learning to Pray in the Age of Technology) (2007), which belong to the *O Reino* (The Kingdom) series, but also others, such as *Uma Menina está perdida no seu Século à Procura do Pai* (A Girl is Lost in Her Century Looking for Her Father) (2014), or the counter-epic *Viagem à Índia* (Journey to India) (2010), show an imaginary space that is out of place in relation to what is apparently 'Portuguese'. In the counter-epic, because it's a question of taking it to its ultimate parodic and self-deprecating levels, at the same time as decaling the formal (and allusively thematic) structure of the Camonian epic *Os Lusíadas*, read through James Joyce's novel *Ulysses*. In the other novels mentioned, we find an abstract space-time (and therefore of an allegorical nature), in which actions take place whose non-sense contributes to, in the end, a single sense: that of the pre-eminence of evil. From a certain point of view, Gonçalo M. Tavares' work can be read as a parallel and a counterpoint to the poetry of metaphysical spirituality that we mentioned above. In a world closed in on its tragedy, evil unfolds its intrigues without any of them even being able to invent an 'other' being. This 'outside of itself' in Portuguese literature, which Gonçalo M. Tavares' narrative displays, finds its highest point in what is basically the direct image of the Holocaust: an 'absence of God' that is, after all, more than the 'death of God'. The cruelty of the eugenic experiments in *Aprender a Rezar na Era da Técnica* doesn't even manage to find a response that matches this idea of evil-for-itself. The last work in the *O Reino* series, *O Osso do Meio* (The Middle Bone) (2020), is extraordinarily clear in this respect: evil, through the solitude of four characters, in an undefined space and time, which can therefore always be the one we read about.

In other series by Tavares, particularly in *O Bairro* (The Neighborhood), with its ten inhabitants and their respective volumes (*O Senhor Valéry* (Mr. Valéry), or *O Senhor Kraus* (Mr. Kraus), for example), we revisit the history, literary and otherwise, of a group of ten authors whose intertextual dialogue with Tavares' work once again densifies through anachronisms. These are impossible 'neighbourhoods', presented to us as challenges to interpretation. The rest of Tavares' work, however, which includes short essays in the style of Montaigne, short stories and scattered works, takes up this set of thematic anxieties and questions the limiting side of what it is to be human after all. In our 'technological' age (Walter Benjamin) and what we have come to recognize as 'AI' (Artificial Intelligence), the threats to the humanity of the human interweave Tavares' fiction into an interrogation from which nationalism seems to have effectively disappeared. This is a cosmos – apparently on its way to becoming chaos.

A curiously similar case is the work of José Gardeazabal: a minimal poet in the work that launched him in 2015, *História do Século XX* (History of the 20th Century); a novelist in *Meio Homem Meio Baleia* (Half Man Half Whale), 2018; *A Melhor Máquina Viva* (The Best Living Machine), 2020, announcing *A Trilogia dos Pares* (The Pairs Trilogy); and a playwright in the *Trilogia do Olhar* (The Gaze Trilogy), a set of 3 dramatic texts published in 2017. There are some differences, however. To begin with, Gardeazabal is governed by a narrative form in fragmented dissolution, from which it is difficult to reconstitute a cohesive interpretative universe. But there are also some similarities between Gardeazabal and Tavares, starting with the allegorical dimension of the fiction. In *Meio Homem Meio Baleia*, we find a journey with an unattainable goal, made along a wall that can be touched, and featuring three characters: the father, his pre-adolescent daughter and the driver. In a world divided by a wall, the journey is to serve

148   *Helena Buescu*

the humanitarian purpose of bringing water to the most vulnerable. But is that really the case? Where are the vulnerable? How do we get beyond the wall? How do you 'give water to the thirsty'? How do you perform 'a miracle of fish without fish'? Parables of discomfort? Moral parables? Political parables?

Philosophical parables, in any case, in which the contemporary world is activated by social and personal inequalities. As in Tavares, the action is abstractly located in a 'Europe' that keeps changing centre, 'back and forth'. And it is in this 'Europe', in which Portugal is integrated (not just geographically), that we read a fiction that, being Portuguese, is more than national. This is a 'lamentation of Western civilization'. With a 'Germany' inside and many other nationalities. Another novel by Gardeazabal, *A Melhor Máquina Viva* (The Best Machine Alive) (2019), is perhaps even harsher. Here, it is capitalist society (i.e. world society) that is directly questioned, through a narrative in which a writer decides to experience extreme poverty for a year in order to write about it. It's not just about material and financial poverty, but rather about all the poverty that affects vulnerable subjects, and in which the world is organized around theft, fatigue, hunger: 'wearing the anonymity of the naked'. 'After all, what is a cosmopolis?' asks one of the characters. There seems to be no way out of it. These are questions that continue in his most recent titles, *Quarentena. Uma história de amor* (Quarantine. A love story) (2021) and *Quarenta e três* (Forty-three) (2022).

Another author where the fragmentary dimension and the conception of the literary as a continuous progression have a major role is Afonso Cruz. His extensive oeuvre includes the *Enciclopédia da Estória Universal* (Encyclopedia of Universal History), whose four volumes (to date) began being published in 2012, and which correspond to a kind of syncretic combination of aphorisms, short stories, very brief essays and prose poems: a mixture of genres integrating the work into a universe of peculiar dispersion. But Cruz's other fictions also offer an idea of fiction that responds to the cosmopolitanism already mentioned here as an orientation to be retained in the current panorama of Portuguese literature. The motto given, in *Enciclopédia...*, by the Library of Alexandria, is significant in this respect. However, we can refer to a series of novels anchored in a journey (to Cambodia), *Princípio de Karenina* (Karenina Principle) (2020); or in a place (Berlin) *Sinopse de amor e guerra* (Synopsis of Love and War) (2021), surprisingly written and published in a period when closure and distance would seem to be the most inviting principles.

Gardeazabal and Tavares in particular take up another anachronistic procedure and make it more complex. As we have seen, Gonçalo M. Tavares organizes his published work into 'sets', which he even gives titles to. He thus recognizes a unity in them that it is up to the reader to read and interpret. We have several series, *O Reino* (now with five novels); the ten titles of *O Bairro* (published by Gallimard in 2021 in a single volume, *Le Quartier, Les Messieurs*); the series entitled *Livros Pretos* (Black Books); the *Colecção Breves Notas* (Brief Notes Collection), to which are added, among others, the *Diversos* (Miscellaneous) (in itself, another possible 'set'). In Gardeazabal, we have 'trilogies', which, although they don't have the same systematic weight as Tavares', do have a similar procedure, above all emphasizing their 'out of time' character, clearly anachronistic and therefore deeply historical.

Several authors, such as Rui Nunes, Afonso Cruz, José Gardeazabal and Gonçalo M. Tavares, have, in the 21st century, taken up the idea of literature as a long project, with different stages. They have thus returned to the tradition, almost erased in the 20th century in Portugal, of a literary process that aims at continuity and a common idea, towards which each individual work converges. It's not a question of serialization, much less the *roman fleuve* like Proust, or Balzac's *Comédie Humaine*: there is no sustained construction of a novelistic continuity that could give the world described any consolidation. Rather, it is a conception of the literary that starts from the idea of the whole as a fundamental structure for literary writing. We can talk, therefore, about what for decades was almost anachronistically referred to as a work, a concept that was replaced throughout the 20th century by that of a text, with different connotations. There is a dialogue here and a hesitation between totality and diversity.

9.3 The current situation

Self-reflexivity was a permanent condition of 21st-century literature in its first two decades. What is literature? Does it have any purpose inside or outside itself? There are those who respond with the apparently derisory value of the literary in a world that is destroying itself, this being one of the 'future challenges'. Luís Quintais is one of these authors. Lobo Antunes is another because nothing in his work offers the possibility of hope. We could also talk, albeit from another point of view, about the poet Barreto Guimarães, as well as some Adília Lopes, in the kitsch disintegration she makes of the contemporary. In poets such as Pedro Eiras (the Dantean trilogy of *Inferno*, *Purgatorio*, and *Paraíso*, published between 2020 and 2022) and João Moita *Miasmas*, 2010; *Fome*, Hunger, 2015), who have been publishing poetry in the last decade, on the other hand, a dystopic world becomes the focal point of lyrical discourse. Is there a future? A Dantean one, in which language interrogates the limits of the representation of the natural world. Rui Lage, with a literary universe spanning from poetry (*Estrada nacional*, National route, 2017) to fiction (*O Invisível*, The Invisible, 2020) to essay, prolongs in his recent title (*O Firmamento*, The Heavens, 2022) an elegiac reflection on the misencounters between the poet and all the elements of the natural world, and Jorge Reis-Sá continues this set of questioning, both in his poetry as in his book of acclaimed short fiction, *A Hipótese de Gaia*, The Gaia Hypothesis, 2022. On what seems to be a tendency that we may connect with natural anxieties typical of our age, the name of Luísa Costa Gomes (*Afastar-se*, Getting away, 2022) must also be mentioned, with her 13 surprising short fictions centred on water, in its material and symbolic diversity. Nature and art come together in all of these reflections.

Nonetheless, this self-reflexivity also brings the possibility of confirming its potential as art in its inter-artistic relations (from a previous tradition) and, primarily, in the aforementioned awareness of literary traditions. This is clear in the works of, for example, Julieta Monginho, Ana Luísa Amaral, Tatiana Faia, Manuel António Pina, Jorge Reis-Sá, Castro Mendes, Maria do Rosário Pedreira or Manuel de Freitas, who reincorporate poets, works, traditions and confront poetry with other arts. Alexandre Andrade, in the minimal short stories he publishes in *Todos Nós Temos Medo do Vermelho, Amarelo e Azul* (We're All Afraid of Red, Yellow and Blue) (2019) does the same thing; as cinema has also done in recent decades, attracting multiple relationships (with writers such as Manuel Gusmão, Manuel de Freitas and Pedro Mexia. Gonçalo M. Tavares, moreover, has also dedicated a paradoxical reflection on Jacques Tati).

Karen (2016), the book for which Ana Teresa Pereira won the biggest literary prize in Portuguese, accentuates this dimension, through the way in which film noir, the various traditions of the Gothic and the inspiration that clearly goes beyond the 'national' give special prominence to a fiction that is in every way mysterious. Something similar

150   *Helena Buescu*

happens in Djaimilia Pereira de Almeida's work, who chooses the visual dimension (in this case, photography) to focus on literature as art, for example in *Pintado com o Pé* (Painted by Foot) (2019). This rapprochement between the literary and the visual is not only due to the common narrative path that partially unites them. It is also, and perhaps above all, due to symbolizing what is increasingly appearing, and on a global scale, as the set of mysteries of the world, which seems unstoppable for humans but transformable by the various kinds of art.

This same self-reflexive theme is carried over into the intertextual dimension. In Gonçalo M. Tavares, for example, who 'cannibalizes', as the Brazilian modernist Oswald d'Andrade has put it, everything that touches him as a writer: other authors, such as Camões, Valéry, Swedenborg, Brecht; the whole complex tradition of the *Mitteleuropa* novel; and even the constant revisiting of history, from the Holocaust and its allegorical avatars, to the Spanish Civil War or the slave trade.

9.4 Future challenges

One of the central issues when considering the idea of 'future' in literature is this: recognizing the emergence of the concept of untimeliness. What happens when what occurs seems to appear 'out of time' is, in my opinion, central as a form and self-reflexive manifestation of the literary – not only in terms of the material circulation of works once they are published, but also the circulation of the thematic and formal material that makes them up. Within the modes of literary circulation, there are those that emphasize such mismatches, thus revealing the temporal and historical gaps that literature is also made of. In fact, this inactual character appears as an illustration of a specific mode of literary circulation and, more broadly, of cultural circulation. It is, therefore, a specifically literary proposal and an instance of self-reflexivity.

We thus have a reflection on identity that passes through cosmopolitanism, for example in Tavares, Rui Nunes or Gardeazabal; in Djaimilia Pereira de Almeida, through the intrinsic violence of human confrontations; in Tolentino de Mendonça, Daniel Faria, Tatiana Faia or Manuel António Pina, through a contemplative and metaphysical poetry revisited by the present; or in Hélia Correia, whose historical imagination doesn't hide the shock that ancient tragedies have on the present. All of this leaves some central questions as future challenges: how can lyrical and even tragic material continue to be relevant in a world that seems to have left any kind of weight behind? Will inter-artistic work see an even greater manifestation in the self-figuration and reflection of the literary? What are the ways in which our present rediscovers its pasts (which ones?) and retells them? These are unanswerable questions, of course. But they are the ones that seem to be most thoughtful when it comes to looking at the literature that is being produced today and that is heading towards the future.

References

Lotman, Jurij Michajlovic, and Boris Andreevic Uspenskij. 1975. *Semiotica e Cultura*. Milan-Naples: Riccardo Ricciardi Editore.
Paul, Gilroy. 2005. *Postcolonial melancholia*. New York: Columbia UP.

10 Portugal in the European Union

Isabel Camisão and Sandra Fernandes

10.1 Introduction

As European integration deepened, the attention of European scholars gradually focused on Member States (MS[1]) and their adaptation to the process of integration (Ladrech 2010). Such a strand of research – labelled Europeanization – was at first essentially concerned with the impact of EU integration on domestic political systems (Graziano and Vink 2012). Claudio M. Radaelli's most cited definition of Europeanization captures well the initial focus of the analyses:

> processes of (a) construction (b) diffusion and (c) institutionalization of formal and informal rules, procedures, policy paradigms, styles, 'ways of doing things' and shared beliefs and norms which are first defined and consolidated in the making of EU decisions and then incorporated in the logic of domestic discourse, identities, political structures and public policies.
>
> (Radaelli 2001, 108)

The underlying assumption, thus, is that EU membership prompted a process of domestic adaptation of national institutions, policies, and politics. This dimension is commonly labelled as top-down Europeanization.

However, as studies on Europeanization evolved, it became clear that this is a multi- (rather than uni-) directional process. Indeed, since EU MS and EU citizens are represented at EU institutions at the supranational level and domestic organized interests found formal and informal venues to influence EU policy-making, it is fair to argue that Europeanization includes also a bottom-up dimension. Even though larger, wealthier states are normally perceived as being more influential in international affairs, the EU Multilevel Governance System, characterized by the dispersal of authority and continuous negotiation among nested governments at the supranational, national, regional, and local levels (Hooghe and Marks 2003), grants all MS opportunities to exert influence, regardless of their dimension and wealth.

Bottom-up Europeanization, therefore, "analyses the domestic level before the EU pressure begins and then follows participation of the country in negotiations at the EU level, ending with the process of implementing EU regulation" (Bandov and Kolman 2018, 138). Actually, both processes (top-down and bottom-up) are often simultaneous, as EU policies and rules are being adopted and implemented and domestic actors are participating in EU governance (Bandov and Kolman 2018), which in turn shapes domestic politics and policies.

DOI: 10.4324/9781003488033-10

This chapter has been made available under a CC-BY-NC-ND license.

152 *Isabel Camisão and Sandra Fernandes*

In this chapter we aim to show that, despite being labelled a small state, Portugal has not only been transformed by the EU, but has also helped to shape the EU, leaving a recognizable Portuguese imprint in important policy areas. By doing this, it is not our intention to claim that Portugal's record in EU's negotiations has always been a story of success. Actually, throughout almost 40 years of membership, there were some "dark periods" that put Portugal's resilience to the test, as was the case of the Eurozone crisis.

The chapter is organized as follows. The next section highlights some important works that studied the process of Portugal's Europeanization. Section 9.2 highlights two issues that gained salience at the EU level during the Portuguese presidencies – the relationship with Africa and the Lisbon Strategy. Section 9.3 explores the role of Portugal in the design of the Integrated Maritime Policy (IMP). Section 9.4 looks at the country's leadership position in setting and implementing environmental targets. The chapter concludes with a tentative inventory of the areas where Portugal can make a difference in the future.

10.2 Portugal's Europeanization: evidences from the literature

There is already a bulk of literature focusing on the changes that have occurred in Portugal during the course of accession to the EU and as a result of its MS status (e.g., Magone 2002; 2004; 2006; Goucha Soares 2009; 2010; Teixeira and Pinto 2012).[2] Indeed, the Portuguese case clearly highlights Europeanization effects, both in terms of institutions, citizens' attitudes, and policy. One consensual conclusion is that EU membership was key for the consolidation of the democratic regime (Vink 2012, 253; Magone 2006). The same is true for other MS (Greece and Spain in the South, but also Central and Eastern Europe countries) that were in the process of democratic consolidation at the time of accession. The need to meet EU's accession conditions (the so-called Copenhagen criteria) paired with the effects of participating in EU's system and having to implement EU's legislation favours a significant relation between accession and democratic consolidation (Pridham 2006). However, this is not an irreversible path, as democratic drifts in Poland and Hungary demonstrate.

Beyond institutional adjustment (affecting not only national executives, but also the parliament, the courts, and interest groups), Portugal also experienced variations in political behaviour and attitudes towards the EU. Ranging from a clear increase in the perception of the benefits of, and in support for, EU membership (from the accession date to the early 1990s) to a slight decrease of both, "without, however, affecting the generalized consensus concerning integration" (Magalhães 2012, 240).

As support for the EU has a non-neglectable utilitarian dimension, arguably some of these variations can be explained by fundamental transformations that have occurred in all domestic policies and in politics as a result of EU membership. The Eurozone crisis was a telling example. As expected, during the peak of the crisis, there was a sharp decrease of public opinion support for the EU.[3] Interestingly enough, however, the crisis did not significantly alter political elite attitudes towards the EU (Magalhães, Cancela, and Moury 2016).

One area that has been impacted by membership was the domestic political discourse. As Jalali (2012) noted, it is clear that EU economic and social development benchmarks often became the domestic benchmarks. This is clearly visible in the determination to meet altogether the economic and budgetary conditions (convergence criteria) of the Economic and Monetary Union, which allowed the country to be a frontrunner state joining the Euro.

Portugal's ability to follow EU's rules granted it the label of "European good student", used by some political parties in the opposition to criticize the Portuguese government for being more concerned with complying with EU's demands than with the potential negative spillovers that might result from this compliance for the Portuguese economy and society. If an important result of accession was the undeniable positive evolution of Portugal's economy, namely in terms of modernization, growth, and overall improvement of the citizens' living conditions, this has not been a linear evolution.Actually, some important asymmetries remain, with the robustness of the Portuguese economy sometimes falling short when compared with the economy of other MS (Magone 2006; Goucha Soares 2009; Amaral 2022; Crespo and Simões 2022).

The transformation affected also foreign policy preferences. Leaving behind the "isolationist-fatalist" attitude (Magone 2002, 225), Portugal has experienced a wide political consensus on foreign policy, strategically balancing the Atlanticist position with the European one (Teixeira 2012), and being an active supporter (not only with words but also with acts) of human rights, democracy, and solidarity (Magone 2006). At the same time, participation in the *fora* of the EU increased its visibility as an international actor, allowing the long-standing traditions and experience of its diplomacy to shine again (Magone 2006)

Conventional narrative, then, tends to demonstrate that despite the magnitude of the challenges ahead, a process of domestic adaptation driven by the EU's accession process and membership made Portugal a far more modern, developed, and democratic country. However, considering that Portugal is a MS for almost four decades, in our opinion, not enough attention was paid to the fact that Portugal also contributed to shaping EU decisions and policies, that in turn triggered domestic adaptation when implemented (bottom-up perspective). Our goal, as noted in the introduction, is to contribute to fill in this gap by mapping areas where Portugal had a notorious influence, particularly in terms of agenda-setting and policy formulation. The selection of the issues is not meant to be exhaustive but rather illustrative of different policy sectors influenced by Portugal and different political windows seized by Portuguese diplomacy and leadership.

Considering that over the last decade the EU has been living in a sort of "crisis mode" (adding to more "perennial" crises such as climate change, the EU was hit by a bank and sovereign debt crisis that escalated to a Eurozone crisis, a refugee crisis, Brexit, the COVID-19 pandemic, the war in Ukraine and the related energy crisis, just to state a few), processes of domestic adjustment were sometimes even harsher and abrupt. What is more, the time for debate and negotiation, which enhance participation and diversify venues of influence, is more limited in crisis times, as crisis response cannot be achieved through "business as usual". Therefore, crisis moments can alter the relation between the EU and its MS, either by making the union stronger or by deepening the divisions. Also, the literature on crises shows that periods of crisis are "critical junctures" (Capoccia and Kelemen 2007), during which it is possible to reform institutions and policies that are normally resistant to change. The EU has seized the opportunity to advance some policy areas, such as the twin green and digital transition (including energy policy). A more volatile and confrontational geopolitical environment has also triggered changes in EU's foreign policy as the EU is striving to offset power loss. We are therefore also interested in seeing if Portugal has been (or can be) an active player in shaping policy change in key domains in such turbulent times.

154 *Isabel Camisão and Sandra Fernandes*

10.3 The Presidency of the Council as a window of opportunity: the "return" to Africa and the Lisbon Strategy

The literature on the EU shows that rotating the Presidency of the Council grants the leading MS an opportunity to push forward pet proposals (Tallberg 2003). Portugal was responsible for driving forward the Council's work on four occasions (first semester of 1992, first semester of 2000, second semester of 2007, and first semester of 2021) and has become particularly skilful in using those periods for shaping the European agenda and policies. While the first Presidency was a learning moment, and an opportunity to demonstrate that the country was up to the MS status (Teixeira and Hermenegildo 2018), the second Portuguese Presidency demonstrated that Portugal had gained the skills and confidence necessary to exert leadership and to influence the process of European integration. Indeed, during the first Presidency (1992), Portugal adopted a more inward strategy and was cautiously finding its way as regards more political issues. In turn, the second presidency revealed a country with a clear idea of what was best for Europe as a whole, keen to defend its vision and with the ability "to mobilize its peers to build the future of the European Project" (Teixeira and Hermenegildo 2018, 79). The following two examples are illustrative of policy entrepreneurship[4]: EU-Africa relations and the Lisbon Strategy.

For historical, geographic, and geostrategic reasons, Portugal is a country particularly aware of the necessity to open Europe to the rest of the world (Silva 2021). Accordingly, bridging the poles of the so-called "strategic triangle", that includes Africa, along with Latin America and Europe, has been an important priority of Portugal's foreign policy at the EU level. The Portuguese goal of pushing forward a Euro-African agenda was (and still is) well known among the other European counterparts (Silva 2021). Actually, Africa, and particularly the Portuguese-speaking Africa, "was chosen, in the first stage of integration, as the main priority as far as foreign policy at European level was concerned"(Vasconcelos 2000, 30). This explains why following accession Portugal chose the development portfolio in the European Commission: "[t]he choice coincided perfectly with the almost exclusively African (95%) orientation of development cooperation" (Vasconcelos 2000, 30).The goal was materialized during the second rotating Presidency[5] (first semester of 2000), which was sought to define "Europe on the Brink of the 21st Century".[6]

Indeed, the "good student" (Cunha 2013) – as Portugal was initially coined, given its position as "excessively deferential toward Community institutions" (Macedo 2003, 170) – gave way to a confident MS that had well-defined priorities not only in the economic and social fields, but also as regards institutional and foreign policy matters. Amid the topics of the latter, the EU-Africa relation featured as the main priority of the Portuguese Presidency (along with the adoption of a Common Strategy for the Mediterranean and the launch of the EU–India Strategy) (Teixeira and Hermenegildo 2018). One crucial milestone would be the organization of the first summit between the two continents. Actually, Portuguese diplomacy had already been working on this goal in the years that preceded the Presidency (Gama 2000; Ferreira-Pereira 2008) which is telling of the shift towards a more proactive stance as regards promoting issues that "echoed the deep roots and identity of the country" (Teixeira and Hermenegildo 2018, 82).

It is also in line with what is expected from policy entrepreneurs that work "(...) well in advance of the time the window opens. Without that earlier consideration and softening up, they cannot take advantage of the window when it opens" (Kingdon 2003, 181). Holding the Presidency of the Council for the second time offered Portugal the

Portugal in the European Union 155

right window of opportunity to further push its pet proposal: "[i]n external matters, the Presidency was noteworthy for the way it reflected the historical and geographical position of Portugal" (Edwards and Wiessala 2001, 45). Portugal's diplomatic efforts paid off, and the first ever EU-Africa summit took place in Cairo (3 and 4 April 2000). The Summit marked the beginning of the formal partnership between the two continents (the EU-Africa Partnership), paving the way for a regular and comprehensive dialogue at the highest political level (ONGD 2021). By then, the negotiations for a new relationship framework between the EU and Africa, Caribbean and Pacific countries were also concluded, leading to the adoption of the Cotonou Agreement.

Portugal's commitment to the EU-Africa agenda did not end with the 2000 Presidency. Actually, it stood up as a top priority of the next two presidencies (2007 and 2021). The third Presidency of the Council, with the motto "A stronger Union for a better world", had three key axes: the reform of the Treaties, the modernization of economies and societies and strengthening of Europe's role in the world (Sócrates 2007). When equating the relations between Africa and the EU, the programme highlighted the ambition to develop a Joint Strategy and to organize the second EU-Africa Summit:

> I would like to draw attention to our presidency's biggest initiative: Portugal proposes to convene the second EU-Africa summit in December. Europe has not had a structured institutional dialogue with Africa for seven years – an incomprehensible failing in European foreign policy. If there is one country that must take a stand against this and do everything to overcome this situation, it is Portugal.
>
> (Sócrates 2007)

Despite "difficult negotiations",[7] the second EU-Africa summit (ONGD 2021, 72), successfully achieved both goals,[8] confirming Portugal's ability to inscribe its pet priorities in the European agenda: "In this context, it [Portugal] proved not only its organizational but also its negotiation skills, and, at the same time, its capacity to project its national interests" (Teixeira and Hermenegildo 2018, 83).

Unsurprisingly, the relationship between the EU and Africa featured again among the priorities of the fourth Portuguese Presidency "(…) with both sides aware of the need to maintain a strategic dialogue to address global challenges (…)" (Portuguese Presidency of the Council 2021a, 11). Specifically, the Presidency took an active part in organizing the 6th EU-African Union Summit. Also, bridging the African agenda with other key priority of Portugal – the Green Europe: promoting the EU as a leader in climate action – the Presidency (along with the European Investment Bank) organized the High-level EU-Africa Green Investment Forum (23 April 2021). The initiative, which was preceded by the so-called Green Talks,[9] brought together representatives of governments and business, international financial and development institutions, civil society and academia, and was described as a "turning point" and an opportunity to turn "the green agenda into a structuring pillar for relations" between the two continents (André cited in 2021. Portugal.EU 2021).[10] The negotiations for the post-Cotonou Agreement were also concluded at the time (Portuguese Presidency of the Council 2021b). Once more, by making a purposeful use of the Presidency of the Council, Portugal was instrumental to maintain Africa into the European Agenda.

In the early 2000s, Portugal's actions were also decisive for setting EU's economic competitiveness benchmarks, striving for levels of competitiveness and employment comparable to the US performance of the 1990s. The "Lisbon Strategy" was adopted during

156 *Isabel Camisão and Sandra Fernandes*

the second Portuguese Presidency of the Council precisely with this purpose. Having the ambition of transforming Europe into "the most competitive and dynamic knowledge-based economy in the world, capable of sustainable economic growth with more and better jobs and greater social cohesion" (European Council 2000), the document was a pillar for economic, social, and later environmental goals.

For Portugal, the aim of the Strategy was aligned with its own European quest for modernization as a way to overcome its peripheral location. Trying to leave behind the image of a sheer net recipient of EU funds, especially considering the massive enlargement that would take place in 2004, the country adopted the posture of a responsible and actively engaged MS. In the 1990s, António Guterres' socialist government focused on social policies and poverty. In line with previous governments, at least since accession in 1986, the national strategy aimed at modernizing and developing the economy to close the gap between Portugal and the other MS.

These economic goals were, however, part of a broader ambition, namely to fully integrate the country and to end its isolation from the core Europe. Access to education and health and scientific and technological development were linked to the consolidation of democracy, all essential conditions for fully-fledged participation in EU dynamics. Starting as one of the lagging-behind states, Portugal fully met the convergence criteria in 1999 to join the euro. As a result, the country gained enhanced legitimacy to negotiate the Lisbon agenda.

The Secretary of State for European Affairs recalls that the Lisbon Strategy was the "big project" of the Presidency, prepared from 1999 to 2000, one that conveyed optimism in the future of the EU, in particular with regard to its external competitiveness (Seixas da Costa in Agência Lusa 2020). Once more, the negotiations behind the scenes confirmed the prestige of Portuguese diplomacy, in particular against the backdrop of a tense environment among MS caused by the first election of a far-right party in Austria.

The careful preparation of a political strategy designed to build consensus on the Lisbon Agenda is visible in the risk that Portugal took ahead of the 2000 Presidency. The *modus operandi* developed in 1999 was threefold. Firstly, the usual EU bureaucracy was circumvented by the direct involvement of MS to avoid signing a document that would have been prepared solely by the European Commission. Secondly, the document gained the support of Romani Prodi, at the time the President of the Commission, who considered the Strategy not only important but timely. Thirdly, an *ad-hoc* "international audit for the Portuguese Presidency" (Sousa 1999) allowed the involvement of experts on the key drivers of the Strategy, i.e., the new economy and the economy of knowledge.

The report and the MS's inputs served as the basis for the draft Strategy that Portugal sent to its counterparts early in the semester of its Presidency. At the time, Sousa noted that Portugal counted on "the prestige it enjoys among its peers in the Union and with the safety of preparatory work that seems not to have forgotten the smallest detail" (Sousa 1999). Later, the author recognizes that the approval of the Strategy, regardless of its achievements, allowed Portugal to convey a different image to the other MS and showcase a high level of performance (Sousa 2002).

This was a paramount task for a small MS that had recently entered a new economic cycle. Portugal aimed at including the topic of European unemployment structural problems within the broader discussion of the transformation of the economy into an innovation and knowledge-based economy. With more than 40,000 pages of documents, the country crafted a patient mobilization that "put the train in motion" and compelled the Commission to support the plan (Sousa 2002). Domestically, the Strategy was presented as a way of improving Portugal's GDP growth (therefore converging to the EU average). The institutional innovation associated with the approval of the Strategy was also indicative of Portugal's political activism and somehow anticipated the following reforms of the Treaties (Guterres 2001).

10.4 From fisheries to a whole ocean approach: a Portuguese-inspired Integrated Maritime Policy

The previous section showed that holding high-level positions at the EU level, such as the Presidency of the Council, enhanced Portugal's ability to influence EU's priorities. This section builds on the same argument by showing that holding the Presidency of the Commission was also instrumental to leave a Portuguese imprint in an important policy sector. One of the chief characteristics of the European Commission (henceforth Commission) is its independency, i.e., the members of the Commission "shall neither seek nor take instructions from any Government, or other institution, body, office or entity" (Article 17.º (3) TEU). That being said, the literature on the Commission suggests that its "presidentialisation" entails a central role for the President (i.e., political leadership), allowing him/her "to stamp [his/her] personal mark in the Commission's work" (Nugent and Rhinard 2019, 209).

The adoption of the Integrated Maritime Policy during the Barroso Commission's first mandate is illustrative of the argument introduced above. According to Kingdon (2003) getting people to recognize the existence of a problem is crucial for influencing the political agenda. The need to substitute the piecemeal approach to the oceans[11] for a truly integrated maritime policy was perceived by Barroso as a priority, thus becoming a mark of his Commission. And, Barroso's solution for the problem was clearly inspired by his experience, first as Minister of Foreign Affairs and then as Prime Minister of Portugal. Due to the high-level positions he held in the Portuguese government, Barroso had the opportunity to participate in the rekindling of Portugal's interest in the oceans, which in turn influenced its vision regarding the need for an EU coordinated approach to maritime affairs.

Barroso himself acknowledged the Portuguese "inspiration" of his Commission proposals regarding maritime affairs in the opening speech of a Dutch conference on the topic:

> As Foreign Minister of Portugal I campaigned for Lisbon as the site for EXPO 98, which was devoted to the theme of the oceans and the future. At that time Portugal hosted several important international conferences on oceans and seas affairs and was instrumental in establishing the UN's 1998 International Year of the Oceans. These experiences convinced me of the importance of both oceans governance and the role of oceans for the future of mankind.
>
> (Barroso 2005, 3)

And again in 2006:

> As a Portuguese, it is only natural that maritime issues are close to my heart. That is why the sustainable use and governance of our oceans has been, for a long time, a matter of considerable importance to me. I find it striking, therefore, that while the oceans are an essential element of life-support for our planet, even influencing

158 *Isabel Camisão and Sandra Fernandes*

our climate, they remain relatively unknown. Equally, their importance to our lives is often underestimated.

(Barroso 2006, 2)

Actually, the reference to the Portuguese inspiration appears often in the discourses of the Portuguese leaders: "In effect, our Country can take pride from having been one of the inspiring countries of the European Commission's initiative, through the work carried out by the Portuguese Ocean's Strategic Commission" (Cavaco Silva 2011).

Building on the above, we argue that Portugal's actions, first at the domestic level, and later at the supranational level, were instrumental for putting the maritime policy high into the EU's agenda, and eventually to prompt policy change at the EU level, particularly during the Barroso Commission. After some years of apparent limited attention to the topic of the oceans, in mid-90s, Portugal "stepped up its action on oceanic diplomacy" (Saliou 2008, 16). Among several initiatives that marked the country's "reconciliation" with the oceans two particular events are milestones worth to singularize.

The first was the World Exhibition that was held in Lisbon in 1998 under the theme "The Ocean, a heritage for the future", commonly known as EXPO 98. The second was the creation of a special committee – Strategic Ocean Committee (SOC) in 2003. SOC, which delineated the first National Strategy to the Sea in three decades,[12] was chaired by a well-known Portuguese specialist in maritime affairs, Tiago Pitta e Cunha,[13] whom during the Barroso Commission, joined the Cabinet of the newly appointed Commissioner for Fisheries and Maritime Affairs in Brussels, precisely to work on the IMP. In a speech in Lisbon during the Portuguese Presidency Ministerial Conference, Barroso noted the importance of Portugal's historical relation with the sea:

> Just two weeks ago, the Commission put forward an Integrated Maritime Policy for the EU. With this new policy, for the first time the EU has forged a genuine strategic approach to Europe's maritime affairs and coastal areas. This policy recognises the important but often forgotten maritime dimension of Europe. A dimension that has played a remarkable role in shaping our history, including the one of our host, Portugal.
>
> (Barroso 2007)

Thus, unsurprisingly, at the EU level, the path for an IMP accelerated during the mandate of the first Barroso Commission. It is true that the Barroso Commission was not the first one to acknowledge the need for policy change in the maritime domain. For example, negotiations over the Marine Strategy Framework Directive (MSFD), which is considered the environmental pillar of the IMP, began in 2002 during the Prodi Commission. Also, in the late 1990s, the question of maritime security was discussed at the EU level, leading to the creation of the European Maritime Safety Agency (EMSA) (2002),[14] a development triggered by serious maritime incidents such as Erika (1999) and Prestige (2002).[15] However, the Barroso Commission purposefully seized the opportunity opened by the growing international awareness regarding the importance of the oceans (and the forming consensus on the need to have a holistic approach to maritime issues) to propose a Portuguese-inspired all-embracing maritime policy.It is worth noting that Barroso's vision for maritime affairs not only influenced policy formulation but also triggered institutional changes. A new portfolio on Fisheries and Maritime Affairs was created, the

Commission's services were reorganized and new administrative and political structures were created, including a Task Force on Maritime Affairs.

The decision to propose an IMP was also in line with other Portugal-inspired policy decisions, namely the above-mentioned Lisbon Strategy negotiated during the Portuguese Presidency of the Council in 2000. Under the Strategy, the EU committed itself to become the most competitive knowledge-based economy in just ten years (European Council 2000). Considering that between 3% and 5% of Europe's Gross Domestic Product (GDP) was estimated to be generated by marine-based industries and services (without including the value of raw materials, such asoil, gas, or fish) and the maritime regions accounted for over 40% of GDP (European Commission 2006, 3), it became evident that the piecemeal approach to EU maritime governance (dispersed between different Commission's services, MS' structures and entities, and private stakeholders) needed to be substituted by a truly integrated maritime governance.

Portugal was relevant not only for agenda-setting but also for policy formulation and decision. Before issuing the proposal for an IMP, the Commission launched a wide consultation on a future maritime policy for the Union, involving a wide range of actors including third-country governments, business representatives, non-governmental organizations, companies, representatives of science and academia, and citizens. During the consultation period, Portugal (along with Spain and France) was particularly active in the process of influencing the shape of the EU maritime policy. The three MS even issued a joint contribution that endorsed the Commission's ideas and was praised by the Commission Task Force on Maritime Affairs (Saliou 2008, 24). The salience of the tripartite positioning paper, but also of the Portuguese diplomacy, was highlighted in a speech by the, at the time, President of the Portuguese Republic:

> Portugal has displayed a clear leadership since the very birth of the Integrated Maritime Policy, supporting the Commission in all the key issues of this policy's development. I recall and emphasize the tripartite positioning paper, containing a view for Europe and the sea, submitted by Portugal, Spain and France, as well as Portugal's diplomatic activity developed during our last presidency of the Union, which I believe decisively contributed for the swiftness with which the December 2007 Council of Europe approved the new maritime policy, presented by the Commission barely two months earlier.
>
> (Cavaco Silva 2011)

The Commission presented its proposal for an IMP, the so-called "Blue Book" package (based on the consultation report and on several working documents), on 10 October 2007, during the third Portuguese Presidency of the Council. Arguably, considering the salience of the oceans for Portugal and the country's renewed activism in maritime affairs since the 1990s, holding the Presidency of the Council offered the right momentum to advocate for an EU maritime policy "[t]he maritime domain calls for an integrated approach. We will work towards the definition of a European Maritime policy to be based on the Action Plan to be presented by the Commission" (Portuguese Presidency of the Council 2007, 5).

Indeed, maritime affairs featured amid the priorities of the 2007 Portuguese Presidency, enabling "substantial progress to be made in this area" (Santos 2021, 47). Among other initiatives, the Portuguese Presidency supported the seminar held by the Conference of Peripheral Maritime Regions and held a ministerial conference to present and discuss the

160 *Isabel Camisão and Sandra Fernandes*

results of the Green Paper. The importance of the Portuguese Presidency's work is highlighted in a Commission's Communication:

> the Portuguese Presidency held a first informal ministerial meeting dealing with maritime policy in the broadest sense. Under the Portuguese Presidency, the Commission's proposal for an Integrated Maritime Policy was also discussed in the General and External Affairs Council, given its horizontal and across-the-board remit.
>
> (European Commission 2008, 6)

Portugal also played an important mediation role between the Council and the European Parliament (EP) in the negotiations on the MSFD, which was crucial for reaching agreement in 2007 on this environmental arm of the IMP. Portugal's active role continued during the phases of implementation and evaluation of the IMP (Santos 2021). More recently, during the last Portuguese Presidency of the Council (2021), maritime affairs featured again in the agenda. For example, a ministerial conference on IMP – A Blue Agenda in the Green Deal – was held in Lisbon (8 June 2021). The meeting stressed the importance of the sustainable blue economy in European economic recovery and the role the IMP must play in a blue, resilient, digital, social, and global Europe,[16] therefore establishing a clear link between the IMP and other chief priority areas of EU's action.

10.4 Multilateral advocacy: climate and energy to punch above its weight

The previous sections have highlighted the role of the Portuguese Presidency to advance the EU agenda – for the EU relation with Africa, the Lisbon Strategy, and the IMP. In this section we build the case of the Portuguese diplomatic activism that acts as a bridge and consensus maker, boosting multilateral engagement on complex and divisive issues. International institutions are a cornerstone for Portugal and its elites, which recurrently promote a more active Europe on the global scene (Silva 2018).

For Portugal, engagement means pragmatism and dialogue with powerful states on a case-by-case basis. The relations with China are an example of this Portuguese pragmatic stance. Lisbon portrays Beijing as an indispensable partner with whom the EU needs to maintain an open dialogue due to their mutual dependence. On the flip side, the image of Portugal as being China's "special friend" in the EU raised criticisms, particularly considering the country's openness to Chinese investments and the acquisition of key assets, namely in the energy sector (Wise 2020). The same pragmatic reasoning, but also historical and cultural ties, explains Portugal's desire to reconnect with India or its drive to enhance relations with Africa, in this case to countervail the increasing Chinese presence on the continent. Portugal has, thus, an active role in advancing pragmatic dialogues in multiple geographies.

Climate change is probably one of the most prominent areas where the importance of Portugal's diplomacy is recognized, particularly as regards its ability to establish broad dialogues within and outside the EU on complex issues that need multilateral engagement. As the current Prime Minister notes, Portugal is one of the EU's most affected countries by climate change:

> we are from the territories that have suffered the most from coastal erosion, we are from the countries that have suffered the most from the increase in drought and we know that we are one of the countries where the risk of forest fires increases the most.
>
> (Governo de Portugal 2022)

Dennisson and Franco (2019) emphasized how climate change and multilateralism are intertwined as a benchmark of Portuguese foreign policy:

> The Portuguese are instinctive multilateralists, and hope that the bloc can help them tackle the challenges of globalisation: from climate change to cooperation on the impact of freedom of movement on Europe.

A global vocation and a diplomacy operating in a "360-degree perspective" have structured Portuguese external action with the country becoming "at ease with multilateralism" (Silva in Agência Lusa 2018) – as per the Minister of Foreign Affairs. Overall, three interconnected pillars structure Portuguese foreign policy and contribute to its participation in several political arenas. Additionally, Portugal's strategic geographical position allows the country to punch above its weight by consistently enacting a global vocation, specifically by being a staunch defender of multilateralism.

Thus, not surprisingly, the external dimension of the 2021 Presidency has been entitled "Global Europe", which was the fifth goal of the agenda. Amid fierce US-China competition and the decline of the relation with Russia, Portugal has a clear understanding that most of the EU's challenges are, indeed, external. Portuguese government initially planned to promote multilateralism as a political value and a principle of EU's action (an ambition postponed by the priority that had to be given to the collective management of the COVID-19 pandemic). This ambition was already present during the 2007 Presidency, which aimed at contributing to a "Stronger Europe for a better world". Against this backdrop, climate change is perceived as one of the domains "where Portugal can lead" (Gouveia 2021) and that allows the country to "surpass a lot its geographical and demographic dimension" (Lobo Antunes 2008). The same happens with energy issues. Both climate and energy were a joint dimension of the 2007 Presidency (Eurocid 2007). In 2021, the moto was more ambitious with the transversal inclusion of the "green agenda" aiming at EU's sustainability, turning the European Green Deal into one of the Portuguese top priorities (Comissão Europeia n.d.).

The Portuguese Presidency facilitated key negotiations with the European Parliament that resulted in the approval of the European Climate Law. The negotiation phase was initially a "challenging task" (Zacarias in Agência Lusa 2021) but it allowed the Portuguese vision to be implemented. Specifically, Portugal wanted a collective methodology to attain carbon neutrality (Zacarias in Agência Lusa 2021). The new legislation defines the goal of neutrality by 2050 and provides for a reduction of 55% in greenhouse gas emissions by 2030, as compared to 1990 levels. At the domestic level, national legislation even anticipated by five years the goal set by the Union for 2050.

Being the fourth producer of renewable energies in the EU (Almeida 2022), Portugal aims to export clean energy to the rest of Europe. Indeed, integrating the Portuguese energy system in the EU is one of the goals of the ongoing Recovery and Resilience Plan (approved to fight the negative effects of the pandemic). In 2022, it has become a top priority for all MS in the disruptive context of the conflict between Russia and Ukraine, in order to redirect the European energy market and cut imports from Russia. The construction of the MidCat pipeline, that would link the Iberian Peninsula to the rest of Europe, namely Germany, was hampered by the French veto on the Pyrenees' route.[17] The Portuguese action to convey a tripartite negotiation with France and Spain ultimately led to the abandonment of the project and the adoption of a Green Corridor

162 *Isabel Camisão and Sandra Fernandes*

in October 2022, including new pipelines for natural and green gas and electrical grids (Silva 2022).

The degraded geopolitical context caused by the war in Ukraine was used by Portugal as a justification to call off of MidCat, despite being a project in which the country had already invested. The project was launched in 2009 by Portugal and revived by the Barroso Commission in 2014 as a way to reduce the dependency on Russian gas. The Portuguese Prime Minister considered that a "historical blockage" was unlocked (Costa in Godinho and Guerreiro 2022). Confirming Portugal's role as an honest broker among MS, the Portuguese President of the Republic mentioned:

> Common sense prevailed because if it was in the interest of Europe and, deep down, it was in the interest of the three [France, Portugal and Spain], because there were differences that were not decisive, there was no reason not to have an agreement.
>
> (Rebelo de Sousa in Godinho and Guerreiro 2022)

10.5 Final remarks

The literature on Europeanization shows that MS undergo a process of domestic adaptation as a result of EU membership (top-down dimension). However, European integration is, in part, shaped by the MS, meaning that Europeanization has a bottom-up dimension that captures the influence of MS (and of subnational actors) over agenda and policy shaping. While extant research on Portugal's Europeanization tends to be focused on the impact of EU on domestic politics, policies, and institutions, our chapter offers a complementary analysis, by mapping the areas and specific examples that are illustrative of Portugal's entrepreneurship.

The consolidation of the EU-Africa (afterwards EU-African Union) partnership is a clear example of an area where Portugal had an active role. The first EU-Africa summit was a result of Lisbon's competent and persistent diplomacy and the Portuguese presidencies of the Council were purposefully used by the country to amplify and consolidate Portugal's African agenda.

The Lisbon Strategy was negotiated in a juncture to address structural issues of the EU, such as high unemployment and low growth. Portugal demonstrated not only its convergence towards the core of the EU, confirming its full legitimacy as an MS, but also its diplomatic capacity to set an agenda (innovation and knowledge-based economy) that was not self-evident at the end of the 1990s. The 2000 Presidency was used instrumentally to implement a tailored-made methodology that was recognized as competent.

Another emblematic example of Portugal's influence over agenda-setting and policy formulation is the EU IMP. The country's long tradition as a maritime state and its renewed activism in late 1990s early 2000s helped to put the oceans governance on the European agenda. Also, it was the Barroso Commission that adopted the IMP. Even though the Commission operates under the principle of independency, Barroso himself recognized the influence of the Portuguese experience (including the government positions he held in Portugal) in the shaping of his own vision for the policy.

Amid several crises (financial bailout, migration, COVID-19 pandemic, etc.), Portugal continues to see itself as a country committed to deepening integration and as a bridging force (see for instance the negotiations for the Multiannual Financial Framework), operating under European liberal and humanist values. However, a change has been looming in the Portuguese mindset: from a dedicated listener and Europe's "good student"

Portugal in the European Union 163

towards an active speaker with a voice that stands out and adds value to the integration project. Although this is not immediately visible in the relations with Russia, this is certainly the case of the relations with China and the transatlantic partnership, in which Lisbon wants to be a game changer for more EU.

Looking ahead, we identify three areas, already in the EU agenda, in which Portugal could have a further impact. These are (a) the rebuilding of the transatlantic relationship; (b) engaging with Africa as the centre of geopolitical competition; and (c) boosting energy diversification including climate change measures, in particular under the RePowerEU programme.

The Trump administration, Brexit, and the war in Ukraine have been the catalysts for policies to create "more EU" in the domains of the Common Foreign and Security Policy and Common Security and Defense Policy, as for instance the Permanent Structured Cooperation in Defense (PESCO) and the European Defense Fund (EDF) launched in 2017. MS understood that strategic and sovereign autonomy needs to be achieved through European capabilities and in close partnership with the United States and NATO. Lisbon has embraced institutional change to boost EU's level initiatives, creating namely the "idD Portugal Defense"[18] in 2020. At the political level, Portugal stands as a fierce supporter of Atlanticism that serves not only as a multiplier of national interests but as a bridge between the North and South Atlantic. It is expected that the intertwining between EU and NATO's engagement will be at the core of Portuguese orientations in the Atlantic at large, enacting its unique strategic location in this geography.

The way Portugal might support the EU's further engagement in the African continent is related to the above-mentioned North-South axis. Having a facilitated dialogue with the Portuguese-speaking countries (including Brazil), Portugal supports the current political understanding that the security of the Atlantic area is a broad task. The global consequences of the Russian war in Ukraine or the climate change agenda already show the urgency to engage with the Global South for common solutions to common problems.

Finally, Portugal aims both at boosting its energy mix and reducing its vulnerable position, pre-existent to the energy crisis caused by the war in Ukraine. Besides domestic measures that are being studied at the EU level as a possible common solution (such as the "Iberian brake" to control market prices), Portugal places itself as a leverage to reduce dependence on Russia. With a deep-water port facility in Sines, a low level of gas in its energy mix, and renewables production, Portugal has the potential to contribute significantly to the goals of RePowerEU.[19] The Plan was adopted in May 2022 to accelerate energy transition in response to market disruption. The Portuguese Prime Minister's persistent advocacy for the urgent adoption of "new European regulations that streamline issuing renewable energy licenses" (Costa in Governo da República Portuguesa 2022) (crucial for speeding up energy transition) showcases the current Portuguese activism in the successive packages of measures adopted in the energy sector and anticipates an important contribution of Portugal to the EU's overall response to the energy crisis.

Notes

1 The abbreviation MS is also used to refer to Member State in the singular.
2 This chapter does not focus specifically on the other intertwined dimensions of Portuguese foreign policy beyond Europeanization. The country is a strong Atlantist, multilateralist and it also frames its foreign policy identity in the Lusophone world (Ministry of National Defense 2013; Fernandes and Silva 2023).

164 *Isabel Camisão and Sandra Fernandes*

3 According to the European Commission (2013) "[t]he view that membership of the EU is a good thing declined most between 2007 and 2013 in (...) Portugal (36%, -19)".
4 The concept of "policy entrepreneur" is an operational definition of the Multiple Streams Framework. To be successful, a policy entrepreneur should have some qualities, namely to have some claim to a hearing (either resulting from expertise, ability to speak for others, or an authoritative decision-making position); to have political connections or negotiation skills; and to be persistent (Kingdon 2003, 180–181). In this chapter, we adopt a "loose" definition of policy entrepreneurship to refer to Portugal's activism and ability to influence.
5 Before the adoption of the Treaty of Lisbon, it was commonly referred to as Presidency of the EU.
6 See Portuguese Presidency of the Council (2021c).
7 According to Louis Michel (2007), member of the Commission, the "summit featured intense, rich, high-quality debates pointing to the new nature of our relationship, and thus its genuinely and essentially political nature". Besides economic partnership agreements, some other "difficult issues" were addressed, including Zimbabwe's situation under Mugabe's leadership and the Darfur humanitarian and security situation, and the uncooperative attitude of the Sudanese Government (Michel 2007).
8 The Joint EU-Africa Strategy and an Action Plan was adopted on 9 December 2007 and the second EU-Africa Summit took place in Lisbon on 8 and 9 December 2007.
9 Over 25 conferences that occurred in Europe and Africa (Portuguese Presidency of the Council 2021b).
10 Cf. Portuguese Presidency of the Council (2021d).
11 Despite the fact that the majority of EU MS are maritime states, EU maritime affairs were for decades essentially synonymous with fisheries. Although this narrow vision of the topic was gradually abandoned, throughout the 1990's maritime issues continued to be perceived essentially as national competences. At the EU level, the question was handled in a fairly fragmented way, under a range of EU policies such as industry, transport, fisheries, or regional policy.
12 "The Ocean, a national goal for the XXI Century" was published in 2004. See Strategic Ocean Committee (2004).
13 For example, Pitta e Cunha was Portugal's representative in the negotiations of UNCLOS. Also, in 2003 he was appointed by the Portuguese Prime Minister to be the coordinator of the Oceans Strategic Commission. See European Parliament (n.d.).
14 The agency was temporarily based in Brussels, but afterwards relocated to Lisbon.
15 These were two major accidents involving single hull tankers (named respectively Erika and Prestige) transporting heavy fuel oils that resulted in large amounts of oil spill into the ocean.
16 See Portuguese Presidency of the Council (2021e).
17 The 3 billion euros gas pipeline was in the making since 2013 and abandoned in 2019, mostly by pressuring environmental forces in France. However, the issue of competition is seen as the main reason for Paris to oppose the pipeline that would curtail both its exports of nuclear-generated electricity and LNG. After the war in Ukraine started in February 2022, the argument of promoting fossil energy in a context of both rupture with Russia and green transition has been key French arguments (Leali and Caulcutt 2022).
18 idD Portugal Defence is a state-owned company under the joint supervision of the Ministry of National Defence and the Ministry of Finance, that "aims to help the Defence Technological and Industrial Base in becoming an international player in the Defence Economy". It acts as an interface between the Armed Forces, companies, universities and research centres and international organisations of which Portugal is a member. See (idD n.d.).
19 See European Commission (2022).

References

Agência Lusa. 2018. "Internacionalização e Multilateralismo são Traços da Política Externa Portuguesa – MNE." *Diário de Notícias,* January 3, 2018. https://www.dn.pt/lusa/internacionalizacao-e-multilateralismo-sao-tracos-da-politica-externa-portuguesa---mne-9021759.html#error=login_required&state=021ea9e5-5afd-4d0d-a9c1-c7d10c7f7d05

Agência Lusa. 2020. "Presidência na União Europeia. Estratégia de Lisboa foi "o grande projeto" de 2000." *Observador,* November 4, 2020. https://observador.pt/2020/11/04/presidencia-na-uniao-europeia-estrategia-de-lisboa-foi-o-grande-projeto-de-2000/

Agência Lusa. 2021. "Presidência da UE. Ana Paula Zacarias afirma que Lei Europeia do Clima marca o início da jornada "rumo a um futuro mais sustentável." *Observador,* June 24, 2021.https://observador.pt/2021/06/24/presidencia-da-ue-ana-paula-zacarias-afirma-que-lei-europeia-do-clima-marca-o-inicio-da-jornada-rumo-a-um-futuro-mais-sustentavel/

Almeida, J. 2022. "Portugal é o quarto país da UE que mais consome energia produzida por renováveis." *Jornal de Negócios,* January 26. https://www.jornaldenegocios.pt/empresas/energia/detalhe/portugal-e-o-quarto-pais-da-ue-que-mais-consome-energia-produzida-por-renovaveis

Amaral, Luciano. 2022. *Economia Portuguesa - As últimas décadas.* Lisbon: Fundação Francisco Manuel dos Santos.

Bandov, Goran, and Nikolina, H. Kolman. 2018. "Research on Europeanization in Literature: From the Top-down Approach to Europeanization as a Multi-directional Process." *Cadmus* 3, no. 5: 234–144. https://cadmusjournal.org/files/pdfreprints/vol3issue5/Research-on-Europeanization-in-Literature-GBandov-NKolman-Cadmus-V3-I5-Reprint.pdf

Barroso, José M. Durão. 2005. "Opening Speech." In *European Maritime Policy Conference: Proceedings.* Dutch Maritime Network.

Barroso, José M. Durão. 2006. "Message from the President of the European Commission." In *Towards a future Maritime Policy for the Union: A European Vision for the Oceans and Seas.* Luxembourg: Office for Official Publications of the European Communities.

Barroso, José M. Durão. 2007. "Key note speech - European Maritime Policy". Speech 07/645, October 22, 2007. https://ec.europa.eu/commission/presscorner/detail/en/SPEECH_07_645

Cavaco Silva, Aníbal. 2011. Address delivered by the President of the Republic at the Conference on the European Union Maritime Strategy for the Atlantic Region Lisbon Conference Centre, November 28, 2011. https://anibalcavacosilva.arquivo.presidencia.pt/?idc=22&idi=59718&action=7&idl=2

Comissão Europeia. n.d. "A luta contra a emergência climática." Accessed October 12, 2023 .https://portugal.representation.ec.europa.eu/estrategia-e-prioridades/principais-politicas-da-ue-para-portugal/o-pacto-ecologico-e-transicao-energetica-em-portugal_pt

Capoccia, Giovanni and Daniel Keleman. 2007. "The study of Critical Junctures. Theory, Narrative, and Counterfactuals in Historical Institutionalism." *World Politics* 55, no. 3: 341–369.10.1017/S0043887100020852

Crespo, Nuno and Nádia Simões. 2022. *Mercado de Trabalho em Portugal - do teletrabalho ao salário mínimo.* Lisbon: Actual Editora.

Cunha, Alice. 2013. "Portugal no Centro da Europa: As Presidências Portuguesas do Conselho da União Europeia (1992, 2000 e 2007)." *Ler História,* no. 64: 163–167. https://doi.org/10.4000/lerhistoria.303

Dennisson, Susi and Lívia Franco, *The instinctive multilateralist: Portugal and the politics of cooperation* (ECFR Policy brief, 2019). https://ecfr.eu/publication/instinctive_multilateralist_portugal_politics_cooperation/

Edwards, Geoffrey and Georg Wiessala. 2001. "Conscientious Resolve: The Portuguese Presidency of 2000." *Journal of Common Market Studies* 30, no. 1: 43–46. https://doi.org/10.1111/1468-5965.39.s1.4

Eurocid. n/d. "Presidência Portuguesa 2007." Accessed November 3, 2022. https://eurocid.mne.gov.pt/portugal-na-europa/presidencia-portuguesa-2007

European Commission. 2006. "Green Paper Towards a future Maritime Policy for the Union: A European vision for the oceans and seas." COM(2006) 275 final Volume II – Annex, 07.06.2006.

European Commission. 2008. "Guidelines for an Integrated Approach to Maritime Policy: Towards best practice in integrated maritime governance and stakeholder consultation." COM(2008) 395 final.

European Commission. 2013. "Eurobarometer, 40 years, Effects of the Economic and Financial Crisis on European Public Opinion." https://europa.eu/eurobarometer/angular/assets/about/EB-40years.pdf

European Commission. 2022. "REPowerEU A plan to rapidly reduce dependence on Russian fossil fuels and fast forward the green transition." May 18, 2022. https://ec.europa.eu/commission/presscorner/detail/en/IP_22_3131

166 *Isabel Camisão and Sandra Fernandes*

European Council. 2000. *Lisbon European Council 23 and 24 March 2000. Presidency Conclusions.* https://www.europarl.europa.eu/summits/lis1_en.htm

European Parliament. n.d. "Tiago Pitta e Cunha." https://www.europarl.europa.eu/meetdocs/2009_2014/documents/sede/dv/sede190313audcvpittaecunha_/sede190313audcvpittaecunha_en.pdf

Fernandes, Sandra and David Silva. Forthcoming. "Portugal in the nuclear realm: A case of broad multilateralization." *International Politics.*

Ferreira-Pereira, Laura Cristina. 2008. "Portugal e a Presidência da União Europeia (1992–2007)." *Relações Internacionais*, no. 20: 131–143. https://ipri.unl.pt/images/publicacoes/revista_ri/pdf/ri20/n20a11.pdf

Gama, Jaime. 2000. "EU-Africa Summit European Parliament Debates." https://www.europarl.europa.eu/doceo/document/CRE-5-2000-04-11-ITM-006_EN.html

Godinho, Rui Miguel and João Francisco Guerreiro. 2022. "Adeus, MidCat. Olá, Corredor Verde. Portugal, Espanha e França com acordo para novo gasoduto." *Diário de Notícias*, October 20, 2022. https://www.dn.pt/politica/adeus-midcat-ola-corredor-verde-portugal-espanha-e-franca-com-acordo-para-novo-gasoduto-15273326.html

Governo da República Portuguesa. 2022. "Prime Minister António Costa at the European Council focusing on the energy crisis." Brussels, October 20, 2022. https://www.portugal.gov.pt/en/gc23/communication/news-item?i=prime-minister-notes-solidarity-and-common-responses-as-the-way-to-overcome-the-economic-and-socia

Goucha Soares, António, "Portugal: An Incomplete Europeanization." (working paper, GHES, Gabinete de História Económica e Social, 2009). https://ghes.rc.iseg.ulisboa.pt/wp/wp382009.pdf

Gouveia, Teresa. 2021. "Where Portugal could lead." ECFR. https://ecfr.eu/article/where-portugal-can-lead-europe-in-2021/

Governo de Portugal. 2022. "Portugal não tem tempo a perder no combate às alterações climáticas." https://www.portugal.gov.pt/pt/gc23/comunicacao/noticia?i=portugal-nao-tem-tempo-a-perder-no-combate-as-alteracoes-climaticas

Graziano, Paolo and Maarten P. Vink. 2012. "Europeanization: Concept, Theory, and Methods." In *The Member States of the European Union*, edited by Simon Bulmer and Christian Lesquene, 31–53. Oxford University Press.

Guterres, António. 2001. "A Estratégia de Lisboa – Uma nova ambição para a Europa." *Europa Novas Fronteiras*, no. 9/10, July–December, https://eurocid.mne.gov.pt/artigos/europa-novas-fronteiras-1 - toc-edi-es

Hooghe, Liesbet and Gary Marks. 2003. "Unravelling the Central State, but How? Types of Multi-Level Governance." *American Political Science Review* 92, no. 2: 233–243. 10.1017/S0003055403000649

idD. n.d. "idD Portugal Defence." https://www.iddportugal.pt/en/

Jalali, Carlos. 2012. "Governing from Lisbon or Governing from Brussels? Models and Tendencies of Europeanization of the Portuguese Government." In *The Europeanization of Portuguese Democracy*, edited by Nuno S. Teixeira and António C. Pinto, 61–84. Social Science Monographs, Boulder (distributed by Columbia University Press).

Kingdon, John W. 2003. *Agendas, Alternatives and Public Policies*. Longman.

Ladrech, Robert. 2010. *Europeanization and National Politics*. Palgrave Macmillan.

Leali, Giorgio and Clea Caulcutt. 2022. "France to look into MidCat pipeline again as energy crunch tightens." *Politico*, September 28, 2022. https://www.politico.eu/article/france-pledges-to-reconsider-midcat-pipeline-amid-iberian-pressure/

Lobo Antunes, Manuel. 2008. "Presidência em balanço." *Relações Internacionais*, 5–10. https://ipri.unl.pt/images/publicacoes/revista_ri/pdf/ri17/RI17_01MLAntunes.pdf

Macedo, Jorge Braga de. 2003. Portugal's European Integration: The GoodStudent with a Bad Fiscal Constitution. *South European Society and Politics*, Vol. 8, Issue 1-1: 169-194

Magalhães, Pedro. 2012. "The Support for European Integration in Portugal: Dimensions and Trends." In *The Europeanization of Portuguese Democracy*, edited by Nuno S. Teixeira and António C. Pinto, 225–249. Social Science Monographs, Boulder (distributed by Columbia University Press).

Magalhães, Pedro, Cancela, João, and Catherine Moury. 2016. "Scattered Clouds in the Horizon of Consensus: Attitudes of Portuguese Parliamentary Elites Towards Europe Before and After the Crisis." *Historical Social Research* 41, no. 4: 173–194. https://doi.org/10.12759/hsr.41 .2016.4.173-194

Magone, José. 2002. "Attitudes of Southern European Citizens Towards Integration." In *Southern Europe and the Making of the European Union,* edited by António C. Pinto and Nuno S. Teixeira, 209-235. Social Science Monographs, Boulder (distributed by Columbia University Press).

Magone, José. 2004. *The Developing Place of Portugal in the European Union.* Routledge.

Magone, José. 2006. "The Europeanization of Portugal (1986–2006) A Critical View." *Nação e Defesa,* no. 115: 9–28.

Michel, Louis. 2007. "Second EU/Africa Summit (Lisbon, 8 and 9 December 2007) (debate)". https://www.europarl.europa.eu/doceo/document/CRE-6-2007-12-11-ITM-016_EN.html

Ministry of National Defence. 2013. "Conceito Estratégico de Defesa Nacional." *Governo de Portugal.* https://www.defesa.gov.pt/pt/comunicacao/documentos/Lists/PDEFINTER_ DocumentoLookupList/Conceito-Estrategico-de-Defesa-Nacional.pdf

Nugent, Neill and Mark Rhinard. 2019. "The 'political' roles of the European Commission." *Journal of European Integration* 41, no. 2: 203–220. https://doi.org/10.1080/07036337.2019 .1572135

ONGD Plataforma Portuguesa. 2021. "The European Union and Africa: Towards a partnership "between equals"?" https://www.plataformaongd.pt/uploads/subcanais2/the_european_union _and_africa_towards_a_partnership_between-equals_englishversion.pdf

Portuguese Presidency of the Council. 2007. "Portuguese Presidency of the Council: A stronger Union for a better world (July–December 2007)." *CVCE.* https://www.cvce.eu/content/ publication/2007/7/4/0d5f5fa9-2aec-409c-b4b1-9180c3aa992d/publishable_en.pdf

Portuguese Presidency of the Council. 2021a. "2021 PORTUGAL.EU Portuguese Presidency of the Council of the European Union, 1 January to 30 June 2021." https://www.2021portugal.eu /media/rohpisqf/portuguese-presidency-en.pdf

Portuguese Presidency of the Council. 2021b. "2021 PORTUGAL.EU, Results." https://www .2021portugal.eu/en/results/

Portuguese Presidency of the Council. 2021c. "Presidency Of The Council of the European Union." https://www.2021portugal.eu/en/presidency/presidency-of-the-council/

Portuguese Presidency of the Council. 2021d. "Portuguese Presidency want a "turning point" in relations between the European Union and Africa." *2021PORTUGAL.EU,* April 22, 2021. https://www.2021portugal.eu/en/news/portuguese-presidency-wants-a-turning-point-in -relations-between-the-european-union-and-africa/

Portuguese Presidency of the Council. 2021e. "Ministerial Conference "A Blue Agenda in the Green Deal." *2021PORTUGAL.EU.* https://www.2021portugal.eu/en/events/ministerial-conference -a-blue-agenda-in-the-green-deal/

Pridham, Geoffrey. 2006. "European Union Accession Dynamics and Democratization in Central and Eastern Europe: Past and Future Perspective." *Government and Opposition* 41, no. 3, Summer: 373–400. https://www.jstor.org/stable/44483159

Radaelli, Claudio. 2001. "The Domestic Impact of European Union Public Policy: Notes on Concepts, Methods and the Challenge of Empirical Research." *Politique Européenne,* no 5: 105–136. https://doi.org/10.3917/poeu.005.0105

Saliou, Virginie. 2008. "Setting the Agenda of the European Maritime Policy: Multi-level transfers of ideas and legitimacy." *Cyprus Center of European and International Affairs,* (Paper No 2008-05).

Santos, Conceição. 2021. "The Integrated Maritime Policy in the European Union and the Portuguese experience over the past 14 years." *Public Policy Portuguese Journal* 6, no. 1: 40–55.

Silva, Augusto Santos. 2021. *Tempo de Agir na Europa – A Presidência Portuguesa de 2021.* Imprensa Nacional-Casa da Moeda.

Silva, Augusto Santos. 2018. "O Futuro da Europa no Mundo." https://www.portugal.gov.pt/ download-ficheiros/ficheiro.aspx?v=%3D%3DBAAAAB%2BLCAAAAAAABAAzNTU3BAD6 UMgFBAAAAA%3D%3D

Silva, Bárbara. 2022. "Gasoduto Midcat dos Pirinéus foi substituído por projetos CelZa e BraMar, diz Governo." *Jornal de Negócios,* October 20, 2022 https://www.jornaldenegocios.pt/empresas /energia/detalhe/gasoduto-midcat-dos-pirineus-foi-substituido-por-projetos-celza-e-bramar-diz -governo

168 *Isabel Camisão and Sandra Fernandes*

Sócrates, José. 2007. "Presentation of the Programme for the Portuguese Presidency of the European Union – Address given by Prime Minister José Sócrates to the Assembly of the Republic (27 June 2007)." *CVCE*. https://www.cvce.eu/obj/address_given_by_portuguese_prime_minister_jose_socrates_to_the_assembly_of_the_republic_lisbon_27_june_2007-en-160cb0aa-055b-4073-95c7-12c80a9c8cd7.html

Sousa, Teresa. 1999. "Uma agenda europeia para a sociedade do conhecimento." *Público*, December 3, 1999.https://www.publico.pt/1999/12/03/jornal/uma-agenda-europeia-para-a-sociedade-do-conhecimento-127314

Sousa, Teresa. 2002. "A "via europeia" para a nova economia: o contributo português." *Janus*. https://repositorio.ual.pt/handle/11144/1956?locale=en

Strategic Ocean Committee. 2004. "The Ocean, a national goal for the XXI Century."

Tallberg, Jonas. 2003. "The Agenda-shaping Powers of the EU Council Presidency." *Journal of European Public Policy* 10, no. 1: 1–19. https://doi.org/10.1080/1350176032000046903

Teixeira, Nuno S. 2012. "Introduction: Portugal and European Integration." In *The Europeanization of Portuguese Democracy*, edited by Nuno S. Teixeira and António C. Pinto. Social Science Monographs, Boulder.

Teixeira, Nuno S. and Reinaldo S, Hermenegildo. 2018. "The Portuguese Presidencies of the European Union - A Preliminary Study." *Portuguese Studies* 34, no. 1, 70–85. https://doi.org/10.5699/portstudies.34.1.0070

Vasconcelos, Álvaro de. 2000. "Portugal: The European Way." In *Portugal A European Story* edited by Francisco Seixas da Costa, Álvaro de Vasconcelos, and Maria João Seabra. Principia.

Vink, Maarten. P. 2012. "Conclusion: Europeanization and Democratization in Portugal – Brother-in-arms or Frères Ennemis?" In *The Europeanization of Portuguese Democracy*, edited by Nuno S. Teixeira and António C. Pinto, 251–261. Social Science Monographs, Boulder (distributed by Columbia University Press).

Wise, Peter. 2020. "Lisbon rebuffs claims Portugal is China's 'special friend' in EU." *Financial Times*, January 20, 2020. https://www.ft.com/content/862c633e-393b-11ea-a6d3-9a26f8c3cba4

Index

Note: Page numbers in **bold** and *italics* indicate tables and figures, and references following "n" refer notes.

AAAS *see* American Association for the Advancement of Science
ABIC *see* Association of Scientific Research Fellows
Abrantes, G. 125, 127
academia, gender inequality in 11, 105, *107*
ACL *see* Lisbon Academy of Sciences
Adjustment Program 35
Agency for Innovation and Technology Transfer (now the National Innovation Agency) 100
Algarve 14
Alice (2005) 126
Amaral, A. L. 143; *Ágora* (*Agora*) 143; Ara (Altar) 143; *Mundo* (*World*) 143
American Association for the Advancement of Science (AAAS) 101
Andor, L. 33, 34
ANI *see* Agency for Innovation and Technology Transfer (National Innovation Agency)
ANICT *see* National Association of Researchers in Science and Technology
António, um rapaz de Lisboa (António, a Lisbon Boy) 130
António Miguel (2000) 128
Aquele Querido Mês de Agosto (*That Dear Month of August*) (2008) 126
Arena (2009) 127
arts 11, 123–136; cinema 125–128; music 134–135; performing 128–130; theatre 130–131; visual 131–134
Arts Institute 128
Arts Support Model 129
Associação Ciência Viva 117
Associated Laboratories 118, 121n26

Association of Scientific Research Fellows (ABIC) 118
Atlantic International Research Centre (AIR) Centre 116
auteur cinema 126

Bafatá Filme Clube (Bafata Film Club) (2013) 127
Bahro, H. 47
Balada de um Batráquio (Batrachian's Ballad) 127
Ballet-Teatro 128
banal nationalism 17–18
Banco Espírito Santo, bankruptcy of 71–72
Baptista, S. 129
Baroque Orchestra 134
Barroso, J. D. 47–48
Barroso Commission 157–159
Bayerlein, B. 47
BE *see* Bloco de Esquerda
Bettencourt, M. 128
Bloco de Esquerda (BE, Left Bloc) 35–38, 40, 45, 54, 55, 57, 58
"Blue Book" package 159
Bombarda, R. M. 131
Botelho, J. 126
Branca de Neve (*Snow White*) (2000) 125
budget transparency 73
Buraka Som Sistema 135
Burmester, P. 134

Caetano, M. 2, 3
Calado, P. 93
Calouste Gulbenkian Foundation (FCG) 121n29; Modern Art Centre 132; Music Service 134; Programa Gulbenkian de Doutoramento em Biologia e Medicina (PGDBM) 121n29

170 Index

capital: financial 69–70; human 10, 68–69, 71, 76; institutional 70–73; managerial 69–70; public 73–75
Cardoso, Dulce Maria 126; *Eliete – A Vida Normal* (Eliete – Normal Life) 143; *O Retorno* 143
Cardoso, Margarida 126
Carvalho, T. 129
Casa da Música 134
Casa de Lava (Down to Earth) (1994) 126
Castile 15
Catholicism 20
CCDR *see* Regional Coordination and Development Commissions
CDS *see* Democratic Social Centre
CDS-PP *see* Social and Democratic Centre-Popular Party
Centeno, M. 8
Cerro Negro (2012) 127
CGTP *see* General Confederation of Portuguese Workers
Chafes, R. 129
child poverty 67–68
Christianity 16, 20
Chuva é Cantoria na Aldeia dos Mortos (The Dead and Others) (2018) 127
cinema 125–128
CLA *see* Council of Associated Laboratories
Cláudio, M. 145
Coelho, P. P. 8, 55
Cohesion Fund 8
Comer coração (Eating heart) 129
Commission for Citizenship and Gender Equality 82
Commission for Social Security Reform 33
Commission Task Force on Maritime Affairs 159
Common Foreign and Security Policy 163
Common Security and Defense Policy 163
Community of Portuguese Language Countries (CPLP) 17
Condado Portucalense 14
Conference of Peripheral Maritime Regions 159
Constelações do Equador (Equatorial Constellations) (2021) 127
Constitutional Court 35, 36
Constitution of the Portuguese Republic (CPR): 1976 6; 1822 21–22; 1982 7; 1989 7; Art. 13 79
Convention on the Elimination of All Forms of Discrimination against Women 80
corporatism 2
Correia, H. 143, 145, 150
Corruption Perception Index 70
Costa, A. 8, 53–55, 57, 88
Costa, P. 125, 126

A Costa dos Murmúrios (The Murmuring Coast) 126
cost containment 10, 29, 30, 32, 33, 39
Council of Associated Laboratories (CLA) 118
Council of Europe 86; Group of States Against Corruption 71
Council of Public Finances 73
Council of the Revolution 5
Court of Accounts 72–73
CPLP *see* Community of Portuguese Language Countries
CPR *see* Constitution of the Portuguese Republic
Cruz, A. 148
Cruz, G.: *Existência* (Existence) 140; *Fogo* (Fire) 140
Cultural Center of Belém 22

da Costa, M. V. 143; *Irene, ou o Contrato Social* (Irene, or the Social Contract) 138, 139; *Memória de Elefante* (Elephant Memory) 138; *Missa in Albis* (Mass in Albis) 138; *Os Cus de Judas* (South of Nowhere) 138
da Silva, C. C. 126
da Silva, V. 33
da Silva Ferreira, M. 129
de Almeida, D. P. 150; *Esse Cabelo* (That Hair) 144; *Maremoto* (Tsunami) 138, 144; *uanda, Lisboa, Paraíso* (Luanda, Lisbon, Paradise) 138
de Azevedo, J. 129
de Carvalho, A. M. 145; *Não se Pode Morar nos Olhos de Um Gato* (You Can't Live in the Eyes of a Cat) 146; *O Gesto que Fazemos para Proteger a Cabeça* (The Gesture We Make to Protect Our Head) 146
de Freitas, M. M. 129, 142
de Mendonça, J. T. 141, 142
Democratic Renewal Party (PRD, *Partido Renovador Democrático*) 60n6
Democratic Social Centre (CDS) 5, 45, 51, 53–55, 57, 58
democratization process 3–7, 9
demographic change 124–125
Dennisson, S. 161
de Oliveira, M. 125; *A Morte Não É Prioritária* (Death is Not a Priority) 145
de Quental, A. 145
de Sousa, A. R. 127
de Sousa, M. R. 48, 88
DeVIR/CAPa 128
Diamantino (2018) 127
Diários da Bósnia (Bosnia Diaries) (2005) 126
Dias, C. 129
dictatorship 3–7

Digital Economy and Society Index 68
Directive for Reconciliation between work and family for Parents 37
discrimination 80, 87, 92–96; by association 93–94; multiple 93
dos Santos, T. 34, 129
dualization 31–34
Dyson, K. 28

Economic and Monetary Union (EMU) 26, 27, 29, 34, 39; budgetary restrictions 33
The Economist's Democracy Index 2022 79
economy 62–77; child poverty 67–68; financial capital 69–70; human capital 68–69; institutional capital 70–73; managerial capital 69–70; public capital 73–75; by the sea 62–64; in 21st century 64–66
EDF *see* European Defense Fund
EEC *see* European Economic Community
EFTA *see* European Free Trade Agreement
El Dorado (2016) 128
electoral system 49–50
Elgie, R. 46
empire 16–17
EMSA *see* European Maritime Safety Agency
EMU *see* Economic and Monetary Union
Enciclopédia da Estória Universal (Encyclopedia of Universal History) 148
Enough (*Chega*) 58
EP *see* European Parliament
equality 79; gender 80–86, 82–86; *see also* inequality
ERC *see* European Research Council
ERDF *see* European Regional Development Fund
ESF *see* European Social Fund
ESS *see* European Social Survey
ethnic superiority 94, *94*
EU *see* European Union
Eurobarometer 18; Eurobarometer on Science and Technology (2001) 116
Europe 2020 Strategy 28
European Central Bank 8, 21, 62, 65
European Climate Law 161
European Commission 21, 35, 62, 65, 68, 71, 74, 157, 158
European Community 66
European Council Recommendation (1992) 33
European Defense Fund (EDF) 163
European Disability Strategy 2010–2020 37
European Economic Community (EEC) 22; funding mechanisms 7–8
European Employment Strategy (1997) 28, 31
European Free Trade Agreement (EFTA) 2
European Green Deal 38
European Investment Bank 155

Europeanization 9–11, 26, 27, 123, 151–153, 162
European Joint Research Council (JRC) 117
European Maritime Safety Agency (EMSA) 158
European Parliament (EP) 81, 160
European People's Party 45
European Pillar of Social Rights 28, 38, 40
European Regional Development Fund (ERDF) 102
European Research Council (ERC) 115
European Social Fund (ESF) 102
European Social Survey (ESS) 18, 89, 91
European Stability Mechanism 28
European Union (EU) 6, 17, 18, 91–92, 99, 101; on child poverty 67, 68; economic and social dimensions, rebalancing 40; on financial capital 70; GDP 62; on gender equality 81; on human capital 68; on institutional capital 71, 72; on managerial capital 70; Portugal in 1, 7–8, 151–164; Presidency of the Council 154–157; Recovery and Resilience Facility 74, 161; Survey on Income and Living Conditions (SILC) 65, 67, 75
European Values Study (EVS) 84, 96n4
Eurozone crisis 8, 9, 39, 152
EVS *see* European Values Study
Excessive Deficit Procedure 28
Expo 1998 22, 88, 157–158
Exposition of the Portuguese World (1940) 18
expressionismo branco (white expressionism) 128

Fantasmas do Império (Ghosts of an Empire) (2020) 126
Faria, D.: *Dos Líquidos* (Of Liquids) 141; *Sétimo Dia* (Seventh Day) 141
Faria e Castro, M. 74
favor laboratoris principle 31, 36, 38, 40n2
FCCN *see* Foundation for National Scientific Computing
FCT *see* Foundation for Science and Technology
Featherstone, K. 28
FEDER (Regional Development Fund) 7–8
Fernandes, J. 131, 140
Fiadeiro, J. 128
Fifth Centennial of Vasco da Gama 22
financial capital 69–70
Fogo-Fátuo (Will-o'-the-Wisp) (2022) 125
Foundation for National Scientific Computing (FCCN) 101
Foundation for Science and Technology (FCT) 100–102, 112, 114–118, *115*, 121n29, 121n32, 121n41; investment *103*, 107

172   Index

Franco, L. 161
Freyre, G.: *Casa-Grande e Sanzala* (*The Masters and the Slaves*) 93
Futsal World Cup (2022) 21

Galeria Zé dos Bois132
Gardeazabal, J.: *Meio Homem Meio Baleia* (Half Man Half Whale) 147; *A Melhor Máquina Viva* (The Best Machine Alive) 148; *Quarenta e três* (Forty-three) 148; *Quarentena. Uma história de amor* (Quarantine. A love story) 148
gender: employment rates 81–82, *83*; equality 80–86, *82–86*; imbalances, in ICT skills 68; pay gap 10, 82, *84*
General Confederation of Portuguese Workers (CGTP) 34, 36
General Workers' Union (UGT) 34, 36, 39
Geringonça reforms (contraption) 35–40, 54
Germany 29, *29*, 34, 68, 70
Gersão, T.: *O Regresso de Júlia Mann a Paraty* (Julia Mann's Return to Paraty) 143
Gilroy, P. 137
Goes, E. 49
Gomes, M. 125, 126
Great Recession of 2008–2011 26, 28, 30, 38, 64
Greece 66, 68, 70
Green Talks 155
GRICES *see* International Relations in Science and Higher Education Office
Griot, T. 131
gross domestic product (GDP) 6, 8–9, 29, 33, 62–65, *63*, 73–76, *76*, 77, 99, 109, 114, 159
Gusmão, M. 140; *Ana* 144; *Aos Peixes* (*To the Fish*) 144; *Dois Homens* (*Two Men*) 144
Guterres, A. 58, 156

Haikus 129
Hangar-Centro de Investigação Artística 132
HDI *see* Human Development Index
HEIs *see* Higher Education Institutions
Helder, H. 141
Henriques, A. 14
Higher Education Institutions (HEIs) 103, 107, 111, 114
A History of Mutual Respect (2010) 127
Horizon 2020 105, 107, *108*
human capital 10, 68–69, 71, 76
Human Development Index (HDI) 79

ICCTI *see* Institute for International Scientific and Technological Cooperation
ICT *see* Information and Communication Technologies
idD Portugal Defence 164n18

IMF *see* International Monetary Fund
immigration 86–92, *87*, *90*, *91*, 124
IMP *see* Integrated Maritime Policy
industrial conditioning' policy 2
inequality 37–39, 76, 86, 94; class 95; gender 82; income 66, 67, 95; market-based 27; social 79, 95, 96, 148; *see also* equality
Inequality Transparency Index 73
Information and Communication Technologies (ICT) 68
Institute for International Scientific and Technological Cooperation (ICCTI) 100
institutional capital 70–73
Integrated Maritime Policy (IMP) 157–160
Interministerial Commission 12n1
internal devaluation (2010–2014) 34–35
International Budget Partnership 73
International Democrat Union 45
International Meeting of Communist and Workers' Parties 45
International Monetary Fund (IMF) 6, 8, 21, 34, 62, 65
International Relations in Science and Higher Education Office (GRICES) 100
International Social Survey Programme (ISSP) 19
Islam 20
ISSP *see* International Social Survey Programme

Jerónimos Monastery 18
job security 31, 32, 34, 39
Jorge, A. 134
Jorge, L. 125; *Misericórdia* 138
Jotta: a Minha Maladresse é uma Forma de Délicatesse (Jotta: My Maladresse is a Way of Délicatesse) (2009) 127
JRC *see* European Joint Research Council

Kingdon, J. W. 157
King Ferdinand 15
King John I 15, 16
Knowledge Society Agency 100
Koolhaas, R. 134
Koretzky, A. 127
Kunsthalle Lissabon 132

Laginha, J. 128
Lamas, S. 127–128
Leston-Bandeira, C. 49
Liberal Initiative (*Iniciativa Liberal*) 58
Licença para criar – Imigrantes nas Artes em Portugal (Licence to Create – Immigrants in the Arts in Portugal) 124–125
Lijphart, A. 50
Lisbon Academy of Sciences (ACL) 100, 118
Lisbon Agenda (2000) 31, 156

Lisbon Metropolitan Orchestra 134
Lisbon Strategy 34, 99, 155–156, 162
literary: circulation 143–144, 150; production 11, 138, 139, 143–145
literature 137–150; comparative 140–149; current situation 149–150; future challenges to 150; imperfect present 137–140
Lobo Antunes, A. 125, 139; *As Naus* (*Return of the Caravels*) 138
Lopes, A. 142–143
Lourenöo, E. 138
Luís, A. B. 125

MAAT *see* Museum of Art, Architecture and Technology
Machado, D.: *A Educação dos Gafanhotos* (*The Education of the Locusts*) 140
Mair, P. 45, 46, 51
managerial capital 69–70
Mantero, V. 128, 129
Marine Strategy Framework Directive (MSFD) 158
market-based inequality 27
Martins, M. 126
Mata, A. G. 127
material deprivation 65–67, 75, 76, 92
Maternity Leave Directive 41n10
Mattoso, J. 15
Maumaus 132
medieval kingdom 14–16
Memorandum of Understanding (MoU) 8, 28, 30, 34, 35
Mendes, L. F. C. 140; *Voltar* (*Going Back*) 140
Mendes, V. 144
Metáfora ou a Tristeza Virada do Avesso (Metaphor or Sadness Inside Out) (2013) 127
A Metamorfose dos Pássaros (The Metamorphosis of Birds) (2020) 127
MFA (Armed Forces Movement) 5
Michel, L. 164n7
minimum wage 34, 36, 38–40
MIPEX (Migrant Integration Policy Index) 79, 87
Miranda, P. J.: *Aaron Klein* 145
Mitteleuropa 11, 145, 146, 150
Moedas, C. 89
Monginho, J.: *Volta ao mundo em vinte dias e meio* (Around the World in Twenty and a Half Days) 140
Monteiro, J. C. 125
Montenegro, L. 89
MoU *see* Memorandum of Understanding
MSFD *see* Marine Strategy Framework Directive
Multiannual Financial Framework 74

multiculturalism 126, 141
multilateral advocacy 160–162
Multiple Streams Framework 164n4
Museu do Chiado 132
Museum of Art, Architecture and Technology (MAAT) 132
music 134–135
NAS *see* National Academy of Sciences
NASTC *see* National Agency for Scientific and Technological Culture
Nataf, D. 6
Natal de 71 (*Christmas 71*) (1999) 126
National Academy of Sciences (NAS) 101
National Agency for Scientific and Technological Culture (NASTC) 117
National Association of Researchers in Science and Technology (ANICT) 118
National Confederation of Solidarity Institutions 35
National Health Service (NHS) 26, 30, 32, 37, 39; sustainability 35
national identification, expressions of 18–21, *19*, *20*
national identity 9, 14–19, 22, 23, 93; reproduction of 17–18
Nationality Law 87
nationalism: banal 18; official 17–18
National Network of Long-Term Care 33
National Strategy for Equality and Non-Discrimination 2018–2030 80–81
National Strategy for Knowledge and Innovation 111
nation-building process 14–16
Neto, J.: *Meridiano 28* (*28th Meridian*) 140
Network of Integrated Long-Term Care 33
NHS *see* National Health Service
no-confidence motion (*moção de censura*) 48
North Atlantic Treaty Organization (NATO) 7
No Quarto da Vanda (In Vanda's Room) (2000) 125
Now the People! alliance 45
Nunes, R. 144; *O Choro é um Lugar Incerto* (Crying Is an Uncertain Place) 146; *Os Olhos de Himmler* (Himmler's Eyes) 146

O Barco (The Boat) 23
Observatory of Science and Technology 100
O Canto de Ossobó (The Song of Ossobó) (2018) 127
O Cordeiro de Deus (The Lamb of God) (2020) 127
O Crime do Padre Amaro (The Sin of Father Amaro) (2005) 125–126
Odete (2005) 126
OE *see* State Budget
OECD *see* Organization for Economic Cooperation and Development

174 *Index*

O Fantasma (The Ghost) (2000) 125
O Fatalista (The Fatalist) (2005) 126
official nationalism 17–18
O Filme da Treta (2006) 126
Onde o Verão Vai: Episódios da Juventude (Where the Summer goes: Chapters on Youth) (2018) 127
Open Budget Index 73
Operation Iraqi Freedom 48
Organic Law No. 1 of 2019 82
Organization for Economic Cooperation and Development (OECD) 6, 33, 50, 69, 73, 110, 114; PISA tests 67, 116
Os Lusíadas 17, 21, 22, 141, 147
Os Madredeus 135
Ourique 15

Padrão dos Descobrimentos 22
party system 45–46; alternation 52; decline in support for two main parties 52–53, *53*; dynamics in 21st century 51–59; innovation 52; new parties, emergence of 58–59; openness 52, 53–58, **56**
PASF *see* Projects in All Scientific Fields
PCP (Communist Party) 3–5, 35–38, 40, 45, 54, 55, 57–59
People-Animals-Nature party (*Partidos-Animais-Natureza*) 58, 59
Pereira, A. T. 145; *Atelier da Noite* (Night Studio) 143; *A Dança dos Fantasmas* (The Dance of the Ghosts); *Karen* 149
Pereira, M. 128
performing arts 128–130
Permanent Structured Cooperation in Defense (PESCO) 163
PESCO *see* Permanent Structured Cooperation in Defense
Pessanha, C. 144
Pessoa, F. 125, 137, 141
Pina, M. A.: *Todas as palavras: Poesia reunida* 142
Pintasilgo, M. de L. 60n4
Pitta e Cunha, T. 158
Platform Workers Directive 40
PM *see* prime minister
PMI *see* Procedure for Macroeconomic Imbalance
Poetas sem Qualidades (Poets without Qualities) 142
policy entrepreneur 164n4
politics 44–60; electoral system 49–50; party system *see* party system; political system 46–49, *49*; political system evolution 50–51; subnational government 50
PORDATA 96n5
Porta Jazz Association 134
Porto Symphony Orchestra 134

"Portugal Space 2030" strategy 116, 118
Portuguese Space Agency 116
poverty 95; child 67–68; income 65; rate 65; threshold 66
Praça do Império 22
PRD *see* Democratic Renewal Party (PRD, *Partido Renovador Democrático*)
prime minister (PM) 47
Princípio de Karenina (Karenina Principle) 148
Procedure for Macroeconomic Imbalance (PMI) 28
Prodi, R. 156
Projects in All Scientific Fields (PASF) 101, *102, 112, 114*
PS *see* Socialist Party
PSD *see* Social Democratic Party
public capital 73–75
public debt 63–65, *63*, 73; interest rates *29*
public expenditure 8, 30, *30*, 33, 39

Quality of Democracy Barometer 79
Quatro Contos (Four Stories) (2020) 127
Quintais, L.: *Angst* 142

race/racism 22, 96n10; racial superiority 94, *94*
Radaelli, C. M. 151
Rafa (2012) 127
R&D *see* research and development
R&DUs *see* Research and Development Units
Recovery and Resilience Plan 2021 (RRP) 38, 39
REDE – Associação de Estruturas para a Dança Contemporânea (Association of Structures for Contemporary Dance) 129
Regional Coordination and Development Commissions (CCDR) 102
Remix Ensemble 134
research and development (R&D): expenditure *104*; Framework Programmes (FP) 105; investment 102, 103, 109
Research and Development Units (R&DUs) 112–114, *113, 114*
Revolution of the Carnations (1974) 2, 3
Rodrigues, J. P. 125, 126
RRP *see* Recovery and Resilience Plan 2021

Sacramento, J. 126
Salaviza, J. 125, 127
Salazar, A. de O. 2, 3
Sammis, E. 6
Sampaio, J. 48
S&T *see* Science and Technology (S&T) policy
Sapinho, J. 126
Saraiva, A. 40n8
Saramago, J. 125; *A Jangada de Pedra* (The Stone Raft) 139

Sartori, G. 45, 47
science 99–119; ambition 112–114, *113*; financial resources 102–103, *103*, *104*; human resources 103–105, *104*, *105*; internationalization 114–116, *115*; outputs 105–109, *106–111*; and society 116–118; specialization 114–116; strategy 111–118; structure of 100–101
Science and Technology (S&T) policy 100, 101
Science Law 118
self-censorship 101
semipresidentialism 46–48
Serralves Foundation Museum of Contemporary Art 131
SGP 28, 31; budgetary rules 38, 40
SII *see* Social Insertion Income
Silva, C. 6, 48
Silva Melo, J. 130
Sinopse de amor e guerra (Synopsis of Love and War) 148
Sita 126
slave trade 22–23, 150
Soares, M. 7
Soares, Z. 131
Social and Democratic Centre-Popular Party (CDS-PP) 8, 34
Social Democratic Party (PSD) 4, 6, 8, 34, 45, 47, 50, 51, 53–55, 57–59, 89
Social Emergency Program (2011) 35
social inequality 79, 95, 96, 148
Social Insertion Income (SII) 33
Social Investment Package (2013) 39
Socialist Party (PS) 4, 5, 7, 34, 36, 38, 45, 47, 50, 51, 54, 55, 57–59
social policies 27–31
social safety net 33, 35
Social Security 92
society 79–96; gender equality 80–86, *82–86*; immigration 86–92, *87*, *90*, *91*; racial and ethnic differences 92–95, *94*
SOC *see* Strategic Ocean Committee
sovereign debt crisis 26, 28, 33, 39, 65, 70, 72, 153
Spinola, A. de 3
State Budget (OE) 101
Statistics Portugal 73
Strategic Ocean Committee (SOC) 158
subnational government 50

Taprobana (2014) 127
Tavares, G. M. 125, 146–147; *Aprender a Rezar na Era da Técnica* (Learning to Pray in the Age of Technology) 147; *Jerusalém*

147; *O Osso do Meio* (The Middle Bone) 147; *Uma Menina está perdida no seu Século à Procura do Pai* (A Girl is Lost in Her Century Looking for Her Father) 147; *Viagem à Índia* (Voyage to India) 141, 147
Teles, L. 127
Tiny, S. 127
Todoli, V. 131
Transparency International 70
trauer (grief) 137
Treaty of Rome 27
The Tree (2018) 127
Trefaut, S. 126
Troika 8, 21, 30, 37; loan 29

UGT *see* General Workers' Union
Understory 126
UNDP *see* United Nations Development Program
unemployment 5, 6, 9, 31–38, 63–65, 92, 95, 156, 162; protection 31, 32, 34, 37
United Nations 69, 80, 87
United Nations Development Program (UNDP) 79
University of Aveiro 134
untimeliness 141

Vasconcelos, C. 127
Veiga, T.: *Camilo Broca* 145; *Embora eu seja um velho errante* (Though I'm an Old Wanderer) 145; *Os Naufrágios de Camões* (Camoes' Shipwrecks) 145
Venice Film Festival 126
Verde, C. 145
Veser, E. 47
Vicente, D. P. 127
Victorino, M. 128
vinculo esterno 27, 28, 38
visual arts 131–134
A Volta ao Mundo Quando Tinhas 30 Anos (Around the World When You Were 30) (2011) 127
Von der Leyen Commission 40

welfare state 26–40
Western Europe: longest dictatorship in 2–3
World Bank 9, 33
World Inequality Database 73

Yvone Kane 126

Zelensky, V. 58